W9-CPO-930

VOLUME 459   JANUARY 1982

THE ANNALS

of The American Academy *of* Political *and* Social Science

ISSN 0002-7162

RICHARD D. LAMBERT, *Editor*
ALAN W. HESTON, *Associate Editor*

GOVERNMENT AND ECONOMIC PERFORMANCE

Special Editor of this Volume

J. ROGERS HOLLINGSWORTH

Professor of History
University of Wisconsin
Madison, Wisconsin

S **SAGE** PUBLICATIONS *BEVERLY HILLS   LONDON   NEW DELHI*

330.4
G721

THE ANNALS

© 1982 *by* The American Academy *of* Political *and* Social Science

PRISCILLA A. ESTES, *Assistant Editor*

Editorial Office: 3937 Chestnut Street, Philadelphia, Pennsylvania 19104.

For information about membership* (individuals only) and subscriptions (institutions), address:

SAGE PUBLICATIONS, INC.
275 South Beverly Drive
Beverly Hills, Calif. 90212 USA

From India and South Asia,
write to:
SAGE PUBLICATIONS INDIA Pvt. Ltd.
P.O. Box 3605
New Delhi 110 024
INDIA

From the UK, Europe, the Middle
East and Africa, write to:
SAGE PUBLICATIONS LTD
28 Banner Street
London EC1Y 8QE
ENGLAND

**Please note that members of The Academy receive THE ANNALS with their membership.*

Library of Congress Catalog Card Number 81-84719
International Standard Serial Number ISSN 0002-7162
International Standard Book Number ISBN 0-8039-1781-3 (Vol. 459, 1982, paper)
International Standard Book Number ISBN 0-8039-1780-5 (Vol. 459, 1982, cloth)
Manufactured in the United States of America. First printing, January 1982.

The articles appearing in THE ANNALS are indexed in *Book Review Index; Public Affairs Information Service Bulletin; Social Sciences Index; Monthly Periodical Index; Current Contents: Behavioral, Social, Management Sciences;* and *Combined Retrospective Index Sets.* They are also abstracted and indexed in *ABC Pol Sci, Historical Abstracts, Human Resources Abstracts, Social Sciences Citation Index, United States Political Science Documents, Social Work Research & Abstracts, Peace Research Reviews, Sage Urban Studies Abstracts, International Political Science Abstracts,* and/or *America: History and Life.*

Information about membership rates, institutional subscriptions, and back issue prices may be found on the facing page.

Advertising. Current rates and specifications may be obtained by writing to THE ANNALS Advertising and Promotion Manager at the Beverly Hills office (address above).

Claims. Claims for undelivered copies must be made no later than three months following month of publication. The publisher will supply missing copies when losses have been sustained in transit and when the reserve stock will permit.

Change of Address. Six weeks' advance notice must be given when notifying of change of address. Please send old address label along with the new address to insure proper identification. Please specify name of journal. Send change of address to: THE ANNALS, c/o Sage Publications, Inc., 275 South Beverly Drive, Beverly Hills, CA 90212.

Origin and Purpose. The Academy was organized December 14, 1889, to promote the progress of political and social science, especially through publications and meetings. The Academy does not take sides in controverted questions, but seeks to gather and present reliable information to assist the public in forming an intelligent and accurate judgment.

Meetings. The Academy holds an annual meeting in the spring extending over two days.

Publications. THE ANNALS is the bimonthly publication of The Academy. Each issue contains articles on some prominent social or political problem, written at the invitation of the editors. Also, monographs are published from time to time, numbers of which are distributed to pertinent professional organizations. These volumes constitute important reference works on the topics with which they deal, and they are extensively cited by authorities throughout the United States and abroad. The papers presented at the meetings of The Academy are included in THE ANNALS.

Membership. Each member of The Academy receives THE ANNALS and may attend the meetings of The Academy. Membership is open only to individuals. Annual dues: $24.00 for the regular paperbound edition (clothbound, $36.00). Add $6.00 per year for membership outside the U.S.A. Members may also purchase single issues of THE ANNALS for $5.00 each (clothbound, $7.00).

Subscriptions. Institutions may subscribe to THE ANNALS at the annual rate: $42.00 (clothbound, $54.00). Add $6.00 per year for subscriptions outside the U.S.A. Institutional rates for single issues: $7.00 each (clothbound, $9.00).

Single issues of THE ANNALS may be obtained by individuals who are not members of The Academy for $6.00 each (clothbound, $7.50). Single issues of THE ANNALS have proven to be excellent supplementary texts for classroom use. Direct inquiries regarding adoptions to THE ANNALS c/o Sage Publications (address below).

All correspondence concerning membership in The Academy, dues renewals, inquiries about membership status, and/or purchase of single issues of THE ANNALS should be sent to THE ANNALS c/o Sage Publications, Inc., 275 South Beverly Drive, Beverly Hills, CA 90212. *Please note that orders under $20 must be prepaid.* Sage affiliates in London and India will assist institutional subscribers abroad with regard to orders, claims, and inquiries for both subscriptions and single issues.

THE EIGHTY-FIFTH ANNUAL MEETING OF THE AMERICAN ACADEMY OF POLITICAL AND SOCIAL SCIENCE

APRIL 23 AND 24, 1982
THE BELLEVUE STRATFORD HOTEL
PHILADELPHIA, PENNSYLVANIA

The annual meeting of The Academy is attended by hundreds of distinguished scholars, statesmen, authors, and professionals in diverse fields, including representatives of many embassies, academic institutions, and cultural, civic, and scientific organizations.

This 85th Annual Meeting will be addressed at each session by prominent scholars and officials and will be devoted to the topic of

INTERNATIONAL TERRORISM

Members of the Academy are cordially invited to attend and will receive full information. Information on Academy membership can be found in each volume of THE ANNALS (see page 3).

- Proceedings of the 85th Annual Meeting will be published in the September 1982 volume of THE ANNALS.

● FOR DETAILS WRITE TO: THE AMERICAN ACADEMY OF POLITICAL AND SOCIAL SCIENCE ● BUSINESS OFFICE ● 3937 CHESTNUT STREET PHILADELPHIA, PENNSYLVANIA 19104

CONTENTS

BOOK DEPARTMENT CONTENTS

INTERNATIONAL RELATIONS AND POLITICS

AFRICA, ASIA, AND LATIN AMERICA

EUROPE

UNITED STATES

SOCIOLOGY

ECONOMICS

PREFACE

During the past decade, there has been a widely held view that the discipline of economics is in disarray. While economists in advanced industrial societies have been quite useful in telling governments what policies not to adopt, they have been much less successful in specifying what governments should do in order to achieve impressive economic performance.[1]

Meanwhile, governments, wishing to achieve impressive economic performance, have had very high expectations from economists. Understandably, policymakers want to predict the consequences that are likely to follow from their policies, but increasingly the discipline of economics has demonstrated that it has a very low success rate in forecasting beyond short-term phenomena.

In all advanced industrial societies, the role of government in shaping economic performance is substantial. While economists play an important role in shaping governmental economic policy, the economists' models are very simplistic, and this is the basic reason that the discipline of economics is in a state of crisis. Whereas conventional economics seeks to explain economic performance with parsimonious theories of factor supply, demand, pricing, and marketing organization, a number of other social scientists have, during the past decade, attempted to explain economic performance by relying on more complex models. One might refer to these noneconomists as the new political economists. Instead of focusing exclusively on economic variables to explain economic performance, the political economists assume that the structure and performance of economic institutions and political institutions are inseparable. In short, the political economist argues that economic performance may be explained only by focusing serious consideration on the social-structural and political-institutional arrangements of the society.

Consistent with this strategy, recent social scientists have demonstrated with cross-national research that there are substantial regularities between the way that power is organized among various groups and the performance of national economies. Specifically, the research has attempted to explain such questions as the following: why do nations differ in their levels of unemployment; in equality in income distribution; and in rates of change in economic growth, productivity, and inflation? And in an effort to confront these questions, one political economy study after another has

---

NOTE: Articles in this issue of *The Annals* were presented at a workshop on "The Role of Government in Shaping Economic Performance," University of Wisconsin, Madison, March 26 and 27, 1981. Funds for the workshop were provided by the Anonymous Fund, College of Letters and Sciences, University of Wisconsin; the Council for European Studies; and the German Marshall Fund. The editor especially thanks Dean David Cronon of the University of Wisconsin for helping to make the workshop possible. Ellen Jane Hollingsworth provided valuable assistance in the editing of the articles.

1. For a discussion of the problems facing the discipline of economics, see *The Public Interest* (special issue, "The Crisis in Economic Theory," 1980).

demonstrated that economic performanc is very much tied to the polity, for example, partisan representation within legislatures and cabinets.[2]

In the articles that follow, there is an effort to explore the role of government in shaping economic policy, and in several of the articles, the authors argue that if one ignores political variables, one cannot understand the economic performance of national economies. Leon Lindberg focuses on the crisis in which the discipline of economics finds itself and points out that if we are to understand national economic performance, it is necessary to alter the way that we study and approach the subject of economic performance. He makes a convincing argument that the political institutions of a society play an important role in shaping levels of inflation, unemployment, economic grants, and economic productivity.

While all advanced capitalist economies in recent years have encountered serious problems of inflation, unemployment, and lagging rates of growth and economic productivity, some nations have better prospects of dealing with these problems than others. My article in this volume argues that variation in economic performance is shaped by differences in the capacity of countries to shape coherent economic policies. In an effort to explain why countries vary in their ability to develop coherent policies, I focus on the history of their underlying social and political structures. It is argued that Sweden, which has a political structure that facilitates coherent economic policies, is likely to be more successful in confronting the economic problems of the 1980s than the United States, which has a political-structural arrangement that places severe constraints on the implementation of coherent policies.

Consistent with this theme, David Cameron suggests that a number of differences in the economic performance among nation-states may be traced to differences in the distribution of political power. Focusing on a number of advanced industrial societies, Cameron demonstrates that as the level of the leftist strength of political systems increases, there are higher levels of employment and lower rates of inflation and economic growth, but higher levels of capital formation. As every variable in the Cameron article is of considerable interest to policymakers in all advanced industrial societies, his article should be carefully pondered by analysts who attempt to predict economic activity without seriously evaluating the role that the political institutions of a society play in its economic performance.

Cameron's article is important in another respect. It is a serious effort to evaluate the new fiscal conservatism epitomized by the victories of Ronald Reagan and Margaret Thatcher. It concludes that contrary to the arguments of the Thatcher and Reagan governments, high levels of government spending and large increases in spending have not caused stagflation.

Donald Hancock also demonstrates that many of the differences ·in the way that economic systems perform may be traced to variation in their political-institutional arrangements. While his analysis focuses on Sweden and West Germany in the post-World War II period, his theoretical argument that the variation in Social Democratic strength influences economic outcomes may be extended to other countries. Political analysts studying a single country over time often fail to perceive that partisanship influences

2. For a discussion of this literature, see J. Rogers Hollingsworth and Robert A. Hanneman, "Working Class Power and Political Economy of Western Capitalist Societies," in *Comparative Social Research* (Greenwich, CT: JAI Press, forthcoming).

economic performance, but when one studies cross-national differences in left-right strength, one has enough variation to discern that the partisanship of societies definitely influences their economic performance.

In a very creative article, Jerald Hage and Remi Clignet raise different types of questions about economic performance, ones all too often ignored in the literature: at the firm level, what type of organizational structure is required by different kinds of technologies in order to maximize profits? And at the societal level, what types of political-institutional arrangements are required by different kinds of technologies if economic growth is to be maximized? In other words, it is not enough to observe that economic performance varies, depending on the partisan distribution of power. Hage and Clignet go much further and specify what types of institutional arrangements are necessary in order to maximize certain types of utilities. Unfortunately, this type of article is all too rare in the social sciences.

Like Hage, Clignet, and myself, Henry Teune confronts the problem of how political structure influences the rate of economic growth. He argues that in advanced industrial societies, decentralized political structures are more conducive to high rates of economic growth than are more centralized arrangements. In this sense, his argument complements that of Hage. Whether decentralized political systems have the capacity to produce the coherence that I argue is necessary for impressive economic performance is problematic. The apparent contradiction between Teune's and my article may be reconciled by recognizing that the centralization-decentralization continuum is a multidimensional concept and that economic growth may be maximized by decentralizing some activities and centralizing others.

While the articles by Cameron, Hancock, Teune, and myself focus on advanced industrial societies, James Caporaso's article deals with the role of the state in shaping economic performance in developing societies. His article, along with that of Hage, points out that the type of state activity required to manage a society with a developing economy is very different from that required by highly developed societies. Both articles acknowledge that as societies move through different stages of development, they will encounter different problems and will require different types of political systems. Unfortunately, the scholarly literature has hitherto not been very precise concerning the type of state that is required to manage a specific type of economy.

What are the economic consequences that follow from government's pursuing particular policies? In varying ways, the articles by Gregory Christainsen and Robert Haveman, Robert Hanneman, and Peter Eisinger confront this type of problem. In recent years, a number of analysts have argued that the proliferation of government regulations has caused a decline in the rate of economic productivity in the United States. In response to this perspective, there has been a great deal of pressure exerted on the federal government to deregulate the economy as a means of increasing the nation's rate of economic productivity. The Christainsen-Haveman article, reporting on many studies that have analyzed the reasons for the decrease in the rate of economic productivity, concludes that very little of the slowdown has been due to the regulatory policies of the American government. Hence, those who expect productivity increases to follow as a result of deregulation of the American economy would appear to be in for a disappointment.

Hanneman, focusing on five Western nations, points out that taxation historically has been an instrument for the management of developed economies, but he argues that as tax systems have become more complex, the capacity to manage economies with the instrument of taxation has become increasingly constrained. As one Western society after another has in recent years confronted a fiscal crisis, the capacity of the state to use revenue policy as a tool to manage the economy has become quite limited—even though the successful performance of economies is dependent on the role of the state. And it is the limited potential of the state to manage economies via fiscal policy that is one reason why Keynesian economics is facing a crisis.

Social scientists have long been concerned with the question of who benefits when services are provided by one of the following sectors: the voluntary nonprofit, the for-profit, or the public sector. There is a fair amount of theoretical literature but little empirical work on who benefits from services being organized in one sector rather than another. Of course, the world is not always neatly organized into these three sectors, for as the article by Eisinger demonstrates, there are occasionally joint ventures between the public and the for-profit sectors. In the United States, it is somewhat common for public and nonprofit welfare organizations to work together. Because joint ventures between government and for-profit sectors are quite common in France, Eisinger, by focusing on this process there, can assess some of the consequences of this type of partnership. Focusing on the French housing market, he demonstrates that in such an arrangement, the for-profit sector becomes the dominant partner, but in a way inimical to the interests of low-income groups. The Eisinger article is of particular interest at the present time, for governments throughout Western Europe and North America are considering either turning over to the private sector services previously performed by the public sector, or participating in joint ventures with the private sector.

As industrial societies face chronic inflation, the scholarly community has focused more attention on the link between increases in the money supply and increases in the rate of inflation. As Milton Friedman and others have argued that substantial inflation is always and everywhere a monetary problem, money policymakers have responded by turning to monetary instruments as a means of managing the economy. John Woolley, in the concluding article, analyzes the monetarists within the United States as a political force. Because monetarism is presently a central part of the Reagan administration's approach to economic policy, the Woolley article should be of special note for those who are interested in the process by which monetarists have mobilized power to support a monetarist policy in the United States.

The articles in this issue of *The Annals* offer a number of conceptual and theoretical insights that are only occasionally noted in the conventional economics literature. First, political and economic behavior are strongly, but variably, related. Satisfactory explanations of economic performance depend on models that incorporate not only economic but also political variables. Second, the process connecting social and political structure to economic performance is complex but discoverable. Several of the articles advance the literature by specifying the conditions under which social and institutional arrangements influence economic performance.

The theoretical insights into empirical analysis of the role of government in shaping economic behavior seem to offer much promise: for economists, clear guidelines for explaining why the same economic variables perform differently in different societies; for researchers in policy studies, a way of operationalizing some of the most important aspects of what might be called the institutional environment in which economic policy is made. With additional work, the insights of the new political economy may bring economists and noneconomists into closer and more productive interaction.[3]

J. ROGERS HOLLINGSWORTH

3. For an elaboration on this point, see ibid.

ANNALS, *AAPSS*, 459, January 1982

The Problems of Economic Theory in Explaining Economic Performance

By LEON N. LINDBERG

ABSTRACT: The analytical, policy, and ethical issues raised by the contemporary crises of economic performance in the United States and the attendant crisis in economic theory might well serve as a critical catalyst for consummating a marriage of political science and institutional economics. Besides generally compatible modes of reasoning about economy and polity, political scientists and institutionalists share two essential perspectives on the problems of explaining economic performance and prescribing government roles in the economy which suggest a common research agenda: (1) a similar dissatisfaction with the epistemological and ideological characteristics of the mainstream economic debate about the policy and performance failures of the 1970s; and (2) some initial distinctive propositions about the institutional, structural, and political determinants of contemporary economic performance in the United States that can be empirically tested and that may serve as an entry point into the academic and policy debates of the 1980s.

Leon N. Lindberg is professor of political science and environmental studies at the University of Wisconsin—Madison. He has held research appointments at the Brookings Institution, the Carnegie Endowment for International Peace (Geneva), the Center for International Affairs at Harvard, and the Center for Advanced Study in the Behavioral Sciences. He is co-director and co-author of a large forthcoming study of the politics and sociology of global inflation and has written widely on energy policy and politics, economic policy, and the political economy of inflation. His books include The Energy Syndrome, Politics and the Future of Industrial Society, Regional Integration: Theory and Research, Europe's Would-Be Polity, *and* The Political Dynamics of European Economic Integration.

THE economic performance problems of the American economy in the 1970s and into the 1980s may have set the stage for a promising intellectual marriage between political science and institutional economics. The offspring would be an interdisciplinary political-institutional paradigm of political economy.

The central aspirations of such a paradigm would be threefold:

—to describe the concrete practices, institutional structures, and working rules that structure economic relationships and the complex interactions between the economy and the political system;

—to view the political economy in terms of organic, evolutionary, and adaptive metaphors that admit of nonteleological logics rather than laws of capitalist development; and

—to build new ethical and analytic foundations for a theory of the state in the economy that seeks justifications for intervention and criteria for the evaluation of policy that see the state as more than "a parameter of the market" or handmaiden to the individual pursuit of self-interest, and that see the state neither as a set of neutral policy instruments nor as an incompetent and imperfectable Leviathan that grows and grows without measure, trampling incentive, enterprise, and liberty.

MAINSTREAM ECONOMICS

Such a paradigm would stand in more or less sharp—and, one hopes, healthy—competition with most of mainstream or neoclassical economics, both as a basis for understanding the allocative and distributive performance of the economy and as the basis for policy prescription with respect to such problems as energy, inflation and unemployment, innovation and productivity, and stagnation and economic progress. Its relationship to Marxian political economy and to the diverse strands of so-called post-Keynesian or neo-Ricardian economics would be more complex and synergistic because these share many of the same intellectual and epistemological traditions as those of political science and institutional economics.[1]

The distinctiveness of mainstream or neoclassical economics lies in its having deliberately and progressively divorced itself from the premises of classical political economy and its concern for long-period growth, distributional struggle, and endemic instability. It derives as well from the mainstream commitment to a logico-deductive style of analysis justified by a "methodological individualism" and a narrow positivist epistemology, and from a self-conscious isolation from the other social sciences and from most of the philosophical controversies of the twentieth century. Social science investigations of bureaucracy, authority, class, and power; the socialist and conservative critiques of individualism and commercialized society; and the doubts about the status of statements of fact and value spawned by existen-

1. Alan Coddington, "Keynesian Economics: The Search for First Principles," *Journal of Economic Literature*, 14:1258-73 (1976); Albert Eichner, *A Guide to Post-Keynesian Economics* (Armonk, NY: M. E. Sharp, 1980); Martin Hollis and Edwin Nell, *Rational Economic Man* (Cambridge: Cambridge University Press, 1975).

tialism, structuralism, language theory, and the theory of uncertainty all have had little influence on modern economics.[2]

PARADIGMS AND POLICYMAKING

Political scientists and institutionalists share another attribute with Marxists and post-Keynesians: effective exclusion from the central academic and policy debates on economic performance and economic policy. None has as yet been very influential in shaping the prevailing view of why American economic performance has faltered, or in assessing the reasons for the declining effectiveness of specific economic policies, or in proposing alternative modes of government action. To some extent this exclusion or lack of influence reflects established intellectual and academic hierarchies. Political scientists have only recently turned their hand to systematic investigation of economy-polity interrelationships as these affect the functioning of the economy. Institutionalists and post-Keynesians—not to mention Marxists—are typically not represented in major economics departments, except in low-status or so-called applied fields. Nor have their analytical and normative concerns been reflected at Brookings, The American Enterprise Institute, or the bevy of new, mostly conservative, think tanks.

Indeed, the crisis in economic policy, and the crisis in economics,

which it has stimulated, has seen much more accommodation in the economics mainstream to what James W. Dean calls the "reactionary" assaults of monetarism, rational expectations theory, and supply-side economics.[3] This swing back to "more fundamentally correct economic ideas," away from the quasi-sociological eclecticism of neo-Keynesians like Arthur Okun and James Tobin, toward "reconstituted reductionism," noninterventionism, and a "new love affair with the market," reveals something important about the kinds of evidence, reasoning, and ethical preoccupations mainstream economics can readily incorporate or accommodate.

The lack of impact upon policymaking doubtless has something to do with the fact that the neoclassical paradigm offers a much more coherent political and ideological justification for capitalist institutions and the market as an allocating mechanism. As James Q. Wilson has observed, "What intellectuals chiefly bring to policy debates, and what chiefly accounts for their influence, is not knowledge but theory." They provide the "conceptual language" and the "ruling examples" (not evidence!) that become the "accepted assumptions" for those in charge of making policy.[4]

Intellectuals framed, and to a large degree conducted, the debates about whether this language and these paradigms were correct. The most influential intellectuals were those who

2. Hollis and Nell, *Rational Economic Man;* Benjamin Ward, *What's Wrong with Economics* (New York: Macmillan, 1972); Robert Solo, *The Positive State* (Cincinnati: South-Western Press, 1981).

3. James W. Dean, "The Dissolution of the Keynesian Consensus," *The Public Interest* (special issue, "The Crisis in Economic Theory"), XX:19-34 (1980).

4. James Q. Wilson, "'Policy Intellectuals' and Public Policy," *The Public Interest,* 64:66 (Summer 1981).

managed to link a concept or a theory to the practical needs and ideological predispositions of political activists and government officials.[5]

It may be no accident that the neoclassical mainstream has been most dominant in economic analysis and in policymaking in societies where ideological liberalism and business power were generally unchallenged. The contemporary swing to the right in economics and public policy is surely more marked—if not mainly confined to—these same societies. Nor is it accidental that economic analysis and practice is more institutional and overlaid with nonmarket considerations where social democracy or paternalistic conservativism is influential and when the status of labor in the society is assured—even if in a functionally subordinate position. I will return to the economic performance implications of these speculations about the relationship between political power and ideology and economic doctrine and policy in the conclusion.

THE DISORDERED STATE OF INSTITUTIONAL ECONOMICS AND POLITICAL SCIENCE

Notwithstanding the gatekeeping roles of established hierarchies and paradigms of so-called normal science and the "demand functions" of dominant elites in the United States for analytical languages more consonant with capitalist power and belief, the lack of influence and effective exclusion of institutional economics and political science from the economic policy debate largely reflects the disordered state of both fields. While we can discern the tentative outlines of a political-institutional paradigm of political economy, it can hardly be claimed that it already exists.

The general outlines of the institutionalist critique of mainstream economics have been visible since the times of Thorstein Veblen and John R. Commons without noticeably progressing toward a generally accepted conceptual vocabulary, a clearly stated set of "puzzles," and some criteria of evaluation, and without generating concrete, cumulative research findings about the ways in which the organizational structures, behavioral predispositions, and power relations within and among firms, industries, and sectors influence economic allocations and the performance of the economy. Nor have most institutionalists come to terms with the needs of a positive theory of the state. Epistemological critiques of neoclassical economics, confident predictions of being the wave of the future, exhortatory essays, and quasi-anthropological descriptions do not a paradigm make.

Political science is itself clearly "between eras," as Charles W. Anderson argues, "casting about for fresh ideas," and "searching for themes that might guide political research."[6] Political economy is currently in vogue but to date has for the most part either taken the form of the application of neoclassical reasoning and ethics to political science, as in public choice theory, or has been part of the broader stream of neo-Marxian analysis, with its

5. Ibid., p. 33.

6. Charles W. Anderson, "Political Theory and Political Science: The Rediscovery and Reinterpretation of the Pragmatic Tradition" (Paper delivered at the Shambaugh Conference on Political Theory, University of Iowa, 1981), pp. 1-2.

own distinctive conceptual formalisms and epistemological preconceptions and with political concerns that do not seem to promise much in the way of new justifications and criteria for state intervention in the capitalist economy. But, as Anderson argues, the approach to empirical inquiry and normative evaluation characteristic of philosophical pragmatism may well constitute the most continuous philosophical tradition of American political science. And this tradition provides a clear bridge to institutional economics, pointing the way to a "new political economy," and distinguishes such a construction from the utilitarianism and positivism of neoclassical economics, as from political economy in the Marxian tradition.

Pragmatic political science was always predisposed toward the positive state, much as economics has always had a bias in favor of the market. In the first instance, American political science was strongly influenced by the Continental —specifically the Bismarckian—model of the state, which it nativized and legitimated by appeal to democratic process. Philosophically, pragmatism had little use for metaphysical doctrines of the state or definitions of its essential purposes. The state ought simply to be regarded as an adaptive mechanism, responsive to public will, which determines its purposes.[7]

LINES OF CONVERGENCE

The political scientist can thus join hands with the institutional economist and the historical sociologist by virtue of their common commitment to viewing economy and polity in cultural context and to contextually deriving evaluative judgments and prescriptions for change, by their sensitivity to tradeoffs

7. Ibid., p. 14.

between group as well as individual interests, and by their sensitivity to the claims of the community. Holistic, organic, evolutionary, and adaptive metaphors characterize both fields. Both approach research from an empirical, historical, and comparative perspective. Indeed, the political scientists who have been working toward a political-institutional analysis of the economy and economic policy come overwhelmingly from earlier backgrounds in comparative politics, historical political sociology, and political development.

Institutional economists seem also to be independently exploring what can be learned from political science and what might be undertaken together. Philip A. Klein writes in the *Journal of Economic Issues*, the institutionalists' "house organ":

The alternative paradigm, which standard economists never tire of demanding of those who feel mainstream economic theory is inadequate for confronting economic problems, could emerge if institutionalists considered more closely than they have the political scientist's approach to understanding the evolving polity.[8]

Political scientists are concerned with the "authoritative allocation of values," but would seldom assume the polity was allocating them in "any predetermined or predefined efficient way." The focus is on "how *in fact* the polity makes allocations," and this involves a full recognition of the importance of conflict and power in the process. The political scientist's normative attachment to "one man, one vote" is not flawed by

8. Philip A. Klein, "Confronting Power in Economics: A Pragmatic Evaluation," *Journal of Economic Issues*, 14(4):878 (Dec. 1980).

TABLE 1
THREE SOCIAL SCIENCE PARADIGMS

	POLITICAL ECONOMY		POLITICAL SCIENCE
	MAINSTREAM ECONOMICS	INSTITUTIONALISM	
Basic outlook	1. Invisible hand (with imperfections) 2. Harmony	1. Cultural conditioning with technological dynamic 2. Conflict	1. Cultural conditioning 2. Conflict
Basic function of system	Allocate scarce resources	Express emergent values of participants through allocative decisions	Allocate values authoritatively
Basic mechanism Assumptions:	Market prices 1. Primarily competitive interaction 2. Automaticity	Interactive value system 1. Power distorts value system 2. Values result from interaction of system and participants	Interactive value system 1. Power distorts value system 2. Values result from interaction of system and participants
Motivation	Self-interest	Perceived self-interest	Perceived self-interest
Assumed distribution of decision-making authority	One dollar = one vote	Control over constellations of dollar votes, reflecting concentrated wealth and power	Control over constellations of one person, one vote reflecting concentrated wealth and power
Objective of system	The end: market equilibrium (all markets cleared)	End-in-view: progress of economy consonant with emergent community values	End-in-view: progress of polity consonant with emergent community values
"Ideal" system	Pure competition	Decision-making process sensitive to changing views of participants in economic process	Decision-making process sensitive to changing views of participants in the political process
Ultimate arbiter of actual system	Consumer sovereignty plus technological progress	Technological change limited by concentrated power and big producer sovereignty	Concentrated power and big unit sovereignty
Result:	Efficiency and progress through producer acquiescence	Manipulated consumer	Manipulated voters
Basic units in system	Households, firms	Individuals	Individuals
Corollary:	Households and firms express demands (wants) and supplies (costs) through prices with optimal technological productivity	Both households' and firms' decisions are the result of power deployment by individuals	All political units' decisions are the result of power deployment by individuals
Result:	Socially ideal resource allocation	x-inefficiency; x-disutility corrupt results of ideal systems (above)	Actual allocation of values deviates from ideal system (above)
Obstacle:	Imperfect knowledge of households and firms	Power blocs deliberately distort information flows	Power blocs deliberately distort information flows
Solution:	Assume it away	Improve information flows to individuals	Improve information flows to individuals

(Continued on p. 20)

TABLE 1 Continued

	POLITICAL ECONOMY		
	MAINSTREAM ECONOMICS	INSTITUTIONALISM	POLITICAL SCIENCE
Welfare assumption	Competitive market equilibria define community welfare (subject to Pareto optimality constraint)	Community welfare as an "end" cannot be defined. The means for moving in the direction of greater community welfare can be discerned in the process	The public interest as an "end" cannot be defined. The means for moving in the direction of greater public interest can be discerned in the process
		There is a means-end continuum that enables the polity or the economy to progress along the continuum despite the absence of a definable absolute end.	

SOURCE: Philip A. Klein, "Confronting Power in Economics: A Pragmatic Evaluation," *Journal of Economic Issues*, 14(4):882-83 (Dec. 1980). Reprinted with permission of the publisher and the author.

any analogue to the mainstream economist's "customary assumption of a given income distribution," nor does the political scientist eschew the question of how values and preferences are, in fact, formed in a society. Klein offers a nice comparison (Table 1) of the structure of mainstream microeconomic theory, institutionalism, and political science to buttress his following conclusion:

If, as I believe, the proper study of political economy is the economy we actually have, then the perspective of political science would appear to point the way toward a reorientation of much of what the economist does. Anthony Downs may have shown what economic logic can do for political science; the potential in the reverse direction may well be far greater.[9]

In my view, the analytical, policy, and ethical issues raised by the contemporary crises of economic performance in the United States and the attendant crisis in economic theory might well serve as a critical

9. Ibid., p. 891.

catalyst for consummating these bonds between political science and institutional economics. Besides generally compatible modes of reasoning about the economy and polity, political scientists and institutionalists seem to me to share two essential perspectives on the problems of explaining economic performance and prescribing government roles in the economy. These suggest a common research agenda:

—a similar dissatisfaction with the epistemological and ideological characteristics of the mainstream economic debate about the policy and performance failures of the 1970s; and

—some initial distinctive propositions about the institutional, structural, and political determinants of contemporary economic performance in the United States that can be empirically tested and that may serve as an entry point into the academic and policy debates of the 1980s.

In the remaining pages of this article, I will be able to offer only a brief sketch of each point.

THE MAINSTREAM DEBATES ON ECONOMIC PERFORMANCE

It is not surprising that the dramatic deterioration of economic performance experienced by the United States in the 1970s should have provoked a reexamination of reigning economic theory and policy prescription. One could hardly expect less of scientists. Yet to a political-institutional analyst, both the main substantive thrust of this reevaluation and the intellectual-cum-political process through which it emerged are perplexing. At the risk of oversimplifying, there seem to be two broad substantive theses competing with each other. The first, associated with the neo-Keynesians, argues that inflation and stagnation and the declining effectiveness of conventional monetary and fiscal policies can be attributed to an unfortunate confluence and cumulation of random events, such as Vietnam, OPEC-I and OPEC-II, and agricultural shortages; inertial forces, such as interest-group rivalries, cost-plus-pricing, wage and price relativities, contract markets, and so on; and policy errors, such as expansive monetary and fiscal policies in 1972-73. No major revisions of the basic neoclassical Keynesian synthesis policy mix is necessary, save the addition of an incomes policy to overcome inertial forces and restore markets.[10]

The second thesis, variously presented by "new classical," monetarist, or supply-side economists, generally attributes performance and policy failure to inflationary expectations, excessive concern with unemployment, and a bias against capital formulation—all the direct result of Keynesian doctrine and the excessive government intervention in the market economy to which they have given rise. The chief policy implication is to urge a drastic retreat from government activism, a fixed monetary rule rather than discretionary fiscal policy, and sharp cuts in government spending.[11]

It is hard to judge which of these theses is the more influential among economists, although the latter is surely in favor in the Reagan administration. Perhaps the outside observer gets an exaggerated view of the extent to which the so-called counterrevolution against the theory and practice of the interventionist state has penetrated the economics profession. Perhaps the renewed devotion to free markets and the conclusion that market failures "pale in comparison with the wastes, distortions, misdirections, and self-serving aggrandizements of government and its bureaucracy"[12] is less widely shared than seems to be the case. Yet there can be little

---

10. See, for example, Alan S. Blinder, *Economic Policy and the Great Stagflation* (New York: Academic Press, 1979); Otto Eckstein, "Economic Choices for the 1980's," *Challenge*, xx:15-27 (July/Aug. 1980); James Tobin, "Stabilization Policy Ten Years

After," *Brookings Papers on Economic Activity*, 1:19-90 (1980); and Richard G. Lipsey, "The Understanding and Control of Inflation: Is There a Crisis in Macro Economics?" *Canadian Journal of Economics* (Nov. 1981).

11. See inter alia the essays in *The Public Interest* (special issue, "The Crisis," 1980). For a moderate monetarist account, see Philip Cagan, *Persistent Inflation* (New York: Columbia University Press, 1979).

12. James M. Buchanan, Introduction to William Mitchell, "The Anatomy of Public Failure: A Public Choice Perspective" (Paper delivered at the Institute for Economic Research, Los Angeles, June 1978).

doubt that the intellectual preeminence of Keynesian macroeconomic analysis and prescription, as of market failure theory, has been sharply challenged and that the general drift back to an earlier and purer economic theory is more powerful than the challenges of institutionalists, post-Keynesians, or Marxians ever were.[13] What is especially troubling to the outside observer is the extent to which conclusions about theory and the relationship between policy and performance seem rooted less in reasoned reflection and concrete research on past policy implementation and more on a kind of atavistic reconversion to truths held independently of specific supporting observation and evidence.

Furthermore, notwithstanding fundamental differences between neo-Keynesian and New Classical thinking about economic performance, their accounts do share certain general orientations common to mainstream economic analysis. Each would be challenged by political-institutional analysts.

1. External shocks to the economy tend to be treated as random and exogenous, rather than as possibly endogenous and systemic, that is, linked to secular transitions in economic structures and the changing distribution of economic and political power.

2. Mainstream economics typically studies change through the assumptions of comparative statics, making comparisons of how resources respond to market signals in various equilibrium states while more or less ignoring the processes of transition from one equilibrium to

13. Dean, "Dissolution of the Keynesian Consensus"; and *The Public Interest* (special issue, "The Crisis," 1980).

another. Political scientists and institutionalists generally argue that there is no certainty that equilibrium is attainable for more than short periods or that transitions will not court collapse, or that uncertainty and instability will not be the dominant behavioral mode of capitalist economics. They would give much more attention to the properties of resilient or robust systems and to the study of change and dynamic adaptation. They would expect adaptive capacities of both private and public institutions to vary from one nation to another and to be important determinants of economic performance.

3. Inertial forces or expectations are viewed essentially as psychological phenomena that can be reversed or broken by policies that induce or force a restoration of marginal economic calculations, rather than as sociological and political trends toward a more symmetrical distribution of power in markets and in access to state policymaking that are not illegitimate and must be met with political means of control.

4. Policy errors are attributable to incorrect economic doctrine, simple miscalculation in a complex and uncertain world, or to the irrational intrusion of political forces, such as special interest groups or electoral pressures, rather than understood as often expressing deep-seated social and political preferences, patterns of influence, business and bureaucratic arrangements, and power and the distribution of political resources.

5. The economic performance record of the postwar period—both good and bad—substantially reflects the influence of so-called Keynesian theory and policy doctrine, rather than being explicable as much in terms of specific histori-

cal and political conditions and the existence or creation of supporting institutional arrangements.

6. One improves policy and performance primarily by adopting better or more correct economic doctrines, as opposed to the view that no such judgment can be made without careful empirical and theoretical study of the specific interactions between policy instruments and the institutions of political and economic society in several nations and historical periods.

7. With varying acknowledgment of the incidence and severity of market imperfections, market-clearing prices retain their special status. Market norms, controls, transactions, and exchanges are seen as basically self-correcting and conducive to efficient allocation and adjustment to changing economic conditions. Fundamental questions are not raised about forces that structure and constrain the choices offered by the market, or about how organizational and ideological factors may systematically influence the productive efficiency of firms, nor is the quality of the market adjustment process in general assessed.

8. The utility and results of government intervention in the economy continue to be judged according to economic theories of what the market leaves undone, rather than according to a distinctive supporting political theory of state intervention in the economy.

9. To the extent that there is systematic analysis of the state and collective decision-making processes more generally, and regardless of whether government intervention is seen as basically benign or inherently flawed, behavioral propositions are deduced from a priori assumptions that subsume the moti-

vations and incentives of politicians and bureaucrats to a simple self-interest-maximizing logic. There is little empirical analysis of the extent to which specific governmental structures—along with structures in the private economy—may help establish regularities in economic policy or economic performance.

TOWARD A THEORY OF THE INSTITUTIONAL STRUCTURE OF THE POLITICAL ECONOMY[14]

In explaining economic performance, both institutional economics and political science would emphasize the interactions among economic agents and group interests and between them and the state. Patterns of economic production and consumption, the economic goals pursued and instruments chosen, and the ability of political authorities to adapt policies and implementation strategies to changing economic and political conditions are largely institutionally constrained or determined. The environment of choice, the social and political matrix within which economic activity is contained, must then be understood on its own terms. We can conceive of the institutional structure of the political economy at three distinct levels: the organization of economic society, the state as a complex organizational system,

14. Much of this section draws from a project I co-directed with Charles S. Maier for the Brookings Institution, *The Politics and Sociology of Global Inflation.* I gratefully acknowledge my debt to Charles S. Maier, Albert O. Hirschman, Robert Keohane, Colin Crouch, John Zysman, Rudolf Klein, David Cameron, Douglas Hibbs, John Woolley, Brian Barry, Michele Salvati, Norbert Kloten, Kozo Yamamura, and Andrew Martin.

and systems of group intermediation and interest representation
linking the public and private sectors.[15] Some propositions about
correlates of economic performance
in the United States and other
nations can be sketched for each.

Economic society

Economic behavior is substantially shaped by institutions and collective interests. The structure and
form of institutions affects production and exchange; feeds back upon
preferences; and affects efficiency,
the economy's adjustment capacity,
and growth potential. Economic
self-interest and voluntary
exchange describe only a portion of
economic reality; conflict, coercion,
and inequality of access to resources
and the struggle for power are at
least as fundamental. The economy
should then be seen as a set of complex, large organizations with multiple motives jockeying with one
another for power and economic
advantage.[16] Institutions are not
simply aggregates of individual
preferences or passive mechanisms
for the transmission of economic
impulses, but constitute a historically specific constraint and opportunity structure that implies an
enduring division of labor and rules
of play, that establishes distinctive
capacities and incapacities, and that

constrains the strategies any individual, economic agent, or political
authority can adopt to achieve its
aims.

This perspective draws specific
attention to how both degrees of concentration and centralized decision-
making—in industrial sectors, trade
associations, finance, or labor unions
—and the dominance-subordination
relationships among business, labor,
finance, and government may serve
as crucial intervening variables in
explaining economic outcomes.
Political-institutional analysis sees
the trend toward the organization of
economic interests to escape market
controls as secular, irreversible, and
implicit in the logic of industrialization, democratization, or capitalist
development. Such a structure of
organizations may subvert pure
market functioning, but a return to
a neoliberal world seems hardly
feasible. One implication is the need
for new forms of political control and
regulation or for arrangements
wherein economic organizations may
be induced to exercise self-restraint.

Among the factors that may help
explain the comparatively poor economic performance of the United
States, as well as the purported economic ineptitude of U.S. government intervention, are the following
four.[17]

15. For an influential statement, see
Peter J. Katzenstein, "Conclusion: Domestic
Structures and Strategies of Foreign Eco-
nomic Policy," in *Between Power and Plenty:
Foreign Economic Policies of Advanced
Industrial States,* ed. Peter J. Katzenstein
(Madison: University of Wisconsin Press,
1978), pp. 295-336.

16. John Zysman, *Political Strategies for
Industrial Order: State, Market and Industry
in France* (Berkeley: University of California
Press, 1977).

17. For some specific references, see John
Zysman, "Decline and Renewal: Industrial
Adjustment in Advanced Societies," unpublished manuscript; Zysman et al., "Financial
Markets and Industrial Policy" (unpublished); Robert Solo, *The Positive State,* chs.
8, 10; David Vogel, "Why Businessmen Distrust Their State: The Political Consciousness
of American Corporate Executives," *British
Journal of Political Science,* 8:45-78 (1975);
Mancur Olson, "The Political Economy of
Comparative Growth Rates," unpublished
manuscript; Hayes and Abernathy, "Managing Our Way to Economic Decline," *Harvard
Business Review* (July/Aug. 1980).

1. Structural Interrelationships Among Business, Finance, and Labor. Capital flows and capital availability to particular sectors or classes of firms may be constrained by the risk-avoidance strategies and propensities of institutional investors and by the separation of industrial and financial management, which institutionalizes a pawn-broker model of industry-finance relationship, rather than a venture capitalist model. The organization of the stock market may benefit financial insiders, stock manipulators, and speculators and may drain funds from productivefirms and discourage the healthy channeling of investment. Productivity may suffer where workers lack job security and responsibility and where labor-management relations are dominated by an insistence on managerial prerogatives and autonomy.

2. The Political Economic Organizational Fragmentation of Business and Finance. Fragmentation across associations of producers—firms, professionals, banks, and unions—may delay innovation and impede the reallocation of resources needed for growth. More encompassing organizational structures are able to internalize part of the external diseconomics of antigrowth policies. Insistence on firm autonomy and the weakness of trade associations results in a lack of corporate leadership and class consciousness and a neglect of the long-range interests of the business system.

3. The Organizational and Behavioral Characteristics of U.S. Corporations as They Affect Investment Strategies and Technological Innovation. The conglomerate corporate form and the preference for horizontal diversification may divert funds from long-range corporate productivity strategies. Managers displacing entrepreneurs and accountants replacing engineers in corporate recruitment strategies may lead to a fatal fascination with short-run profitability over long-term growth and to an emphasis on financial and marketing strategies over technological innovation. Corporations, as large organizations, have routinized planning in ways that downgrade technological innovation or militate against risky investments.

4. Economic Performance is Some Function of the Distribution of Forms of Economic Organization and Market Relationships Across Industries and Sectors, and the Extent to Which Government Policy Recognizes Their Distinctive Behavioral Characteristics.[18] The decentralized, market-directed form that corresponds to the world of neoclassical models organizes a relatively small proportion of production, distribution, and consumption. Decentralized market-segmented, organizational market-negotiated, and politically directed market forms are much more prevalent, and each has different propensities and problems with respect to the incidence and controllability of externalities, price instabilities, technological invention, and product and process innovation. These different behavioral patterns imply different regimes and methods of policy intervention to optimize economic performance: employment, price stability, productivity and the costs of externalities, and so on. To confront the diversity of market forms characteristic of any complex modern economy implies the politi-

18. Robert Solo, *Economic Organizations and Social Systems* (Indianapolis: Bobbs-Merrill, 1967); idem, *The Postive State*, ch. 8.

cal and organizational capacity to deploy a diversity of policy tools and to innovate in institutional design.

The state

Any given state is a complex organizational system, with distinctive relationships to groups seeking access to state power.[19] These mold the objectives political authorities seek as well as their ability to control or coordinate the various policy structures within the state. Policymakers do not have a free choice in the use of the instruments of policy. Some will be limited to indirect and global instruments to influence aggregate demand and the money supply, whereas others may also dispose of direct and selective instruments of intervention, influencing manpower skills, price and wage behavior, and industrial structure generally or by sector and region. As John Zysman notes, the state can intervene in the economy as regulator, administrator, or player.[20] The player state can enter the industrial life of companies and influence their strategies. To be a player the state must not only be organized to make specific discretionary decisions, but must also be linked to business via its influence over the financial system and the flow of credit.

Some political authorities will be able to coordinate the settings of several related policy instruments, whereas in other nations—like the United States—economic policy-making is fragmented into autonomous subgovernments in which part of the bureaucracy, associated legislative committees, and dominant client groups effectively control specific instruments and prevent coordinated or sustained policy.

Some other possible implications for economic performance include the following:

1. Industrial readjustment to rapidly changing technological and competitive conditions may be less costly both economically and politically if active state coordination is used to provide security guarantees and side-payments to affected parties.

2. The ability to maintain reasonable price stability and employment levels may depend on accepting the need for a permanent incomes policy implying the ability to integrate labor organizations into decision-making at firm, industry, and government policy levels.

3. Optimal investment and technological innovation may depend on the ability of government to influence or guide private investment decisions with more than general tax incentives or disincentives.

Group intermediation and interest representation

In each nation a distinctive set of sociocultural norms and established institutional relationships between the public and private spheres defines the limits of legitimacy and the standard modes of state intervention in the economy. Mediating groups and systems of tripartite, or corporatist, interest representation can serve as vital avenues of information flow, and as repositories of decision-making authority and leg-

19. Albert Stepan, *The State and Society* (New Haven: Yale University Press, 1978); Robert Solo, *The Positive State;* Frances Piven et al., "Governing Coalition and Precarious Resources: Structural Change in the State" (unpublished); Katzenstein, *Beyond Power and Plenty.*

20. John Zysman, *The State as Economic Player* (forthcoming).

itimation.[21] Equally important is the extent to which there is a measure of symmetricality of influence among the institutions of so-called civil society—for example, the extent to which labor's demands for recognition and organizational security are secured and cannot be unilaterally changed by either government or business.

Among the implications for economic performance are the following:

1. Interest-group vetoes and policy immobilism will be more important causes of policy incoherence where there is a legally and culturally sanctioned differentiation between the public and private sectors.

2. The adequacy of particular policy instruments and forms of intervention varies with changes in the balance of political forces as well as with changes in economic structure, suggesting that forms of political representation will influence the efficacy of different forms of intervention.

3. The distribution of economic resources, status rewards, societal legitimacy, and relative access to the policymaking process between business and labor may be so unequal as to constitute a permanent source of contraint on economic policy and performance.

CONCLUSION

What if research should confirm the shared perception of many political scientists and institutional economists that lagging industrial adaptation and stagnant economic development in the United States are closely linked to institutional and organizational characteristics of market actors, a weak state, and the absence of effective cultural and sociopolitical linkages between the state and civil society? If so, then the 1980s may reveal that paradigms serving the power needs and ideological predispositions of dominant elites in the United States may not hold the key to the puzzles of our declining economic performance. Andrew Shonfield made this point more than 15 years ago in *Modern Capitalism* when he linked our generally poor post-World War II economic performance to a political and ideological commitment to unreconstructed capitalism that produced consistently incompetent handling of business cycles. More recently political scientists David Vogel, Charles E. Lindblom, and David Cameron have traced economic performance problems to the ideological hegemony of a uniquely free and unconstrained capitalist class and to the privileged position of business.[22] One can only speculate about the political and ideological evolution that may be necessary to give political-institutional variants of political economy greater persuasiveness among policy intellectuals or policymakers.

21. For a general discussion, see essays in Philippe Schmitter and Gerhard Lehmbruch, *Trends Toward Corporatist Intermediation* (Beverly Hills, CA: Sage Publications, 1979).

22. David Vogel, "Why Businessmen Distrust Their State"; Charles E. Lindblom, *Politics and Markets;* David Cameron, "Does Government Cause Inflation? Taxes, Spending and Deficits," in *The Politics and Sociology of Global Inflation,* eds. Leon N. Lindberg and Charles S. Maier (forthcoming).

The Political-Structural Basis for Economic Performance

By J. ROGERS HOLLINGSWORTH

ABSTRACT: Focusing on France, Great Britain, Sweden, and the United States, this study attempts to answer two basic questions. First, how does one explain the variation across these countries in the organizational structure and the power of the working class? Second, for the period since 1950 how does variation in the organizational structure, the power of the working class, and the structure of the state influence such economic performances as inequality in the distribution of income and rates of change in economic productivity? Whereas the discipline of economics generally explains these performances with economic variables, this article is distinctive in demonstrating that political variables are also important. The findings indicate that the encompassing group structure of Swedish labor unions has maximized equality in income distribution and high rates of change in economic productivity while the fragmented and nonencompassing group structure of American labor has had the opposite effect. Sweden and the United States are polar opposites, with the British and French cases falling between the two extremes on most variables.

J. Rogers Hollingsworth is professor of history and chairperson of the Program in Comparative World History at the University of Wisconsin, Madison. His recent publications, research, and teaching have concentrated on the study of comparative public policy. He is presently involved in studying economic and social policies in Western Europe and the United States.

NOTE: The author gratefully acknowledges financial assistance for research for this article from the American Scandinavian Foundation.

THIS article is concerned with the way in which the political institutions of highly industrialized capitalist societies influence their economic performance. Specifically, the research focuses on the impact of political institutions on the distribution of income and changes in levels of economic productivity. This research does not confront the vast literature in economics that attempts to explain income distribution and levels of economic productivity. There are many variables that influence performance, and even though this study argues that the political institutions of countries influence the distribution of income and economic productivity, the intent of this study is not to put forth a monocausal explanation. Rather, its purpose is (1) to demonstrate that specific types of political-institutional arrangements constrain these particular types of economic performance and (2) to explain why these institutional arrangements vary across countries. It will be the task of another article to confront the question of whether the political explanation competes with those economists have already developed or can be integrated into the economics literature.

This article focuses on income equality and economic productivity, goals desired by an increasing share of the citizenry in all advanced industrial capitalist societies. Some social scientists characterize the basic political problem of a capitalist society as one of maintaining the legitimacy of the society's basic institutions by generating greater inequality while simultaneously facilitating further economic growth and productivity. Obviously, there is an inherent tension between

these two goals, and there has been substantial variation in the success with which countries have been able to maximize both goals simultaneously. The ability to maximize several economic performances simultaneously requires a political system with the capacity to develop coherent policies. But the ability of political institutions to implement coherent policies is not simply due to the fact that they may have leaders who are highly intelligent, very well educated, and sensitive to their countries' historical trends. Rather, the ability of a society to implement coherence in public affairs reflects the basic social, economic, and political structures of that country.

Demonstrating how variation in the evolution and structure of interest groups impacts on economic performance, this study attempts to validate the following hypotheses, which are derived from political science, political sociology, and economics.[1]

1. For example, see Theodore J. Lowi, *The End of Liberalism: Ideology, Policy and the Crisis of Public Authority* (New York: Norton, 1969); Kwang Choi, "The Political Economy of Comparative Growth Rates" (Ph.D. diss., University of Maryland, 1979); idem, "A Statistical Test of the Political Economy of Comparative Growth Rates Model" (Paper delivered at the Eastern Economic Association, May 10-12, 1979); Grant McConnell, *Private Power and American Democracy* (New York: Knopf, 1966); Robert J. Lieber, "Interest Groups and Political Integration: British Entry into Europe," in *Pressure Groups in Britain*, eds. Richard Kimber and J. J. Richardson (London: Dent, 1974); Robert Hanneman, "Long-Run Changes in Economic Inequality in Britain, France, and Germany, 1850 to 1970: A Political-Sociological Explanation" (Ph.D. diss., University of Wisconsin, 1979). The following paper by Mancur Olson was especially helpful and explicitly contains several of these hypotheses: "The Political Economy of Comparative Growth Rates," in *U.S. Economic Growth from 1976 to 1986: Prospects, Problems, and Patterns, Studies Prepared for the*

1. During the early stages of industrialization, organized interest groups in most societies are poorly developed and do not greatly impede the flow of capital and labor from one sector of the economy to another. As a result, the potential for high rates of economic growth and productivity is higher than would otherwise be the case.

With lower-income groups poorly organized, income distribution is more highly skewed in favor of the top-income deciles than would be the case were lower-income groups highly organized and in possession of considerable political power.

2. Narrowly based interest groups that do not control a sizable share of the society's resources will have an adverse net effect on the rate of economic productivity and growth by limiting the movement of resources. Examples of narrow-based interest groups are manufacturers' associations, professional associations, labor unions, and cartels. Narrow-based interest groups lead to the repression of labor-saving innovations, featherbedding, fair trade laws, monopolies, and tax loopholes, most of which tend to hold resources in inefficient use and to rob societies of output, thus constraining productivity.

3. There is an inherent logic to the number and density of narrowly based interest groups. The longer the period in which a region or a country has had an industrial economy, the more numerous and dense the narrow-based interest groups—unless the society has suffered from political instability, totalitarian governments, and outside invasions, which tend to limit the density and

Use of the Joint Economic Committee, Congress of the United States (Washington, DC: U.S. Government Printing Office, 1976).

number of organized interest groups. The more numerous and dense the narrowly based groups, the greater the negative effects on the level of economic productivity.

4. The more numerous and dense the highly organized interest groups in a fragmented and decentralized political system, the more they supplant the power of political parties and government, place constraints on the mobility of labor and capital, build rigidities into the economy, slow down economic growth and productivity, generate inflationary pressures, and prevent the implementation of coherent economic policies. A derivative hypothesis is as follows: a highly centralized political system with little fragmentation will better be able to contain the negative economic effects of numerous small but well-organized interest groups and will be in a better position to engage in the formulation and the implementation of a coherent macroeconomic policy.

5. Highly encompassing organizations will pursue policies that are less restrictive than those pursued by narrow-based interest groups. Highly encompassing interest groups, those which have a large percentage of the society's population, will propose policies that tend to be consistent with the common interests of the society, policies that promote high rates of growth and productivity, relatively high levels of income equality, and low rates of unemployment.

6. The more successful the working class is in mobilizing political power in highly industrialized societies, the more coherence there is in implementing policies that promote both equality of income distribution and increases in economic productivity. While the relationship

TABLE 1
PERCENTAGE OF LABOR FORCE WHO WERE LABOR UNION MEMBERS

COUNTRY	PERCENTAGE UNIONIZED			
	1940	1950	1960	1970
Sweden	35	52	61	75
Great Britain	33	44	44	45
United States	13	22	22	23
France	26	22	14	17

NOTE: The author thanks Robert Hanneman, Wilmot James, and Michael Shalev for assistance in compiling these data.

between working-class power and income equality tends to be linear, the relationship between increases in working-class power and increases in economic growth and productivity is not linear. Only after the working class has mobilized power beyond a certain threshold can it coherently pursue both. If 40 percent or less of the working class are organized into unions— especially if the unions are fragmented into numerous groups— there will be no positive effects on increases in levels of productivity.

To test these hypotheses, the research focuses on Great Britain, France, Sweden, and the United States during the years between 1950 and 1975. This article will demonstrate not only how group structure has impacted on economic performance during these years, but also why there is variability in group structure in these four countries.

An effective measure of the power of the working class is the percentage of the labor force that is organized into unions. Table 1, which provides data on the percentage of the labor force that was organized in the four countries between 1940 and 1970, reveals that 75 percent of the Swedish labor force was organized

into unions in 1970, 45 percent in Britain, 23 percent in the United States, and 17 percent in France. And between 1945 and 1969, Social Democratic or Socialist parties were in the executive branch of government 100 percent of the time in Sweden, 50 percent in Britain, 25 percent in France, and not at all in the United States. Clearly, the working class was more successful in mobilizing its power in Sweden and Britain than in France and the United States.

Table 2 ranks the four countries on rates of change in economic productivity for the years between 1950 and 1975. The United States and Great Britain had the lowest rates of change, while France and Sweden substantially outperformed the Anglo-American countries. Sweden's rate of change was higher than that of the other three countries, more than twice as high as that of the United States. While Great Britain has had one of the most unimpressive rates of economic growth in Western Europe since World War II, it nevertheless had an increase in productivity more than 75 percent higher than the United States during the years 1967 and 1975. Sweden is the only one of the four countries that had both high levels in the rate

TABLE 2
ECONOMIC PRODUCTIVITY: OUTPUT PER EMPLOYEE-HOUR IN MANUFACTURING
IN 1950-75 (average annual percentage change)

COUNTRY	OUTPUT PER EMPLOYEE HOUR		
	1950-75	1950-67	1967-75
Sweden	5.2	4.9	5.7
France	4.8	4.9	4.6
Great Britain	3.1	3.0	3.2
United States	2.5	2.7	1.8

SOURCE: U.S. Department of Labor, Bureau of Labor Statistics, *Productivity and the Economy* (Washington, DC: U.S. Government Printing Office, 1977), p. 98.

of change in productivity and relatively high equality in the distribution of income.

In Table 3, whether the data are analyzed with Gini coefficients or an Atkinson index, whether the unit of analysis is for individuals or standardized by households, and whether one analyzes the data on a pre-tax or post-tax basis, Sweden is the country that has the most egalitarian distribution of income, followed by the United Kingdom, the United States, and France. These three tables are summarized in Figure 1, which also describes the interest-group structure in each country. The remainder of this article is concerned with presenting, country by country, a historical-structural explanation for the economic performance measures already described.

SWEDEN

Because of its success in maximizing both an egalitarian distribution of income and high rates of change in productivity, Sweden is the archetype with which the other countries will be compared.[2] The

2. The following materials on Sweden have been very useful: Walter Korpi, *The Working Class in Welfare Capitalism: Work,*

explanation for the performance of the Swedish economy on the two dependent variables is diagrammed in Figure 2. The diagram attempts to explain why Sweden has encompassing groups that have attained a strategic position to dominate the country's political institutions, focusing on the critical variables of the timing and the speed with which the country industrialized, its size in population and area, and the extent to which it has had a history of linguistic, religious, and social cleavage.

Not only did Sweden industrialize late, but it is a small, ethnically and linguistically homogeneous Protestant country. Sweden's indus-

Unions, and Politics in Sweden (London: Routledge & Kegan Paul, 1978); Richard Scase, *Social Democracy in Capitalist Society* (London: Croom Helm, 1977); idem, ed. *Readings in Swedish Class Structure* (London: Pergamon Press, 1976); Andrew Martin, "Labor Movement Parties and Inflation: Contrasting Responses in Britain and Sweden" *Policy,* 7:427-451; idem, "Sweden: Industrial Democracy and Social Democratic Strategy," in *Worker Self Management in Industry: The Western European Experience,* ed. G. David Carson (New York: Praeger, 1976); idem, "The Dynamics of Change in a Keynesian Political Economy: The Swedish Case and Its Implications," in *State and Economy in Contemporary Capitalism,* ed. Colin Crouch (New York: St. Martin's Press, 1979); John D. Stephens, *The Transition from Capitalism to Socialism* (New York: Macmillan, 1979).

TABLE 3
MEASURES OF INEQUALITY IN INCOME

		PRE-TAX			POST-TAX		
		INDIVIDUAL		INDIVIDUAL		HOUSE SIZE	
	YEAR	GINI	ATKINSON*	GINI	ATKINSON*	GINI	ATKINSON
Sweden	1972	.342	.097	.302	.077	.271	.063
United Kingdom	1973	.344	.098	.318	.083	.327	.088
United States	1972	.404	.138	.381	.122	.369	.113
France	1970	.416	.142	.414	.141	.417	.143

SOURCE: *Income Distribution in OECD Countries* (OECD Occasional Papers, July 1976).
*e = 0.5.

trialization developed in a nonurban setting, based largely on iron and timber. Unlike Britain and Germany, Sweden had neither a large landowning class nor a sizable urban artisan class. Sweden's industry developed with a high degree of product specialization and centralization, with an economy dominated by a small number of relatively noncompeting employers. In the context of rapid industrialization with a high degree of capital concentration, a small artisan class, and a small middle class, Sweden's working class tended to organize but into industrial unions. The small number of large firms that dominated the Swedish economy facilitated centralized employers' organizations and the highly centralized economy encouraged centralized labor organizations. And these two highly centralized systems ultimately made possible economy-wide bargaining. The fact that the working class was given the right to participate in electoral politics only at a very late date made it very politically conscious, somewhat in contrast to the British and American cases, where the participation problems were solved at an earlier stage.

When a Social Democratic party emerged in Sweden, unlike those of most European countries, it was highly integrated with the working-class labor unions. Secure with a large working-class base—and this is critical—the Swedish Social Democratic party did not have to make serious compromises with center parties in order to gain power. With its cohesive power, Sweden's Social Democratic party was ultimately able to demand and get from the state extensive welfare services, which included pensions, unemployment insurance, national health care, housing, and family subsidies. This has permitted Sweden to have one of the best-developed and most progressively financed welfare states in the world.

But contrary to popular assumptions, the most significant aspect of the Swedish welfare state is not its consumption and governmental transfer policies. Rather, it is the development of a comprehensive and very coherent labor market and wage policy aimed at reducing the inflation-unemployment tradeoff, while simultaneously equalizing income distribution and generating high rates of change in economic productivity.

The leaders of the LO (the Confederation of Trade Unions or Landsorganization) and the Swedish

FIGURE 1
CLASSIFICATION OF COUNTRIES BY ECONOMIC PERFORMANCE

		LOW	HIGH
INCREASES IN ECONOMIC PRODUCTIVITY	LOW	UNITED STATES Many narrow-based interest groups, with labor poorly organized in a fragmented, decentralized, weak state.	GREAT BRITAIN Many narrow-based interest groups, though labor has a moderately high level of organization. The state is relatively weak but has a fairly high level of centralization.
	HIGH	FRANCE Relatively few narrow-based interest groups, with labor poorly organized. Highly centralized and strong state.	SWEDEN Highly encompassing groups, with labor highly organized. Highly centralized and strong state.

Social Democratic party recognized around 1950—much earlier than in other Western democracies—that fiscal and monetary tools were not adequate to maintain economic expansion and high unemployment without inflation. Sweden in the early 1930s under Social Democratic leadership had been the first country to implement a Keynesian-type policy for generating aggregate demand. By the 1950s, however, when there was finally emerging a political consensus in the United States to the effect that monetary and fiscal policies were "necessary tools" for the conduct of macroeconomic policy, the Swedish Social Democratic party recognized what even Keynes had acknowledged: the management of aggregate demand by fiscal and monetary policy was not an adequate tool for coping with the problems of a capitalist economy over the long run. Similarly, with regard to incomes policies, the Swedes had already discovered as early as the 1940s and the early 1950s that wage freezes and wage controls were artificial and unworkable ways of repressing inflationary pressures.

Significantly, the Swedes understood the implications of Keynes even better than most Western economists who labeled themselves Keynesians. Keynes in the last part of *The General Theory of Employment, Interest, and Money* recognized that in the long run a comprehensive socialization of investment would prove the only means of securing an approximation of full employment. By the early 1950s, the Swedish Social Democrats realized that some significant institutional change would ultimately be necessary in order to maintain full employment, that a new stage of capitalism would by necessity eventually emerge, whereby there must be a socialization of investment capital.

The Swedes have been able to recognize the inadequacies of certain macroeconomic policies and to develop new institutional mechanisms for managing an economy earlier than their counterparts in other advanced industrial capitalist societies. Sweden has been able to do this, for it has a less complex economy, it is a smaller country, and its leaders have had sufficient power to generate innovative policies that are considerably coherent. On the other hand, larger countries with more complex economies and more frag-

FIGURE 2
VARIABLES INFLUENCING SWEDEN'S INCOME INEQUALITY

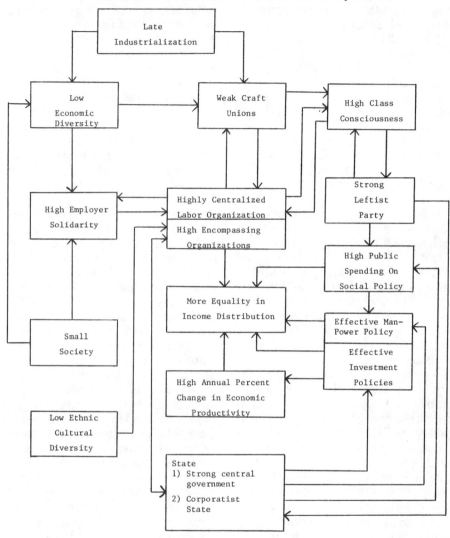

NOTE: The relationship among all variables in this diagram is positive.

mented political structures have not had the ability to generate, implement, and evaluate complicated and coherent macroeconomic policies.

The problem for Sweden was how to carry out policies in which full employment, a high level of income distribution, and a highly efficient economy were given equal priority. Sweden's Social Democratic leadership decided in the early 1950s that the task of maintaining economic expansion, low unemployment, and income equality without stimulating inflation required economic structural change. With fiscal policy and trade union wage pressure, they would squeeze the profits of weak and inefficient firms. In their bargaining, the LO would demand equal pay for equal work across the economy, regardless of the ability of a company to pay. This policy, known as the wage policy of solidarity, would obviously drive down the profits of weak and inefficient firms and force them out of business. The workers released from these companies were provided alternative jobs through an active labor market policy consisting of job retraining, unemployment moving costs, and extensive information on employment possibilities and public work jobs. The strategy was to reduce structural unemployment and to shift workers to high productivity and high wage sectors—to upgrade average wages and the overall productivity of the Swedish economy while reducing the inflationary impact of high employment. It is important to note that manpower policy rather than wage restraint became the basic means of dealing with the unemployment-inflation problem. With its high level of centralization, the LO has negotiated wage agreements with the even more highly centralized employers' federation, the SAF, a process unthinkable without a high level of centralization on the part of both negotiating parties.

Both before and after World War II, the Swedish Social Democrats adopted the view that state planning and cooperation with the business community were necessary in order to bring about the necessary structural changes to achieve the "maturation of capitalism." However, the Social Democrats believed that to achieve their goal of an efficient economy, not all investment decisions should remain in the private sector. To promote some socialization of investment, they resorted to a vast pension program under quasi-public control, with funds used to channel investment to selected target areas.

The attempts of the state to maximize investments that steer capital investment away from stagnant sectors in order to stimulate economic expansion, high employment, and income equality, have made Sweden's economic performance impressive. In certain respects, the state's manpower policy and managed pension fund are the crux of Sweden's welfare policy. Control over vast investment resources has allowed the state to engage in selective investment designed to enhance continued economic growth.

The convergence of interests of trade unions, the Social Democratic party, and big business led to programs that have satisfied the short-term interest of the trade unions and the short- and long-term interests of Sweden's large industrial corporations. As smaller and less productive firms have been forced out of business, the concentration of private economic power has increased, making Sweden the country with the most concentrated capital among the world's highly industrialized societies. These policies have been relatively successful in counteracting recessions in business cycles and in making Swedish industry more competitive in the world marketplace. The consequence has been substantial economic growth, low unemployment, and low income inequality, resulting in one of the higher standards of living in the world, if not the highest. Swedish policymakers have not only been innovative with policy proposals, but they have been fortunate in having the political power to develop and implement coherent macroeconomic policies.

FRANCE

Why are France's particular governmental economic policies so different from Sweden's? Primarily, this is because the social and economic institutions of France have placed limits on the mobilization of working-class power, which in turn has set real constraints on the structure of the state and its policies. Unlike Sweden, which industrialized rapidly, France's process of industrialization has been a long one.[3] By the end of World War II, at least one-third of the French population still depended on the land for their existence. France's agricultural population was not a landless, proletarian one; it was a property-owning peasantry with distinct conservative values. The rural character of the population did much to preserve cultural and linguistic diversity in the country, and

3. The following materials on France have been helpful: Stanley Hoffman et al., *In Search of France* (New York: Harper & Row, 1963); Jean Blondel, *Contemporary France: Politics, Society, and Institutions* (London: Methuen, 1974); H. W. Ehrmann, *France* (Boston: Little, Brown, 1968); Jack Barbash, *Trade Unions and National Economic Policy in Western Europe and the United States* (Madison: University of Wisconsin Press, 1970); D. W. Brogan, *The Development of Modern France* (London: Hamilton, 1940); Val Lorwin, *The French Labor Movement* (Cambridge: Harvard University Press, 1968); John D. Stephens, *The Transition from Capitalism to Socialism;* Ezra N. Suleiman, *Politics, Power and Bureaucracy in France* (Princeton, NJ: Princeton University Press, 1974); idem, *Elites in French Society* (Princeton, NJ: Princeton University Press, 1978).

this cultural diversity has worked to retard the mobilization of working-class power.

The cultural diversity and the slow industrialization process of France are reflected in economic structures very different from the highly centralized and less complex economy of Sweden. While France has historically had a few large, dynamic business enterprises, the economy until World War II was dominated by small businesses, especially family-operated ones, with archaic and paternalistic labor relations. Until recent years, the overwhelming majority of French employers refused to recognize unions or to enter into negotiations with employees, and this has led to a great deal of radicalism among some French employees.

It is here that the Church comes into play. As many studies have demonstrated, the Protestant Reformation left a permanent stamp on the political life of Europe, in that religious issues have been reflected in working-class politics. Socialist or leftist parties and labor unions have had to compete with the Catholic-dominated parties and unions, thus creating a fragmented working class. Many workers from very religious backgrounds have accepted Catholic unions, meaning that the French working class has long been divided between the Communist and Socialist left and a smaller segment of the Catholic moderates.

Among the more industrialized countries of the West, France has one of the smallest percentages of its labor force as union members—approximately 17 percent in 1970. Unlike Swedish labor, French labor is made up of weak confederations that are also divided by region and industries. The French unions have few strike funds because dues are very low. Most French people, as part of their peasant- and family-dominated recent past, have remained deeply suspicious not only of the state and the government, but also of labor union leaders.

It is the fragmentation and weak mobilization of working-class power that is an important factor in differentiating French social and economic policies from those in Sweden or even Britain. At crisis points, the French Left has taken power and has instituted welfare statist reforms—for example, the short-lived Popular Front period during the 1930s and the period immediately following World War II. Both periods were characterized by Socialist-Communist cooperation in the government, along with temporary increases in the level of trade union membership; but there were no permanent gains for the labor movement.

Moreover, France has long had a communication gap between its partisan political elite and the state bureaucratic apparatus, so that when the Left has been able to mobilize political power, it has had great difficulty in implementing its policies. The French governmental bureaucracy has long had close established contacts with the elites in large business establishments, who shared similar backgrounds, especially in education. Organized labor, small business, party leaders, and even cabinet ministers have failed to be effective forces in shaping social policy in the face of a highly institutionalized, independent, and often inflexible power structure consisting of top-level bureaucrats and economic elites. In sum, the situation in France is a good example of what happens when social policies are created by Social-

ists in coalition with other parties but are administered by conservative forces for long periods of time. An important consequence of this type of structure has been a very regressive tax system and widespread tax evasion. Several studies indicate that the French state is so regressively financed that its social policies have redistributive biases toward upper-income groups. In sum, the basic social and institutional structures of French society have been responsible for its high degree of inequality.

But these and other French institutional arrangements are also responsible for the high rates of change in industrial productivity that France has attained in the postwar period. The elite within the French bureaucracy has been the key factor in shaping the policies that have resulted in high rates of economic growth and productivity. Relatively insulated from pressure groups and Parliament and unable to reach into the most remote corners of society, the French bureaucracy has had the power to develop unified and coherent policies for shaping growth in the French economy. Obviously, the French state is not omnipotent in the economy, but through the nationalized banks, the Banque de France, and such state institutions as Credit National, the state has been able to play an extremely important role in shaping coherent investment decisions.

Centralized state planning has acquired a relatively high level of legitimacy and has been able to guide high productivity because of the deeply ingrained antimarket tradition that fears the so-called waste of competition and prefers to mobilize and allocate economic resources through close cooperation between public and private sectors at a centralized level. Moreover, the elite structure of the state bureaucracy and the largest business firms are not highly differentiated. Not only have most of the top elites in the state bureaucracy and the largest business establishments attended the same grandes écoles, but the very top graduates of certain grandes écoles are recruited into a elite institution known as the Grands Crops. A unique institution, the Grands Corps has promoted close cohesion of French elites in all sectors of the society. It has led to a small elite structure that is highly centralized, closed, cohesive, and fundamentally conservative.

The key to understanding the success of French economic planning is the symbiotic relationship between the elites in the state administrative machinery and the large firms: the same type of person manages both. There is a homogeneity in the educational and professional backgrounds of the French elite. As a result, the type of hostility between the public and private sectors that is still strong in Britain and the United States is a thing of the past in France.

Just as members of the French administrative elite have attempted to concentrate political and administrative power, they have, in the postwar period, also promoted the concentration of capital in the private sector through mergers. Indeed, France, largely due to government prompting, has had the highest rate of mergers and has developed one of the most centralized economies in Western Europe. And the more that mergers have occurred, the closer the ties between big business and the state have become. It is the concentration of both economic and political power

that has permitted the French to engage in systematic and efficient planning.

France resembles Sweden in that both countries have carried out extensive planning in developing and implementing social and economic policies. But unlike the Swedes, the French have not had a planning process that is very democratic. Because the French bureaucracy enjoys considerable independence and autonomy from political parties, the French planning process often resembles an elitist conspiracy carried out in the public interest. But unlike the Swedes, the French have not achieved equality and high levels of economic productivity simultaneously. The French bureaucrats have opted for sustained economic growth and have been extraordinarily successful in achieving it, but have a rather poor performance in developing policies designed to achieve a more equitable distribution of income.

GREAT BRITAIN

Great Britain, of course, falls between the cases of Sweden and France in terms of the mobilization of working-class power.[4] It is partly

4. For further elaboration on some of the British materials, see Martin, "Labor Movement Parties and Inflation"; J. L. Nicholson, "The Distribution and Redistribution of Income in the United Kingdom," in *Poverty, Inequality, and Class Structure*, ed. Dorothy Wetterburn (London: Cox & Wyman, 1974); Stephen Blank, "Britain: The Politics of Foreign Economic Policy, the Domestic Economy, and the Problem of Pluralistic Stagnation," in *Between Power and Plenty*, ed. Peter J. Katzenstein (Madison: University of Wisconsin Press, 1978); S. H. Beer, *Modern British Politics* (London: Faber & Faber, 1965); Colin Crouch, *The Politics of Industrial Relations* (Manchester: Manchester University Press).

for that reason that social and economic policies are less coherent in Britain than in Sweden. It is also for that reason that Britain has achieved less income equality than Sweden, but has achieved greater income equality than France or the United States.

The explanation is again a complicated, historical one. First, in contrast with Sweden, Britain is a larger country, the concentration of capital has been lower, the structure of the economy has been more diversified, and industrial production has been less specialized. Second, Britain industrialized before any other nation and developed at a moderate pace. In light of these considerations, structural conditions that have placed constraints on policy coherence may be explained.

The pattern of industrialization in Britain led to the initial development of strong craft unions. Unlike the situation in Sweden, the lag between the era of union organizing and the final development of a leftist party—the Labour party—was very long, perhaps due to the relative openness of the British political system. The suffrage extensions in 1867 and 1883 and the strength of craft unions meant that working-class political participation was more liberal- than socialist-oriented. It was not until 1918 that the Labour party adopted even a very moderate socialist stance.

Because Britain is larger and has a longer tradition of craft unions than Sweden, Britain has had a less centralized trade union movement and a more fragmented working class than Sweden. At the beginning of the 1970s, there were over 500 different labor unions in Britain. Faced with the best-organized conservative party in any capitalist democracy, the British Labour party has had much more difficulty retaining the allegiance of union members. If the British Labour party had the same level of support among skilled, semi-skilled, and unskilled workers as the Swedish Social Democratic party has had since the mid-1920s, Labour would have won every election since the twenties. With these considerations in mind, one can understand why the Labour party has had much less coherence in its policies and has behaved differently from Sweden's Social Democratic party.

Time after time, the Labour party in Britain has generated rhetoric acceptable to its followers, but has attempted to carry out programs demanded by their opponents. This does not mean that there have been no differences between the two parties. There is considerable evidence that when the Conservatives have been in power, sizable elements within the party have been prepared to slow down the expansion of welfare services, to make the tax system less progressive, to introduce user fees if public services were free, and to introduce a means test for a number of unrestricted services.

In Britain, as in America, the tendency of the two major parties to converge toward the center has severely restricted the element of political choice. Britain has had party competition without product differentiation. As a result, the case for innovative and coherent policymaking in Britain goes begging. Britain in the 1960s and the 1970s has been unable to deal with the same basic crisis: the problem of modernizing the economy, renewing the industrial infrastructure in depressed regions, providing a more dynamic economic leadership, and increasing rates of productivity.

Another reason the British have had difficulty in developing and implementing coherence in macroeconomic policy is that the business community has long been very fragmented and decentralized. The potential for effective economic planning is greatly enhanced when a centralized governmental sector can work with a highly centralized business sector. But in contrast with the highly centralized business community of Sweden, the British business community has been much more diversified and decentralized. In contrast with that of France, there is poor cohesion between the administrative and business elites, meaning that the two British sectors are quite differentiated and that there is poor communication between them.

In contrast with the French and Swedish systems, the British system is an example of a parliamentary democracy that industrialized over a long period of time and that demonstrated a policy preference for low industrial concentration, few restrictions on economic competition, and strategies for noninterference and laissez-faire in the economy. Whereas the French administrative and business elite have emerged from a strong antimarket tradition, the British elite are products of a system that has long had a tendency to assume that market economics contains all the theoretical principles one needs. The British, with their more fragmented and decentralized economy, have tended to rely on the more traditional tools of managing aggregate demand.

THE UNITED STATES

Also in contrast with Sweden, American society has a low level of labor organization, an extremely large and complicated economy, and low coherence in its social and economic policies. More important for understanding the different roles of government in influencing economic performance, the American political system is very large, fragmented, and decentralized.[5] On almost every variable in Figure 2, the United States is at the opposite end of the continuum from Sweden. The result is an American economy with high levels of unemployment, sagging levels of productivity, high levels of inequality, and low rates of economic growth.

The United States is a large, ethnically diverse country that industrialized at a pace greater than that of Britain but less than Sweden. Because the political system at the time of industrialization was more open than in Britain or Sweden, a unified, leftist labor party did not develop in America. Instead of creating its own party, the American labor movement has tried to

5. For further elaboration of the perspective developed herein for the United States, see J. Rogers Hollingsworth, "Political Development in the United States," in *Crises of Political Development in Europe and the United States*, ed. Raymond Grew (Princeton, NJ: Princeton University Press, 1978), pp. 163-95; Walter D. Burnham, *Critical Elections and the Mainsprings of American Politics* (New York: Norton, 1970); Lowi, *The Decline of Liberalism;* Edward R. Tufte, *Political Control of the Economy* (Princeton, NJ: Princeton University Press, 1978); Douglas A. Hibbs, "Political Parties and Macroeconomic Policy," *American Political Science Review*, 71:1467-87; Andrew Martin, *The Politics of Economic Policy in the United States: A Tentative View from a Comparative Perspective* (Beverly Hills, CA: Sage Publications, 1973).

influence and mobilize support for the more leftist of the two major parties. The ethnic diversity of America fragmented and divided the labor movement, reduced the power of labor, but ultimately facilitated the narrow-based interests of the American Federation of Labor (AFL).

In general, American political parties, especially at the national level, have not had the discipline and the organization to formulate a social program in the interests of any major group, primarily because the party structure has been a coalition of local groups with a social basis varying from constituency to constituency. The labor movement, dominated by craft unions with little sense of potential mobilization, did not agree on social policy. Here and there, working-class groups achieved success at the local or state level, but historically American labor has developed few coherent policies at the national level.

Unlike the Swedish party system, American political parties have tended to mirror all of the contradictory forces in American society, causing party elites to engage in constant compromises to hold the parties together. As a result, neither of the two major parties has been very successful in developing coherent policies for solving the nation's problems. Third parties, which tend to be programmatic with coherent policies, have been dismal failures in American history. As no single segment or group in American society has completely dominated either of the two major political parties, critical choices about American society have been made outside the party structure. Powerfully organized economic interests have been able to play a major role in shaping economic and social policies in the United States, for they have tended to exert power through their economic domination in the market rather than through political domination of the party system.

Against this background, it is hardly surprising that some of the more important economic policy proposals of organized labor have met with little success. Organized labor, which has been weakly organized by Scandinavian standards, has not been able to get a comprehensive pension or a national health insurance program, even with Democratic administrations.

It is true that the working class has been attracted more to the Democratic than to the Republican party during most of the last half century. But the Democratic party is not a working-class party in the sense that the Swedish Social Democratic party is or even the British Labour party. The Democratic party has been a fragmented, loose coalition for arranging compromises among its different interests. Thus there has been little coherence to the formation of public policy by American political parties. Of course, the sheer size of the country and its decentralized federal system have also contributed to the lack of consistency and coherence in party policies. It has been the failure of the Right or the Left to dominate social and economic policy that explains the constant contradictions and the inconsistencies in American economic policies.

The size, the diversity, and the complexity of American society are all important reasons that political decisions represent momentary compromises, or appear to be chaotic and contradictory, whereas the Swedes, with their homogeneity and much smaller scale, can afford to be more consistent, more global, and much more macroeconomic in their policy concerns.

One might observe the meaning of these contrasts by reflecting on how different the U.S. response has been to manpower policy. American trade unions have devoted much less concern to long-term structural problems than their Swedish counterparts. Instead, Americans have tended to deal with many manpower policy issues by emphasizing the mismatch between different qualities and skills of labor and the willingness of people to supply labor effort in complementary proportions. Unemployment is attributed to the desires and motivations of the individuals clashing with available work opportunities. Americans and Britons are increasingly told that in order to lower unemployment there must be some dismantlement of the welfare-state apparatus. The public is informed that minimum-wage laws, unemployment insurance programs, and income maintenance programs create and support an artificially high wage structure that over the long run compresses the share of profits, reduces investment, lowers productivity, and cuts down the potential for jobs. Thus the emphasis in manpower policy is quite dissimilar to that of the Swedish programs.

Because of the large, diverse, fragmented, and decentralized structure of the American political system, the state has not been able to engage in the same type of formalized economic planning activity that has been possible in some of the more centralized capitalist societies since 1945. Nor has the state been able to place effective controls on investment decisions. As a result, billions of dollars flow out of the country, and a lack of investment capital hinders productivity increases. Whereas the British and American governments still attempt to conduct macroeconomic policy by engaging in the short-term incremental management of demand—that is, altering the relationships among large aggregates by means of the control of credit, levels of government spending and taxation, and so on—the more centralized governments of France and Sweden have been able to mobilize sufficient power to shape supply-type decisions.

The American effort to engage in the short-term incremental management of demand, however, has not been one with much coherence to it. Much of the macroeconomic policy shaped by Washington has resulted in a political business cycle, with economic policies made by presidential administrations eager to receive favorable responses at the ballot box. Herbert Stein, in a detailed study of fiscal policy in twentieth-century America, argues that one of the major explanations for public decisions in American macroeconomic policies is whether the choice was made in an election year or not.[6] For example, every administration between 1945 and 1976 attempted to manipulate the short-term course of the economy in order to improve its political party's standing in the next election.

While a major assumption of modern economic stabilization theory is that macroeconomic fluctuations are the result of economic market behaviors, the historical evidence demonstrates that there has been a systematic relationship

6. Herbert Stein, *The Fiscal Revolution in America* (Chicago: University of Chicago Press, 1969).

between macroeconomic policy and American electoral politics since World War II. The result has been in contrast with some of the more centralized states of Europe: macroeconomic policies lacking in coherence, policies that over the long term are inflationary, and policies that have been poorly designed to improve levels of productivity and to develop a more efficient use of the nation's labor resources.

CONCLUDING OBSERVATIONS

Each of these four countries has a distinctly different style in its approach to economic policies. By undertaking a comparative and historical analysis, however, it has been possible to discern configurations and patterns of behavior that an analysis of only one country would not have permitted. The advantage of comparative analysis is that it permits one to identify systematic patterns of behavior among structural variables. As a result of the analysis, it is now possible to develop four propositions about the relationships among working-class power, centralization of the state and the economy, and the economic performance variables of income distribution and change in the levels of productivity. They are as follow:

—If there is high working-class power in a society with a centralized state and with a centralized economy, there is likely to be low inequality in the distribution of income and high increases in productivity, as in Sweden and Norway.

—If there is weak working-class power in a society with a centralized state and with a centralized economy, there is likely to be high inequality in the distribution of income and high increases in productivity, as in France and Japan.

—If there is high working-class power in a society with a centralized state and with a decentralized economy, there is likely to be low equality in the distribution of income and low increases in productivity, as in Great Britain.

—If there is a weak working-class power in a society with a decentralized state and with a decentralized economy, there is likely to be high inequality in the distribution of income and low increases in productivity, as in the United States and Canada.

The reader should understand that these propositions are intended to apply only to advanced industrial capitalist societies.

Thus far, the emphasis has been on variations across the four countries. However, one should not lose sight of their similarities. While there are still vast differences in Europe and North America in political, social, and economic structures, as well as differences on all types of indicators concerning the quality of life, the variation has narrowed during the twentieth century. Political, social, and economic structures have become more similar, as have many policy outcomes. These societies are facing more similar problems, and citizens across societies increasingly have similar expectations.

Partly as a result, each state is now confronted with serious social, economic, and fiscal problems. For more than 25 years, each state of Western Europe and North America has had public expenditures rising far more rapidly than its gross national product. There is increasing evidence that the electorates on both sides of the Atlantic are becoming disenchanted with the performance of political elites. Under these circumstances, there has been pressure for governments to emphasize short-term considerations instead of the medium or long-term interests of their economies.

But even if the problems these countries are facing are quite similar, one should expect variation in the ability of governments to cope with the problems inherent in Western capitalism. Those societies, such as Sweden and France, that have strong centralized states are likely to have the capacity to mobilize the power necessary to develop and implement the policies necessary to deal with the present crisis. On the other hand, those societies whose political institutions are primarily products of a particular brand of modern liberalism—the United States and Great Britain—are likely to adjust less well to their present economic difficulties. In these societies, there is an absence of powerful public authority sufficient to contain the escalating entitlement claims. Unlike the Swedes and the French, the British and American states must operate within the constraints inherent in individualistic and market-oriented philosophies. To manage the capitalist economies in these states, political decision makers rely heavily on the use of disincentives—taxes—and incentives—subsidies, tax allowances, and so on. If the past is a guide to the future, no group in Britain or in the United States is likely to dominate the incentive and disincentive system during the next quarter of a century, with resulting policy incoherence. In short, these two systems are not well equipped to deal with the impending problems facing Western capitalism.

At the very time that Western societies are losing confidence in the ability of governments to manage short-term events, the necessity increases for government to become even more involved in the affairs of society and to engage in long-term management of the economy. In some respects, governments have less room and less time to maneuver in dealing with economic affairs than did their predecessors, due in part to the tight interrelationships among the community of nations, to the fact that national boundaries are more permeable by international shocks, and to the loss of economic autonomy of nation-states. More than ever before, a high degree of responsiveness, skill, and policy coherence is needed to coordinate the complexities confronting the world system of states, and those states that are lacking in the capability of responding with coherence in their approach to the future are not likely to deal well with their economic and social problems.

ANNALS, *AAPSS*, 459, January 1982

On the Limits of the Public Economy

By DAVID R. CAMERON

ABSTRACT: This article examines the validity of the assertion that low growth, high unemployment, and increasing inflation were all produced by excessively high levels and large increases in public spending. The article presents a systematic analysis of the relationships among 19 nations between increases in spending and lower rates of economic growth, higher unemployment, increases in deficits, and inflation. The article concludes that, contrary to the conventional macroeconomic wisdom, high levels of spending and large increases in spending have not caused stagflation—the obvious implication therefore being that fiscal conservatism will have little beneficial effect on the economy. And the article concludes that, again contrary to conventional wisdom, a large and expanding welfare state may be compatible with, and beneficial to, a capitalist economy.

David R. Cameron is an associate professor of political science at Yale University, where he has taught since receiving his Ph.D. from the University of Michigan in 1976. Prior to his studies in Ann Arbor, he received master's degrees from the London School of Economics and Political Science and from Dartmouth College. He teaches and writes in the field of comparative political economy.

T HROUGHOUT most of the advanced capitalist world, the 1970s was a decade of increasing unemployment, accelerating inflation, and decreasing economic growth. As annual rates of unemployment rose and inflation occasionally approached or exceeded 10 percent, and as the rate of growth in the volume of gross national product more frequently approached zero or even sank to negative figures, an old political-economic ideology emerged as the new conventional wisdom, instructing citizens and policymakers that the assorted economic miseries were the product of government—in particular, the rapid expansion, to excessive levels, of government spending. In one advanced capitalist democracy after another, conservative governments came into office in the late 1970s and early 1980s pledged to revitalizing the economy by cutting spending, trimming deficits, controlling the money supply, and increasing investment through reductions in individual and corporate income taxes. While the Reagan and Thatcher governments have been the most enthusiastic and determined practitioners of such "voodoo" economics, the attraction of monetarism and fiscal austerity as a response to macroeconomic weakness has been widespread. For example, in Sweden, Denmark, the Netherlands, Belgium, and Japan—all nations in which government spending grew rapidly in the 1970s—centrist and conservative governments sought to reduce government spending, or at least slow the rate of increase. Even governments controlled by nominally leftist parties—for example, that of the Federal Republic of Germany—were not immune to the claims made on behalf of fiscal conservatism.

While tax reduction is an essential objective of the conservative fiscal orthodoxy that is increasingly prevalent in the United States and elsewhere, it is not the only objective and, indeed, may not even be the most important one. As Reagan's masterful use of the media and his office as a bully pulpit demonstrates, both spending and tax reductions are viewed as policy prescriptions for larger problems in the economy, such as rising unemployment, accelerating inflation, decreasing economic growth, and low capital investment.

Since the public economy has encountered political limits and since those limits are most often rationalized and legitimated by claims about the reputed adverse impact of government spending and taxing on macroeconomic performance, it is desirable to put the new conservative fiscal orthodoxy to the test. If, as the Reagan and Thatcher governments argue, most of our contemporary macroeconomic ills are by-products of excessive levels and rates of growth in government spending—particularly spending for social programs—and taxing, then a large and increasing public economy may indeed be fundamentally incompatible with a well-functioning capitalist economy. If high interest rates, low levels of investment, rapid increases in the money supply, inflation, low growth, and unemployment are all caused by high levels of and rapid increases in government spending, the public economy may confront limitations of a structural nature, that is, limitations that are inherent in the reproductive requisites and logic of a capitalist economy. On the other hand, if the contemporary macroeconomic disorders are not the product of high and increasing levels of government spending and high taxing or deficits—if, in other words, the new conventional wisdom of fiscal conservatism is simply wrong—one would doubt whether any inherent limitations to the expansion of the public economy exist. In fact, it might well be the case that a large and increasing public economy is, contrary to the new fiscal orthodoxy, not only compatible with but beneficial to capitalism.

I propose to evaluate the new conservative fiscal orthodoxy's argument that a large and growing state sector is fundamentally incompatible with the capitalist form of economic organization. The discussion will proceed in several steps. In the next section I examine the magnitude and extent of change in total government spending throughout the capitalist world in the last two decades. Next comes a consideration of whether increases in spending have been associated with decreases in the rate of economic growth and increases in the magnitude of budget deficits. The analysis will then focus on whether, as the new conventional wisdom claims, the decreases in growth and increases in deficits have contributed, in turn and respectively, to high levels of unemployment and inflation. There follows a discussion of capital formation, a critical determinant of macroeconomic performance, and the last section considers whether—as the conservative fiscal orthodoxy claims—a large and expanding public economy causes low and decreasing rates of capital formation. The article concludes with a brief discussion of some of the implications of the analysis.

THE INCREASE IN GOVERNMENT SPENDING: MAGNITUDE AND PARTISAN SOURCES

During the last two decades, government spending has increased in all the advanced capitalist nations. By the late 1970s, total government spending (including transfer payments as well as final consumption expenditures) at all levels of government represented an amount equivalent to roughly one-third of gross domestic product (GDP) in the United States. The so-called wildly excessive increase in spending that so concerned the Reagan administration in fact represented less than five additional percentage points of GDP between the early 1960s and late 1970s. Table 1 demonstrates that in both current size and extent of growth, the American public economy pales in comparison to those elsewhere. In most of the smaller nations of Europe, for example, government generally spends between 50 and 60 percent of GDP.[1] In the larger European nations—even those governed by conservative and center-right parties during much of the recent past—government now spends about 45 percent of GDP. Even Japanese government—usually viewed as underdeveloped in fiscal terms, relative to governments of other advanced capitalist nations—spends and distributes almost as large a share of the nation's economic product as does government in the United States. Its aggregate spending grew much more rapidly, relative to the entire economy, over

1. For a discussion of the unusually large increase in the public economy in the small European nations, see David R. Cameron, "The Expansion of the Public Economy: A Comparative Analysis," *American Political Science Review*, 72(4):1243 (Dec. 1978).

TABLE 1
TOTAL GOVERNMENT SPENDING IN 19 NATIONS

	TOTAL GOVERNMENT SPENDING AS A PERCENTAGE OF GDP,	INCREASE IN TOTAL GOVERNMENT SPENDING AS A PERCENTAGE OF GDP,	
	1977-79	1960-63 to 1970-73	1970-73 to 1977-79
Sweden	59.7	13.1	14.4
Netherlands	57.7	11.9	10.2
Norway	51.3	11.3	8.0
Denmark	51.1	13.8	8.1
Belgium	49.2	7.8	10.5
Ireland	49.0	9.0	9.4
Austria	49.0	5.5	8.7
Germany	46.4	5.1	7.2
France	45.0	2.2	6.5
Italy	44.8	6.9	6.5
Britain	43.8	5.8	4.1
Canada	40.3	6.8	3.9
Switzerland	40.1	5.9	9.7
Finland	39.1	5.0	6.8
Greece	34.6	5.6	5.1
United States	33.4	3.5	1.2
Australia	31.7	3.1	5.4
Japan	30.5	2.5	9.5
Spain	28.5	5.1	5.5

SOURCE: *OECD Economic Outlook, 29, July 1981* (Paris: OECD, 1981), Table H8, p. 138, updated and amended with data reported in OECD, *Economic Surveys,* for individual countries.

the two decades than did spending in the United States.

While government in every advanced capitalist nation increased its share of the aggregate economic product during the last two decades, the most pronounced increases occurred at different times in different nations. Table 1 presents a disaggregation of the total change during the two decades since 1960. If each nation had experienced a constant rate of increase throughout the 20 years, the increase in the 1970s would have been roughly 65 percent as large as that which occurred between 1960-63 and 1970-73. Table 1 demonstrates, however, that in almost every nation the rate of increase in total government spending, as a proportion of GDP, accelerated in the 1970s. In several—Sweden, Ireland, Belgium, Switzerland, Austria,

Germany, Japan, and France—spending increased more between 1970-73 and 1977-79 than between 1960-63 and 1970-73, in spite of the shorter period of time covered in our measure of change in the 1970s. Only two nations, Canada and the United States, experienced a dramatic deceleration in the rate of increase in total government spending in the 1970s.

These data on recent changes in government spending provoke a host of questions: Why do the nations vary so widely in the extent of government spending? Why did some nations, and not others, experience large increases in spending? Why did the rate of increase in spending accelerate in the 1970s in some nations and decelerate in others? One of the central arguments in comparative political economy concerns the extent to which differences among nations in various domains of public policy, including total government spending—as well as spending for social programs, taxation, nationalization, price stabilization, and employment—reflect differences in the partisan composition of government and, by inference, the social constituencies and ideological predispositions of government. For example, did the acceleration of spending in Austria, Germany, and Australia in the 1970s occur because the Social Democratic and Labour parties came to power (albeit briefly in Australia) after several years or decades of conservative rule? If so, what accounts for the very marked increase in some nations where government was controlled by conservative parties—for example, in Japan in the 1970s and the Netherlands in the 1960s? What can be said, on balance and in general, about the impact on the fiscal size of government of partisan control? Does it matter whether leftist parties govern? If so, how much does it matter?

Regression analysis, reported elsewhere,[2] of data for the 19 nations included in Table 1 reveals that both the magnitude of increase in total government spending over the past two decades and the present size of the public economy depend, to a considerable degree, on the partisan composition of government. Nations in which leftist parties frequently controlled government were much more likely to have experienced large increases in total spending and to have relatively large public

2. This article represents an abbreviated version of the paper with the same title delivered by the author at the Annual Meeting of the American Political Science Association, New York, Sept. 1981. All of the statistical analyses reported here, as well as the documentation of the data used in the analyses, are contained in that paper.

economies than were nations in which centrist and rightist parties frequently governed. On average, for each additional year during 1960-79 in which leftist parties, rather than centrist or rightist parties, formed the government, total government spending increased by nearly one percentage point of GDP.

GOVERNMENT SPENDING AND ECONOMIC GROWTH

Having briefly surveyed the pattern of variation and change in government spending in the 19 nations, we can return to the primary concern of this article: the extent of the relationship, if any, between extensive and increased spending by government and the several macroeconomic afflictions present in most of the advanced capitalist world in the late 1970s and early 1980s. Is the new conventional wisdom—the resurrected orthodoxy of fiscal conservatism—correct in attributing most of the blame for decreasing rates of growth, increasing levels of unemployment, and accelerating rates of change in prices to the expansion of the fiscal role of government? Is there, in other words, a fundamental tension or incompatibility between capitalism and a highly developed fiscal role for the state? Is the capitalist form of economic organization therefore likely to impose limits on the extent and continued increase of government spending?

The expansion of government spending, as a proportion of GDP, was not the only development during the past two decades that occurred in every nation throughout the advanced capitalist world. All nations experienced, simultaneously, a dampening of the rate of economic growth. In the early 1960s, the average rate of growth in real GDP in the 19 nations was 5.7 percent per year. By the late 1970s the average had dropped to 2.7 percent, and in several nations—Sweden, Denmark, Belgium, and Britain—the volume of GDP increased by less than 2 percent a year.[3]

Were the two processes of long-term change related? If they were, was the decrease in the average rate of growth a cause or a consequence of the increase in government spending relative to GDP? That unusually large increases in spending by government, relative to increases in aggregate economic product, may contribute to decreases in the rate of economic growth is suggested by the relation between economic growth and the partisanship of government. Nations in which leftist parties frequently governed—and in which, as a result, total spending increased rapidly and reached high levels—were much more likely to have lower rates of growth than nations in which nonleftist parties usually ruled. Considering the average rate of growth throughout the two decades, each year of government by a leftist party diminished the rate of growth by about one-tenth of one percent, while each year of government by a rightist party increased the growth rate by about one-tenth of one percent. These one-year partisan effects are hardly overwhelming. But they become quite significant when one considers the cumulative impact of uninterrupted government by leftist or nonleftist parties over a decade or more.

Given the covariation of both increases in spending and decreases in growth with the frequency of con-

trol of government by leftist (or nonleftist) parties, it is plausible that a causal relationship exists between spending and growth. Without attempting to disentangle the multiple connections between economic growth and increased state expenditure, it suffices to notice that a strong inverse relationship exists between the two. The nations in which total spending was most extensive and in which spending had increased most rapidly in the 1960s and 1970s tended to have, relative to other nations, lower rates of economic growth. There is, for example, a sizable negative correlation among the 19 nations between the average percentage of GDP spent by government over the two decades and the average rate of growth in real GDP ($r = -.58$).

If one arbitrarily assumes that the inverse relationship between growth and spending reflects only the impact of the latter upon the former (an admittedly simplistic assumption), it is possible to estimate the magnitude of decrease in economic growth associated with an increase in spending. In spite of the strong correlation, the magnitude of decrease is quite insignificant: An increase in total spending of one percentage point of GDP between the early 1960s and late 1970s lowered the growth rate in the late 1970s by only five one-hundredths of one percent. Thus a very dramatic increase in spending, in the range of 20 percentage points of GDP—a magnitude of increase that occurred in a few nations such as Sweden, the Netherlands, and Denmark—would have reduced the rate of economic growth by only one percent.

GOVERNMENT SPENDING AND BUDGET DEFICITS

As government spending increased over the last two decades,

3. The data are reported in Organisation for Economic Cooperation and Development (OECD), *Economic Outlook, 22* (Paris: OECD, 1977); and OECD, *Economic Outlook, 29* (Paris: OECD, 1981).

so did public revenues as a share of GDP. But as Downs, writing at the beginning of the period, might have predicted, the increase in revenues did not keep pace with the increase in expenditures.[4] The result was not, however, that which Downs anticipated—budgets that would be "too small"; rather, a growing portion of the increase in expenditures was financed by deficits, that is, by public borrowings. In the early 1960s 12 of the 19 nations were experiencing chronic budget deficits, although only two, Ireland and Canada, experienced deficits in excess of three percent of GDP. By the late 1970s, however, 17 of the nations were in chronic deficit and the number in which the aggregate deficit exceeded three percent of GDP had increased to 10. And in several nations—Ireland and Italy especially, but also Japan, Switzerland, Belgium, and Britain—the deficits exceeded five percent of GDP and evoked in some the sense of an acute fiscal crisis.

Given the passion and rhetoric of the American debate over balanced budgets,[5] it is interesting that the nations that experienced the largest increases in aggregate budget deficit over the two decades were by no means those with the weakest economies. In fact, some of the nations in which the reliance on deficit financing increased dramatically—Japan, Germany, and Switzerland—were among the leaders in macroeconomic performance. It is also interesting to note

4. Anthony Downs, "Why the Government Budget Is Too Small in a Democracy," *World Politics*, 12(3):541 (July 1960).

5. See James M. Buchanan and Richard E. Wagner, *Democracy in Deficit* (New York: Academic Press, 1977); Aaron Wildavsky, *How To Limit Government Spending* (Berkeley: University of California Press, 1980); and Milton and Rose Friedman, *Free To Choose* (New York: Harcourt Brace Jovanovich, 1980).

that, contrary to much of the rhetoric of opponents of federal spending in the United States, American government has throughout the period, especially in the 1970s, been much less in deficit than most nations, including many whose economic performance became the subject of envy and emulation. It is interesting to note that, again contrary to much rhetoric, the United States is the only nation in which the size of the budget deficits, as a proportion of GDP, has decreased over the two decades.

What have been the relationships among the 19 nations between the extent and rate of increase in spending and the extent and rate of increase in deficit financing? While nations with high levels of spending in the late 1970s were hardly more likely to incur large deficits than nations with low levels of spending (r = .12), there was—as fiscal conservatives claim—a strong positive relationship between the magnitude of increase in spending and the size of the increase in the deficit. While this relationship was quite strong throughout the two decades (r = .35), it became markedly stronger in the 1970s (r = .60). Thus by the 1970s we estimate that 39 percent of every additional percentage point of GDP in government spending was financed by deficit.

Thus far we have identified a series of relationships that seem quite congruent with the claims of the new fiscal conservatism: total government spending has increased, relative to the economy as a whole, in all nations, especially in those governed by leftist parties; the increases in spending were associated, both within and between nations, with the diminution of economic growth; and the increases in spending prompted, especially in the 1970s, an increase in the reliance on deficit financing.

If this analysis is correct, it would seem to be only a short step to the conclusion drawn by proponents of fiscal conservatism—that the stagflation of contemporary capitalist society has been produced by the unchecked expansion in government spending. For is it not widely accepted—indeed, is it not a macroeconomic truism—that high and increasing unemployment is generated by low economic growth? And is it not part of the conventional macroeconomic wisdom that, both by driving up the costs of borrowing—that is, interest rates—and by causing central banks to increase the supply of reserves and money, budget deficits generate price inflation? If these widely held beliefs accurately depict the relationships that exist in the economy, then the obvious solution to the contemporary maladies of unemployment and inflation would lie in the prescription offered by the new fiscal orthodoxy: reduce unemployment by raising the long-term rate of economic growth; reduce inflation by reducing the size of budget deficits; increase growth and reduce deficits by reducing government expenditures.

THE GROWTH-UNEMPLOYMENT RELATIONSHIP

Before accepting the diagnosis and prescription of fiscal conservatism, one should consider the validity of the last steps in the argument. Does sustained low growth in fact cause unemployment? Do budget deficits cause inflation? If either relationship does not in fact exist, or exists in a very modest form, those searching for the cause of stagflation may be forced to look at something other than low growth, budget deficits, and ultimately the extent of government spending.

Is there a relationship between sustained low rates of economic growth and high unemployment? Such a relationship is likely, if for no other reason than that almost every nation experienced an increase in unemployment in the last two decades, at the same time that each experienced a decrease in the rate of economic growth. Among the 19 nations there is a consistent inverse relationship between growth and unemployment, indicating that as the long-term rate of economic growth decreased, which it did in all nations during the two decades after 1960, the rate of unemployment increased. While correlation coefficients between various measures of growth and unemployment are quite modest—in the range of .1 to .4—regression analysis reveals a sizable effect. For example, a difference among the nations of one percent in the growth rate of GDP during 1977-80 was associated with a difference of seven-tenths of one percent in unemployment. Moreover, there was virtually a one-to-one trade-off between economic growth and increasing unemployment in the 1970s. Thus a drop of one percent in real economic growth in the late 1970s increased the proportion of the total labor force that was unemployed by eight-tenths of one percent.

One can estimate the net effect on unemployment of the increase in expenditures, mediated by economic growth. An increase in total government spending of one percent of GDP between 1960-63 and 1977-79 reduced the rate of growth in 1977-80 by 0.05 percent; a decrease in the rate of growth of one percent in turn increased the level of unemployment in 1977-80 by eight-tenths of one percent. Therefore, an increase in total spending equivalent to one percent of GDP increased unemployment by 0.04 percent. In other words, the mediated effect of increased expenditure on unemployment is virtually zero; even an increase in spending over the two decades of 20 percentage points of GDP would have increased unemployment by less than one percent. The claim made on behalf of fiscal conservatism that increased spending harms the rate of employment must be judged as true. But largely because of the very weak relationship between increased spending and lower economic growth, the harmful effects on employment are almost invisible.[6]

The effects of increased public spending on unemployment, via economic growth, are not only miniscule but may be entirely offset by direct partisan effects. Various studies have noted that government by leftist parties, compared to government by nonleftist parties, is associated with a lower rate of unemployment.[7] We find a moderate relationship between the frequency of government control by leftist parties in 1960-79 and the rate of unemployment in 1977-80 (r = -.33). Regression analysis reveals that one year of government by leftist parties was associated with a reduction in unemployment of two-tenths of one percent during 1977-

80. The effect is not overwhelming, but it is visible—particularly if one compares the differential effect of government by leftist parties, compared with that of nonleftist parties, over a long period. This direct partisan effect on unemployment clearly exceeds any indirect effect on unemployment associated with the impact of increased government spending—also a product of leftist-dominated government—on economic growth.

THE DEFICIT-INFLATION RELATIONSHIP

Perhaps there is no macroeconomic cliché more widely accepted, by both citizens and policymakers, than that which attributes inflation to budget deficits—deficits that are the product of rapid increases in spending. Thus the new fiscal conservatism asserts that in order to reduce inflation, budget deficits must be cut—an act that is invariably assumed to require cutbacks in spending.

Do deficits cause inflation? When one systematically compares, across nations, the magnitude and increase over time in the budget deficit of all government with a measure of inflation, defined as the acceleration in the rate of change in prices over time, one finds no indication that deficits contribute to inflation.[8] At most, each percentage point of GDP in deficit added one-tenth of one percent to the long-term increase in prices. Given that most nations in the late 1970s experienced deficits in the range of two to six percent of GDP, there is no reason to believe

6. One reason for the absence of an effect, of course, is the fact that some of the increase in spending is often devoted to programs to facilitate employment—for example, job training. Also, a considerable portion of the increase may be used to expand public-sector employment.

7. See, for example, Douglas A. Hibbs, Jr., "Political Parties and Macroeconomic Policy," *American Political Science Reveiw*, 71(4):1467 (Dec. 1977); and David R. Cameron, "Politics, Public Policy, and Economic Inequality: A Comparative Analysis" (Paper delivered at the Conference on the Role of Government in Shaping Economic Performance, Madison, Wisconsin, March 1981).

8. For an elaboration of this point, see David R. Cameron, "Taxes, Spending, and Deficits: Does Government Cause Inflation?" in *The Politics and Sociology of Global Inflation*, eds. Leon N. Lindberg and Charles Maier (Washington, DC: Brookings, forthcoming).

that the deficits contributed more
than an additional half of one percent in the increase in average rates
of change in prices.

The strongest test of the relationship between deficits and inflation
compares the variation among
nations in the magnitude of increase
in deficits during the two decades
after 1960 with the variation in the
magnitude of increase in average
rates of change in prices. Put to this
test, the conventional wisdom that is
endorsed by the new fiscal conservatism fails miserably. Increased
deficit financing was not positively
associated with the acceleration of
prices. In fact the relationship was
of moderate strength and negative.
Nations with the largest increases in
deficits, as a percentage of GDP,
tended to be the ones in which average rates of price change increased
least rapidly. It is of course true that
some nations with large and increasing deficits—Ireland and Italy, for
example—did experience a substantial acceleration in average rates of
price change over the two decades.
But it is also true that several
nations in which the rate of change
in prices increased very little over
the two decades and actually decel-
erated in the 1970s—Germany,
Japan, and Switzerland, for
example—also experienced large
increases in deficits throughout the
two decades.

Why is the conventional wisdom
wrong in attributing inflation to
large and increasing budget deficits? Many economic reasons could be
adduced. For example, as any good
monetarist knows, increases in the
money supply depend on whether
deficits are monetized rather than
on the simple existence of deficits.
Even very large deficits are not
monetized if real interest rates are
significantly greater than zero and
if potential borrowers, domestic or

foreign, exist. Furthermore, inflation is influenced at least as much by
supply shocks—for example, the
increases in oil prices in 1973-74 and
1979-80—as by any expansion of
demand such as that associated with
the money supply.

In addition to the numerous economic reasons that deficits do not, in
any systematic and cross-nationally
comparable way, cause inflation,
there are some reasons that are
more inherently political. One of
these involves the relationships
between the partisanship of government, the magnitude of increases in
the real earnings of workers, and the
so-called social wage.

Recalling that leftist-dominated
governments generally presided
over larger and more rapidly
expanding public economies than
those dominated by nonleftist parties, and recalling also that large
increases in spending were associated with increases in deficits, one
might expect a positive relationship
between the frequency of leftist control of government and inflation.
That expectation would be reinforced by the knowledge that leftist
governments tended to reduce
unemployment compared to governments dominated by nonleftist parties. For those who believe in the
traditional Phillips curve—namely,
that inflation is a function of the
increase in money wages, that the
increase in money wages is a function of the bargaining power of
labor, and that the bargaining
power of labor varies inversely with
the rate of unemployment—if
leftist-dominated governments
dampen the rate of unemployment
then they unavoidably cause some
increase in the rate of change in
prices.[9]

9. A. W. Phillips, "The Relation Between
Unemployment and the Rate of Change of

Contrary to the inherent logic of the Phillips curve and to the findings of Hibbs,[10] control of government by leftist parties is not associated with higher rates of inflation. In fact the reverse is true. The nations in which leftist parties have governed most frequently experienced smaller increases in the rate of change in consumer prices over the long term than did the nations that were most frequently governed by centrist and rightist parties. The correlation between the extent of control of government by leftist parties during 1960-79 and the acceleration in the average rate of change in consumer prices between the early 1960s and late 1970s is -.29. On average, each year of leftist party government lessened the long-term increase in the rate of change in prices by about two-tenths of one percent. In contrast, each year of government by centrist or rightist parties was associated with an acceleration of inflation by one-tenth to two-tenths of one percent.

Why is it that, contrary to scholarly wisdom, leftist governments were apparently more successful than those formed by centrist and rightist parties in dampening inflation, in spite of their propensity to increase spending? The reason is quite simple: inflation accelerated less dramatically in nations in which leftist parties dominated government because Social Democratic and Labour governments were more successful than those formed by other parties in inducing wage restraint by labor. A critical reason that wage restraint could occur was the willingness of leftist governments simultaneously to increase the social wage—that is, to provide expanded social services, including employment, through the public sector—in exchange for wage moderation.[11]

When one examines the relationship among the 19 nations between the measure of inflation over the past two decades—the increase in the average percentage change in prices between 1960-63 and 1977-79—and comparable measures of long-term change in the earnings of manufacturing workers, one observes a close association. There is a very high correlation across the 19 nations between the extent of inflation—that is, the increase in the average rate of change in prices—and the extent of increase in the average rate of change in nominal earnings of workers ($r = .96$). Each additional percentage point of increase in hourly earnings in the late 1970s, relative to the average rate of increase in the early 1960s, increased the average price change by seven-tenths of one percent. However, since much of the increase in nominal earnings may simply represent compensation for past or present increases in the cost of living, it is preferable to consider the change in real earnings, that is, nominal earnings minus the current rate of inflation. The variation among nations in the increase in average rate of change in real earnings is a very powerful predictor of inflation. While the correlation coef-

Money Wage Rates in the United Kingdom, 1861-1957," *Economica*, 25(100):283 (Nov. 1958).

10. Ibid.; Hibbs, "Political Parties and Macroeconomic Policy," p. 1473. See also idem, "Communication," *American Political Science Review*, 73(1):185 (Mar. 1979).

11. This argument is quite compatible with the critique of corporatism and corporatist arrangements as forms of wage restraint. See Leo Panitch, "Recent Theorizations of Corporatism: Reflections on a Growth Industry," *British Journal of Sociology*, 31(2):159 (June 1979).

ficient is somewhat less than that found with change in nominal earnings (r = .68), the regression coefficient is far stronger; thus an increase of one percent in the average rate of change in real earnings is associated with an increase in inflation in excess of one percent. Without necessarily subscribing to a monocausal, wage-push theory, the acceleration or deceleration of rates of change in earnings certainly appears to represent a significant source of cross-national variation in inflation.

If wage restraint—defined as modest increases or even decreases in the average rate of change in real earnings—is a powerful determinant of the stabilization of rates of change in prices over the long term, under which types of government is wage restraint most likely to occur? For a host of reasons—including differences in class bases, organizational links to union federations, and general sympathy or antipathy toward labor—one might predict that even if leftist governments occasionally tried to moderate wages—for example, by integrating labor into the policy process through corporatist institutions and arrangements—it would be governments formed by nonleftist parties, especially those on the right, that would most vigorously pursue wage restraint. Lacking information on intent, we can judge only by actual results. By that criterion, the prediction is clearly wrong. Across the 19 nations, there is a strong association between the extent of control of government by leftist parties and the extent of wage restraint, defined as a decrease or relatively modest increase in the average rate of change in the real earnings of workers between 1960-63 and 1977-79. However, the nations in which

governments frequently were controlled by leftist parties experienced the smallest increases in the average rate of change in real earnings between the early 1960s and the late 1970s. The relationship between the measure of partisanship and the magnitude of increase in real earnings is strong (r = -.66), and I estimate that one year of government by leftist parties reduced the average rate of change in real earnings by three-tenths of one percent.[12] In contrast to the deceleration in the rate of increase in real earnings in the nations in which leftist parties most frequently governed—Austria, Denmark, Norway, and Sweden—the rate of change in real earnings tended to accelerate most dramatically in nations that were usually dominated by rightist parties. The correlation between the long-term increase in the rate of change in real earnings of workers and a measure of the extent of control of government by rightist parties during 1960-79 is .59.

How could governments dominated by leftist parties restrain the

12. The only dramatic exception to the tendency of nations in which leftist parties frequently governed to experience marked decelerations in rates of change in earnings of workers is Britain. Largely because the average rate of increase in Britain was much lower in the early 1960s than in other nations in which leftist parties frequently governed, the average rate of change decreased much less between the early 1960s and late 1970s. Nevertheless, during each of the three periods of Labour party government since 1945, incomes policies—devoted above all to restraining increases in wages—were implemented with the acquiescence of the TUC. In each case, the TUC leadership was eventually forced, by wage militancy at the base, to withdraw its support of those policies. See Leo Panitch, *Social Democracy and Industrial Militancy* (Cambridge: At the University Press, 1976); idem, "Trade Unions and the Capitalist State," *New Left Review*, 125:21 (Jan./Feb. 1981).

rate of increase in workers' earnings without alienating a significant portion of their traditional core constituency, the unionized working class?[13] One way of doing so was to increase government spending, especially spending on social programs, to compensate for the forsaken gains in wages. As evidence of leftist governments' use of the social wage to compensate for wage restraint, one observes a strong inverse relationship between the extent of increase in the average rate of change in workers' real earnings and the level and extent of increase in total government spending between 1960-63 and 1977-79. The smallest increases in the average rate of change in real earnings occurred in the nations in which spending reached high levels and increased at rapid rates during the 1960s and 1970s. The strongest inverse relationship involves spending for social security and social assistance in the 1970s; each additional percentage point of GDP by which social spending increased in the 1970s reduced the rate of change in real earnings by eight-tenths of one percent ($r = -.55$).

The findings on the relationship among the partisanship of government, wage restraint, and the social wage as a mechanism of compensation for wage moderation suggest a view of the political economy in advanced capitalist societies that is

quite unlike that of many of the new fiscal conservatives. Rather than being incompatible with and harmful to capitalism, a large and expanding welfare state may be beneficial and helpful to a capitalist economy and to the very groups that are often most critical of it. Why? Because by socializing collective bargaining to a degree and offering a social wage as an inducement for wage moderation by workers, the highly developed welfare state assists in limiting labor's share of national income, thereby increasing corporate profits and the funds available for capital investment.[14]

GOVERNMENT SPENDING AND CAPITAL FORMATION

Lurking in the background of the discussion thus far has been a subject that is dear to those who espouse fiscal conservatism and who oppose the continued expansion of the public economy and the welfare state. It may be true, some would argue, that an expanded welfare state can induce wage restraint and dampen inflation. It may be true that

13. Some would argue that the leftist parties have not been able to avoid that fate, and that the alienation of the working-class constituency contributed to the electoral erosion that Social Democracy has suffered in Norway, Sweden, Denmark, and Britain. But others remain skeptical; see, for example, John D. Stephens, "The Changing Swedish Electorate," *Comparative Political Studies*, 14(2):163 (July 1981).

14. The difference between the argument presented here and arguments that identify wage restraint as the essential characteristic of corporatist arrangements in contemporary capitalism is that we do not confine the effort to induce wage restraint to those periods when organized labor participates in corporatist arrangements; rather wage restraint is viewed as an essential objective of most, if not all, governments in capitalist societies at all times, whether or not corporatist integration of labor is used in an effort to make wage restraint more palatable to labor. See, in addition to the works by Panitch already cited, Gerhard Lehmbruch, "Liberal Corporatism and Party Government," in *Trends Toward Corporatist Intermediation*, eds. Philippe C. Schmitter and Gerhard Lehmbruch (London: Sage Publications, 1979), pp. 147-83.

increases in spending are not inflationary, even if funded by public
borrowings. But that avoids the
essential issue. The issue is capital
formation—that is, investment.
Capital accumulation and investment are the most fundamental requisites of capitalist economies. It is
not the effects of spending on growth
or those of growth on unemployment
or those of deficits on inflation that
matter most and that may necessi-
tate limitations on government
spending. It is instead the necessity
to curb the flow of funds to the public sector—through either tax
revenues or payments for deficit-
generated securities—that would
otherwise be invested in capital
goods.

According to this argument, it is
not because the public economy
encounters a ceiling or upper limit
at some particular fraction of GDP
that it must inevitably cease to
grow, relative to the private economy. Rather, it is because the expansion of the public sector at some
point begins to deprive the economy
of capital that limits appear. Thus if
limits to the size of the public economy are appearing now, it is because
the advanced capitalist nations are
starved for investment funds—
partly because of previous increases
in state revenues to pay for
increased spending and partly
because of the massive flow of funds
during the 1970s and 1980s from the
advanced capitalist nations to those
of OPEC. At some point, the argument asserts, the basic reproductive
mechanism of a capitalist economy
—accumulation and investment—
will reassert itself, perhaps after
sustained economic deterioration so
erodes citizens' confidence in incumbent officials that they turn to new
leaders who have campaigned on

programs that explicitly endorse
increased accumulation and investment.

That capital investment does
indeed represent a critical determinant of macroeconomic performance in advanced capitalist society
cannot be disputed. Among the 19
nations during the 1960s and 1970s,
one observes a consistently strong
relationship between the rate of capital investment—defined as the proportion of GDP represented by gross
fixed capital formation—and the
rate of economic growth, unemployment, and inflation. Each additional
percentage point of GDP invested in
fixed capital between 1960 and 1979
increased long-term economic
growth by 0.2 percent, reduced
unemployment by three-tenths of
one percent, and reduced the rate of
acceleration in price changes by
nearly one percent.

When one examines the variation
among the nations in the average
proportion of GDP invested in fixed
capital during 1960-79, one feature
is of special interest: among the 19
nations, Britain and the United
States experienced the lowest rates
of capital formation throughout the
two decades. Given that fact, it is not
surprising that each experienced a
low rate of growth relative to the
other 17 nations, a high and/or
increasing rate of unemployment,
and an increasing rate of inflation.
The relatively low rates of capital
formation in Britain and the United
States may reflect the fact that
governments in both nations continued to espouse a liberal, internationalist foreign economic policy—a
legacy of the era when each, at different historical periods, was the
dominant power in the world economy. Because of their commitment
to a liberal international order, both

continued to tolerate and encourage massive exports of capital rather than domestic investment.[15] And because both nations' governments were unwilling or unable to direct a relatively large share of the economic product into investment, it is perhaps not surprising that voters—sensitive to some of the macroeconomic manifestations of the domestic crisis of accumulation in each nation[16]—elected conservative governments that were led by the most articulate proponents of the new fiscal conservatism.

Both the Reagan and the Thatcher governments dedicated themselves to increasing capital investment. If each succeeds in doing so, and to a marked degree, we would expect the rate of economic growth to increase in Britain and the United States; we would also expect the rates of unemployment and inflation to decrease. However, both governments have simultaneously fought inflation with a strict monetary policy. One common result has been a rapid increase in interest rates. One consequence of high interest rates has been a substantial decrease in demand for goods that require financing—housing and automobiles, for ex-

15. See Peter J. Katzenstein, "Conclusion: Domestic Structures and Strategies of Foreign Economic Policy," in *Between Power and Plenty*, ed. Peter J. Katzenstein (Madison: University of Wisconsin Press, 1978), pp. 295-336, for a discussion of the propensity of Britain and the United States to adopt a liberal, internationalist foreign economic policy and to encourage capital exports.

16. See, among the vast number of studies documenting the tendency of citizens to punish incumbents for poor economic performance, Edward R. Tufte, *Political Control of the Economy* (Princeton, NJ: Princeton University Press, 1978); and James E. Alt, *The Politics of Economic Decline* (Cambridge: At the University Press, 1980).

ample—and a substantial increase in the cost of raising investment capital via debt-financing. That, in turn, has generated economic stagnation or recession in both nations, reflected in near-zero or negative rates of economic growth and increases in unemployment. It is certainly plausible, if not probable, that the effect on investment of the generous tax cuts for business and those with high incomes that were enacted by the Thatcher and Reagan governments, in 1979 and 1981, respectively, was more than offset by the adverse effect on investment of high interest rates and strict monetarism.

To what extent, if any, did the increases in government spending and taxing over the last 20 years contribute to low or decreasing levels of capital formation? The answer is mixed. The proportion of GDP that was invested in each nation in the late 1970s was not related in any significant way to the proportion of GDP represented by total government spending—or by total government revenues, spending on social security and social assistance, and personal income taxes and employees' social security contributions. For example, the correlation among the 19 nations between the proportion of GDP invested in fixed capital in 1977-79 and that spent by government during those years was .01. The correlation between the increase in government spending between 1960-63 and 1977-79 and the decrease in fixed capital formation during the same period was only .01. However, when one examines the relationships between the measures of change in the 1970s one finds some indication that the expansion of the public economy began to dampen the rate of capital formation. For example, between 1970-73 and 1977-79 the extent of increase in total government spending was more closely related ($r = .16$) to the extent of decrease in fixed capital formation, and an increase of one percent of GDP in the former was associated with a decrease of two-tenths of one percent in the latter. Similarly, an increase in personal taxes equivalent to one percent of GDP in the 1970s lessened the increase in investment by one-half of one percent; an increase in total government revenues of one percent of GDP lowered investment by four-tenths of one percent; and an increase in spending on social security and social assistance in the 1970s reduced the proportion of GDP that was invested by more than six-tenths of one percent.

The growing tendency of increases in social spending and taxes to erode investment suggests that, while it is impossible to specify limits to the fiscal role of the state in any precise manner, continued expansion in public spending and taxing is likely to extract higher social and economic costs—in terms of unemployment, slow growth, and inflation—because of diminished investment. Nevertheless, if one believes that the size and expansion of the public economy and welfare state confront limits only when they drastically impede the accumulation and investment of capital, most of the advanced capitalist world appears to be some distance from those limits. Even in the midst of large increases in government spending, many nations—for example, Japan, Austria, Norway, Denmark, Ireland, Belgium, France, Spain, Canada, and even Britain and the United States—experienced increases or only slight decreases in

the rate of capital formation over the two decades.

In a few nations, however—most notably, Germany, Italy, Switzerland, Sweden, and the Netherlands —the marked increase in government spending coincided with significant drop rate of capital formation during the two decades. The experience of these nations suggests that the public economy has approached, in size relative to the entire economy, the limits implied here—that is, limits imposed by the fundamental requisites of a capitalist economy. In Sweden and the Netherlands, in particular, one finds evidence that the expansion of government spending to the range of 60 percent of GDP has hindered and contributed to the decrease of investment. In both of those nations, the dramatic expansion of government and social spending has been accompanied by marked decreases in the rate of capital formation in the 1970s. That being the case, it is not perhaps coincidental that the Social Democratic and Labour parties, as well as other parties, have turned their attention to schemes of forced saving—schemes that usually were initiated as plans to give workers and/or unions control of enterprises but that evolved, even before adoption, into schemes designed, first and foremost, to facilitate capital formation.[17] The advocacy of

17. For a telling indication of the evolution and thrust of the plans, consider the title of a recent article by the architect of the Swedish plan: Rudolf Meidner, "Capital Formation Through Employee Investment Funds: A Swedish Proposal," in *Labor Relations in Advanced Industrial Societies: Issues and Problems*, eds. Benjamin Martin and Everett M. Kassalow (Washington, DC: Carnegie Endowment for International Peace, 1980), pp. 161-71.

employee investment funds by the LO and Social Democrats in Sweden, of the similar VAD by the Dutch Labor party, and of Economic Democracy by the Danish Social Democrats represents, for some, a radical challenge to the most basic premises of capitalism, with their eventual implementation, should that in fact occur, signaling the initial phase in the democratic transition to socialism.[18] For others, the advocacy of such schemes only demonstrates the inevitable necessity for all parties, including leftist parties, that are committed to parliamentary democracy to maintain capitalism by inducing wage restraint and facilitating investment.[19] Whether one views such

proposals as brilliantly conceived instruments for transforming capitalism or as schemes to legitimize and institutionalize long-term programs of wage restraint and capital formation depends, ultimately, on one's ideology and claim to unique insights into the future. What can be said, however, is that the identity of the nations in which such plans have entered the public debate is quite predictable: they have become part of the agenda of politics in those few nations in which the expenditure requirements of the public economy have so increased that they have threatened the reproductive requirements of the capitalist economy. A few nations have experienced such dramatic increases in government spending that the generation of capital has been impeded. But most have not, and in these nations the public economy has expanded without hindering capital formation and, in all likelihood, will continue to expand in the foreseeable future.

18. See, for example, Gösta Esping-Andersen, "From Welfare State to Democratic Socialism: The Politics of Economic Democracy in Denmark and Sweden," in *Political Power and Social Theory*, vol. 2, ed. Maurice Zeitlin (Greenwich, CT: JAI Press, 1981), pp. 111-40.

19. Whether one views it as heretical, paradoxical, or natural that Labour parties should induce wage restraint and advocate programs of capital formation depends, of course, on one's notions about the historical role of Social Democracy. For one interpreta-

tion, see Adam Przeworski, "Social Democracy as a Historical Phenomenon," *New Left Review*, 122 (July/Aug. 1980).

ANNALS, *AAPSS*, **459**, January 1982

The Political Management of Economic and Social Change: Contrasting Models of Advanced Industrial Society in Sweden and West Germany

By M. DONALD HANCOCK

ABSTRACT: In countries characterized by a tradition of an active rather than a passive state, such as Sweden and West Germany, politics constitutes an important autonomous factor in determining policy choices and hence economic and social outcomes over time. The key actors in this context are political parties and their aligned or affiliated interest groups. During the postwar period the Social Democrats initiated a policy shift toward neo-Keynesian expansionist economic measures in an effort to sustain growth and minimize unemployment in both countries, whereas the more conservative Christian Democrats were responsible for implementing a less interventionist policy based on social market economic principles during the formative years of the Federal Republic. As a result of these policy similarities and differences—buttressed by the contrasting role of organized labor in the two countries—Sweden and West Germany have experienced both convergence and continued divergence with respect to their economic and social performance. An important consequence is that they appear to have evolved different types of corporatism—with concomitant implications for both the comparative study of advanced industrial societies and democratic theory.

M. Donald Hancock is professor of political science and director of the Center for European Studies at Vanderbilt University. He has studied in Sweden and Germany and obtained his Ph.D. in 1966 from Columbia University. He is the author of Sweden: The Politics of Postindustrial Change *(1972), a forthcoming book on West German politics, and various articles and chapters on both countries. He is the past president of the Society for the Advancement of Scandinavian Studies, co-founder of the Conference Group on Nordic Society, and co-chairman of the Council for European Studies.*

NOTE: Research support for this article was provided by the University Council at Vanderbilt University and the German Academic Exchange Service (DAAD) in Bonn.

THROUGHOUT much of the postwar period, Sweden and West Germany have constituted what many outside observers consider to be exemplary, if contrasting, models of advanced industrial society: the former because of its extensive social services and historical reputation for political compromise, the latter because of the combination of political stability and material prosperity that distinguish the Federal Republic of Germany (FRG) so sharply from previous German regimes. Since the mid-1960s, however, both countries have experienced recurrent destabilizing tendencies that seem to social pessimists to portend an end to the welfare state or a structural crisis of capitalism.

Such tendencies include sluggish economic growth, a seemingly intractable inflationary spiral, recurrent labor unrest, and the advent of ad hoc groups and/or splinter parties protesting central tenets of national policy. As a result, political leaders in both countries, as elsewhere, have been compelled to reconsider basic strategies of system change in their efforts to sustain economic growth while maintaining the range of social services established during more halcyon years of rapid material expansion.

These successive changes in postwar Swedish and West German performance offer a useful opportunity to test the relative significance of economic and political factors in determining system outcomes. This article seeks to show (1) that in advanced industrial, or postindustrial, societies such as Sweden and the Federal Republic of Germany, economics and politics have become increasingly interdependent and therefore mutually causative of system change, but (2) that political parties and interest groups nonetheless play an autonomous role with respect to economic and social performance at critical junctures in the development of nations and especially in countries characterized by an active rather than a passive state.[1] In the conclusion I will consider the theoretical implications of contemporary divergence between Sweden and West Germany for the evolution of postindustrial society.

ECONOMIC AND SOCIAL
PERFORMANCE IN
INTERNATIONAL PERSPECTIVE

The first step in determining the extent to which economic and political factors account for system outcomes in Sweden and the Federal Republic is to examine their levels of economic and social performance in comparison with those of other advanced democracies, such as members of the Organisation for Economic Cooperation and Development (OECD). The performance variables include the following:

1. Economic Development, as measured by the average annual volume of growth in the gross domestic product (GDP) and per-capita GDP. West Germany sustained the highest annual growth rate among Western European

1. These assumptions are based on recent comparative studies: Edward R. Tufte, *Political Control of the Economy* (Princeton, NJ: Princeton University Press, 1978); Francis G. Castles and Robert McKinley, "Does Politics Matter? An Analysis of the Public Welfare Commitment in Advanced Democratic States," *European Journal of Political Research*, 7:169-86 (1979); David Snyder, "Institutional Setting and Industrial Conflict: Comparative Analyses of France, Italy and the United States," *American Sociological Review*, 40:259-78 (June 1975).

members of the OECD from 1950 to 1960, while Sweden maintained a respectable average rate. During the 1960s the West German rate slowed marginally, while the Swedish rate increased, although it still lagged behind that in the Federal Republic. During the 20-year period from 1950 through 1970, both countries consistently outpaced the average annual rate of growth in the United Kingdom and the United States.

More recently, in response to the tenfold increase in the price of petroleum products since 1973 and the accompanying global inflationary spiral, the growth rate has declined in both Sweden and West Germany —as it has in all OECD countries, with the exception of Norway. In terms of per-capita income, Sweden has ranked among the wealthiest industrial democracies throughout the postwar period. West Germany's per-capita income has risen even faster than Sweden's since 1951, increasing from approximately half of the Swedish level to five sixths of it by 1978.

2. Unemployment Levels. With the beginning of largely continuous economic growth in the late 1940s, both Sweden and West Germany sustained internationally low levels of unemployment throughout the 1950s and most of the 1960s. The unemployment rate rose briefly in both countries during the mid-1960s, fell to less than two percent by the end of the decade, and then began to diverge from 1974 onward—rising to nearly five percent in the Federal Republic while fluctuating around two percent annually in Sweden.

3. Average Annual Rate of Inflation. West Germany and Sweden both sustained lower average

annual increases in inflation than other OECD countries during the 1960s and the 1970s, with the Federal Republic maintaining in each instance the next lowest or lowest level among the OECD countries. Sweden's rate reached 9.3 percent in the 1970s, while the Federal Republic average was 5.9 percent.

4. Frequency of Industrial Conflicts. Sweden and West Germany again stand out as exceptional among the advanced democracies because of their relatively low incidence of industrial conflicts. This is not to say that both countries are immune to labor disputes; on the contrary, dramatic labor-management conflicts have occurred in recent years in each of them. Nonetheless, industrial conflicts are noticeably less severe and less frequent in both Sweden and the Federal Republic than in other industrial nations. When they have occurred, strikes in Sweden and West Germany have typically involved conflicts concerning collective bargaining processes rather than political confrontations with state authorities.

5. Levels of Public Welfare. As conceptualized by Francis Castles, public welfare—defined as "a fundamental improvement in the condition of the working class"[2]—consists of a minimum of three empirical measures: (1) public spending on public education, (2) current transfer payments as a percentage of the GDP, and (3) infant mortality per 1000 live births. On system performance, Sweden and the Federal Republic diverge markedly. As indicated in Table 1, Sweden outranks West Germany in all three

2. Francis G. Castles, *The Social Democratic Image of Society* (Boston: Routledge & Kegan Paul, 1978), p. 50.

TABLE 1
MEASURES OF COMMITMENT TO PUBLIC WELFARE

COUNTRY	CURRENT TRANSFER PAYMENTS AS A PERCENTAGE OF GNP (1977)*	PUBLIC SPENDING ON PUBLIC EDUCATION AS A PERCENTAGE OF GNP (1977)†	INFANT MORTALITY PER 1000 LIVE BIRTHS (1979)‡
Austria	20.6	5.5	17
Belgium	22.0	6.6	14
Canada	12.4	8.0	14
Denmark	15.8	6.7	9
France	24.8	5.8	11
Germany	19.5	4.2 (1976)	17
Japan	9.2	5.4	9
Netherlands	30.9	8.4	10
Norway	24.6	7.6	11
Sweden	24.4	8.4	8
Switzerland	15.3	5.2	11
United Kingdom	15.3	6.2	14
United States	11.6	6.4	15

*OECD Economic Surveys, 1980.
†UNESCO (United Nations Educational, Scientific, and Cultural Organization) Statistical Yearbook, 1980 (Paris: UNESCO, 1980), pp. 674-77.
‡World Bank, World Development Report, 1979, p. 167.

categories; it spends substantially more on a proportional basis on both education and social services, including pensions and unemployment benefits, while maintaining the world's lowest level of infant mortality. In contrast, the Federal Republic's investment in social services is average among industrial democracies, but ranks low in percentage expenditures in education and among the highest in the number of infant deaths.

PARTIES, INTEREST GROUPS,
AND ELECTORAL OUTCOMES

In international comparison, West Germany and Sweden thus emerge as highly affluent nations with relatively low levels of unemployment and industrial conflict. They differ in the Federal Republic's greater success in maintaining a lower than average rate of inflation and Sweden's greater commitment to public welfare.

Economic analysis suffices to explain some of these achievements, but given the historical legacy of state activism in both Germany and Sweden in important areas of economic and social policy, political-ideological analysis must necessarily supplement economic models in accounting for performance patterns in the two countries.[3] The principal actors that have played the key role in determining long-term system outcomes are political parties and their aligned interest groups. Their relevance can be demonstrated in the policy priorities and legislative-administrative choices made since World War II.

Since 1945 successive Swedish governments have consistently pur-

3. See Thomas Anton, Administered Politics: Elite Political Culture in Sweden (Hingham, MA: Martinus Nijhoff, 1980); and Kenneth Dyson, "The Ambiguous Politics of Western Germany: Politicization in a 'State Society,'" European Journal of Political Research, 7:375-96 (1979).

sued interventionist economic and expansive social policies, while federal government officials in West Germany adopted a more activist stance only in the mid-1960s. These policy contrasts are directly attributable to the fact that the Swedish Social Democratic Party (SAP) governed either alone or as the senior partner in various coalition governments from 1932 to 1976, while the Social Democratic Party of Germany (SPD) acceded to national office only in 1966. The SPD did not assume primary responsibility for national policy until 1969, when party leaders formed a coalition government with the more conservative Free Democratic Party (FDP).

As moderate left parties representing primarily working-class and lower-middle class strata, both the SAP and SPD are committed ideologically to basic democratic socialist values affirming the idea of socioeconomic progress, social security, compensatory social justice, and generalized notions of economic democracy. Both parties initially advocated national economic planning and selective nationalization as means to promote economic recovery in anticipation of a global recession in the immediate postwar period; but by the late 1940s in the case of the SAP, and by the mid-1950s in the case of the SPD, they largely abandoned the notion of centralized economic control over private enterprise in favor of a qualified system of market economies. In practice, this meant that the SAP and the SPD became advocates of neo-Keynesian economic principles —including active government measures to sustain economic growth and promote full, or at least maximum, employment.

National trade union movements in both countries staunchly support democratic socialist values: the Swedish Federation of Trade Unions—the LO, founded in 1898—and the German Federation of Trade Unions—the DGB, established in 1949.[4] The LO and the DGB are similar in that each is a national peak association unifying the major industrial unions in its country: 25 in Sweden with a combined membership of 2.1 million and 17 in West Germany with a membership of 7.8 million—both totals are for 1979. At the same time, they differ with respect to four important characteristics:

1. Politically, the LO is directly affiliated with the SAP, whereas the DGB is only aligned with the SPD. Thus there is considerable overlap between the top leadership and rank-and-file membership between the SAP and the LO; no comparable overlap exists between the SPD and the DGB. As a result, the LO is in a position to influence SAP policy directly; DGB leaders, in contrast, must rely on indirect channels to influence party goals and national legislation.

2. The LO represents a substantially larger percentage of the

4. Increasingly allied in recent years with the LO in support of interventionist measures is Sweden's other major trade union federation, the Central Organization of Salaried Employees, (TCO), which in 1979 claimed a membership of 1,012,797 white-collar workers organized in 24 national unions. For a good description of the TCO's structure and its political activities, see Christopher Wheeler, *White Collar Power* (Urbana: University of Illinois Press, 1975). The German Federation of Trade Unions claims institutional and ideological roots dating from the 1840s and is an amalgamation of separate Social Democratic, Catholic, and liberal trade union movements established during Germany's imperial era (1871-1918).

Swedish work force than the DGB has been able to mobilize in West Germany: approximately 60 and 22 percent, respectively.

3. Functionally, the LO exercises substantially more direct leverage on the labor market than its West German counterpart, through its authority to negotiate nationwide collective wage agreements with the Swedish Federation of Employers (SAF). In contrast, the DGB plays at most an advisory and coordinating role in West German wage negotiations, with actual agreements reached on a decentralized basis between the regional offices of the various trade unions and employer groups.

4. In programmatic terms, the LO has consistently pressured the SAP to implement macroeconomic and social reforms designed to achieve greater equality between organized labor and private capital, whereas DGB leaders have concentrated much of their lobbying efforts on a relatively more limited—though still significant— vision of codetermination *(Mitbestimmung)* on the micro level of industrial democracy. Thus both the DGB and the LO are important sources of party initiatives to affect system outcomes. But in comparative terms, the LO is in a more strategic position to influence policy choices in Sweden than is the DGB in the Federal Republic.

Sweden's and West Germany's nonsocialist parties and interest groups predictably affirm greater government restraint vis-à-vis private economic forces. Even before the end of wartime hostilities, leaders of the three nonsocialist parties in Sweden—the Agrarians, since 1959 known as the Center Party, the Liberals, and the Conservatives—

declared their opposition to economic socialization in favor of government deregulation and maximum reliance on private enterprise. Bourgeois spokespersons in occupied Germany were slower to articulate a comparable antisocialist ideological stance, but by the late 1940s leaders of both the liberal FDP and the conservative CDU/CSU (political party in West Germany and associated party in Bavaria) adopted similar rhetoric. By 1950, the CDU/CSU officially embraced a distinctive economic program. As articulated and practiced by the first economics minister of the Federal Republic, Ludwig Erhard, the *Soziale Marktwirtschaft* rested firmly on the fundamental principle of private ownership, but accorded the federal government the right to intervene selectively in the economy to encourage competition and to provide welfare benefits and price supports to those individuals, such as the disabled, retired persons, and farmers, for whom "market forces did not provide . . . what the community regarded as fair or sufficient incomes."[5]

Loosely aligned with the Conservatives, the CDU/CSU, and to a lesser extent the liberal/center parties in Sweden and West Germany, are the leading employer and high-level professional interest associations. The most important of them include Sweden's SAF, the Federation of Industries (SIF), and the Central Organization of University Graduates (SACO/SR). West Germany's equivalent organizations are the Federation of German Employers (BDA), the Federation

5. Allan G. Gruchy, *Comparative Economic Systems*, 2d ed. (Boston: Houghton Mifflin, 1977), p. 146.

of Industries (BDI), and the Federation of Free Professions. National farmers' unions, on the other hand, are divided in their political loyalties—with most Swedish farmers traditionally supporting the Center Party, while a majority of West German farmers and their interest-group spokespersons identify with the CDU/CSU.

Electoral outcomes determined the capacity of these major political parties and their aligned/affiliated interest groups to determine national economic and social policy. In Sweden, the Social Democrats maintained their claim to executive leadership throughout the initial postwar period until a gradual decline in their electoral vote compelled them to invite the Agrarians (Center) to join a coalition government from 1951 to 1957.

In response to strong prodding from the LO, party leaders initiated legislation in 1957 to establish a new supplementary pension system (ATP) designed, in part, to extend the SAP's appeal among middle-class voters.[6] The Social Democrats' eventual victory in the ATP controversy was followed by an increase in popular support for the party, especially during 1964-68. Thereafter, SAP leaders were able to retain

6. Supplementary pensions were designed to augment standard retirement benefits by providing individual workers with approximately four-fifths of their annual income during the most productive years of their lives. As a matter of ideological principle, the SAP and the LO insisted that the new system should be compulsory and should be collectively administered. Nonsocialist spokespersons, in contrast, advocated a voluntary arrangement. The dispute and its outcome are summarized in M. Donald Hancock, *Sweden: The Politics of Postindustrial Change* (Hinsdale, IL: Dryden Press, 1972), pp. 214-24.

cabinet office with the indirect support of the Left Party-Communists until 1976. The Social Democrats lost narrowly to the nonsocialist bloc that year and again in 1979, but managed, even in opposition, to exercise pivotal legislative influence in key policy areas such as energy and taxation.

In the Federal Republic, the Christian Democrats in 1949 established the first of a succession of coalition governments with the FDP and a variety of splinter parties. Under the leadership of Konrad Adenauer the CDU/CSU increased its percentage of popular electoral support from 31.0 in 1949 to a peak of 50.2 in 1957. Christian Democratic strength subsequently declined, resulting ultimately in the transition in 1969 to SPD-FDP executive dominance. Despite their loss to the social-liberal coalition in the elections of 1969, 1972, 1976, and 1980, the Christian Democrats have consistently amassed a substantially larger share of the popular vote than the Conservatives in Sweden. Whereas the Swedish conservatives rarely carried even 20 percent of the vote, in the Federal Republic the CDU/CSU continued to attract around 45 percent of the electorate. This factor, as noted in the final section of this article, has had important consequences for continued divergence in West German and Swedish economic and social performance.

POLICY CHOICES AND
SYSTEM PERFORMANCE:
TO THE MID-1960s

Sweden's SAP and West Germany's CDU/CSU utilized their cabinet status to pursue contrasting economic and social policies from the late 1940s to the mid-1960s.

Rather than rely on market forces alone as a sufficient stimulus to material growth, Swedish government officials implemented interventionist measures to promote price stability and full employment in accordance with SAP-LO programmatic tenets. Central features of this policy, shaped by a prominent LO economist, Gösta Rehn, included restrictive fiscal measures to discourage consumer demand and thus inhibit inflationary pressures; an active labor market policy to retrain and relocate persons out of work; and regional policies and government subsidies to encourage industrial expansion in areas of high unemployment, for example, in the northern provinces. In addition, the LO and its member unions adopted a solidaristic wage policy whereby workers were accorded approximately equal pay for equal work, regardless of the relative profitability of particular industrial sectors. The dual purpose of the solidaristic wage policy was to restrict wage inflation caused by the payment of higher wages in more profitable firms and to encourage economic rationalization by compelling firms with low profit margins to increase productivity or cease operation.

The government's activist economic policies were accompanied by SAP initiatives to expand social services and to reform the nation's elitist school system. The cabinet introduced a sweeping revision of the country's public welfare programs in the early 1950s, established a national health service by the middle of the decade, and sponsored a variety of measures to enhance educational opportunities for lower-middle and working-class youth. Given their direct access to policymakers and their centralized authority on the labor market, LO leaders pursued a complementary strategy of macroeconomic and social change by endorsing the SAP's reform initiatives and seeking through regular bargaining sessions with the SAF to achieve a continuous improvement in wages and employee benefits. The LO also sought a symbolic move toward industrial democracy by negotiating an agreement with the SAF to establish a network of works councils at the factory level in 1946. Their purpose was to encourage productivity rather than radically modify labor-management relations. The LO's and SAP's determination to press for a collective system of ATP benefits during the latter part of the 1950s, noted previously, was further confirmation of the Swedish labor movement's determination to pursue a coordinated strategy of active system change instigated from above.

Christian Democratic economic policies and reform objectives differed substantially from those of the Swedish Social Democrats. Chancellor Adenauer bargained successfully during the critical first decade of the Federal Republic's existence to abolish most external economic controls and to achieve the gradual elimination of regional tariff barriers and other restrictions on trade. His economics minister, Erhard, and other administrative officials simultaneously acted on the party's declared social market economic principles to stimulate economic reconstruction through a combination of monetary and fiscal restraint—designed to curtail domestic inflationary pressures and engender international confidence in the new deutsche mark (DM)—and tax incentives to encourage high levels of savings and investment at the expense of individual consumption. Far less reliance was placed on active labor market measures and no appeal was made to unions to implement a solidaristic wage policy.

Sweden's and West Germany's different strategies of economic management and social reform yielded the somewhat diverse patterns of system performance noted in Table 1. The abolition of most domestic and external economic controls, combined with the transfer of $1.4 billion in Marshall aid funds to West Germany and a significantly smaller amount of American loans to Sweden, helped set into motion parallel processes of economic growth. The Federal Republic's GDP nearly doubled by 1957 to 216.4 billion DM. Sweden's GDP rose during the same period from 39.59 billion kronor to 58.96 billion. Sustained economic expansion during the 1950s and early 1960s was accompanied in both cases by a steady increase in the size of the national labor force and a corresponding decline in the percentage of unemployed persons. Industrial workers in both Sweden and West Germany responded to their improved working conditions—as measured in both material terms and their new institutional opportunities to influence management decisions—by practicing a degree of labor peace through the mid-1960s that was matched only by the other Scandinavian countries.

In contrast with the two countries' broadly similar patterns of economic achievements is Sweden's divergence from West Germany with respect to the former's greater degree of state activism. Largely as a result of the Social Democrats' choice of more active labor market and social policies, the government's share of the GDP was correspondingly larger than in the Federal Republic, rising from 16 percent in 1960 to 28 percent by 1977. In comparison, public consumption as a percentage of the GDP in the Federal Republic increased from 14 percent to 20 percent during the same period.[7] The implementation of the ATP supplementary pension program further enhanced the economic leverage of the Swedish government by generating an important new source of public investment capital through the creation of a series of trust funds under social control.

DESTABILIZING TRENDS:
THE POLITICAL RESPONSE

A sudden pause in international economic expansion and the simultaneous advent of unanticipated forms of mass protest action during the mid-1960s helped prompt significant policy and institutional changes in both countries—most visibly in the short run in West Germany, but potentially of a more sweeping nature in Sweden. In the Federal Republic, foreign demand for West German exports began to fall as early as 1965, causing a drop in the country's GDP from 559.1 billion DM in 1966 to 557.9 billion DM in 1967. Ominously, the unemployment rate jumped from 0.7 percent in 1965 to 2.2 percent in 1967. Sweden likewise experienced an increase in the unemployment rate caused by a similar decline in foreign demand, with the annual rate increasing from 1.6 percent in 1966 to 2.2 percent by the end of 1968. But the government was able to act promptly to extend public support for subsidized labor and retraining programs to prevent a comparable economic downturn, as in the Federal Republic. Thus Sweden's GDP expanded steadily from 140.71 bil-

7. World Bank, *World Development Report, 1979* (Washington, DC: World Bank, 1979), p. 135.

lion kronor in 1965 to 154.92 billion in 1968.

Public protest movements began in both countries with student criticism of American foreign policies in Southeast Asia and proceeded by the end of the decade to include the proliferation of ad hoc citizen groups and multiple forms of worker discontent. The revival of ideological conflict in Sweden and West Germany, as well as other advanced nations, was rooted in complex causes, including generational and value changes, increased public awareness of the contradiction between democratic ideals and the reality of persisting socioeconomic inequality, and opposition to existing or contemplated public policies.

The immediate response to the incipient economic and political crisis in the Federal Republic was the formation of the CDU/CSU-SDP grand coalition in the fall of 1966—an event that legitimized the SPD's claim to executive office and set the stage for a fundamental shift in national economic policy. Under Federal Chancellor Erhard, the grand coalition moved toward greater state economic activism by introducing a sweeping Law for Promoting Stability and Growth in the Economy. The bill defined four principal economic objectives to be pursued jointly by the federal government and private economic groups: the maintenance of stable prices, full employment, external financial equilibrium, and adequate economic growth. To achieve these goals, the bill called for a five-year financial plan relating "the projected development of federal revenues and expenditures . . . to the nation's economic and social priorities."[8] In addition, the 1967 law

8. Gruchy, *Comparative Economic Systems*, p. 154.

prescribed the introduction of a new informal institutional arrangement known as concerted action *(Konzertierte Aktion)*, involving voluntary consultations among representatives of the federal ministries of economics and finance, the Council of Economic Experts, the Federal Bank, employer associations, and union officials on means to maintain stable economic growth.

The federal government acted on its new authority to enact short-term anticyclical measures to increase public expenditures for housing and road construction and reduce business taxes. These expansive measures brought immediate results. Economic growth was restored at an annual rate of five percent by the end of 1967, with the unemployment level falling once again to less than one percent through 1971.

Popularly acclaimed for engineering the federal government's adoption of a more active economic role, the Social Democrats increased their share of the electoral vote from 39.3 percent in 1965 to 42.7 percent in 1969 to become the senior government party. In coalition since then with the FDP, the SPD continued under chancellors Willy Brandt and, after 1974, Helmut Schmidt to pursue a neo-Keynesian policy of active fiscal measures to counter cycles of economic boom and recession.

IN PURSUIT OF
INDUSTRIAL AND ECONOMIC
DEMOCRACY

The rise of the SPD to power and its implementation of a more interventionist economic policy thus precipitated a partial convergence with respect to the political management of economic change in West Germany and Sweden. Henceforth, both governments pursued increasingly similar macroeconomic measures, although Sweden has retained a larger public sector and its traditionally more comprehensive range of social services. The two countries experienced continued divergence, however, as a consequence of organized labor's contrasting response to the deeper social issues that had triggered the renewed ideological controversies of the mid-1960s.

Leaders of both the DGB and the LO interpreted the resurgence of rank-and-file labor militancy during the late 1960s and early 1970s—militancy that took the form of an increased number of industrial conflicts in both countries—as an expression of worker agitation to extend the institutionalized power of organized labor. They differed, however, in their reform strategy to achieve that objective. In the Federal Republic, DGB and member union officials petitioned the SPD-FDP coalition to implement their long-standing demand to extend parity codetermination beyond the iron, steel, and coal industries. After lengthy consultations on alternative models of codetermination within coalition ranks, the social-liberal coalition responded by submitting a compromise bill to parliament in 1975 that empowered workers and shareholders each to select half of the members of the supervisory boards of joint stock companies employing 2000 and more wage earners. The proposal, approved in 1976, fell just short of mandating full parity between labor and capital in that it stipulated that each supervisory board must elect its chairperson by a two-thirds vote. Since the chairperson could not be chosen in defiance of the shareholders, the effect was to ensure the

continued dominance of private capital. Union leaders greeted the legislation as "an expansion of the rights and influence of workers and their unions," but have vowed to continue their efforts to achieve full parity in the future.

In contrast to the DGB's emphasis on extending industrial democracy, the LO embraced a reform strategy that encompasses a more radical transforming vision of macroeconomic democracy. Through their alignment with the SAP, the LO pressured the Swedish government to enact during the 1970s a succession of bills designed to enhance the collective influence of labor in the private sector. Among them were laws passed in 1972, 1974, and 1978 permitting workers the right to elect two representatives to the boards of Sweden's larger industrial firms; the transformation of the traditional rights of employers to assign and dismiss employees into a joint prerogative of labor and management; and the adoption of a Swedish version of codetermination that accords unions a significantly stronger voice in "the direction of allocation of work, personnel management, supervision of work, and [the] working environment."[9]

The culmination of the LO's determined drive to achieve economic democracy is its effort to introduce a new system of employee funds as the next major institutional reform in Sweden. Beginning with a 1975 proposal authored by Rudolf Meidner, a senior LO economist,[10]

9. Nils Elvander, "Sweden,"·in *Towards Industrial Democracy: Europe, Japan and the United States*, ed. Benjamin C. Roberts (Montclair, NJ: Allanheld, Osmun, 1979), p. 145.

10. Rudolf Meidner, in collaboration with Anna Hedborg and Gunnar Fond, *Löntagarfonder* (Stockholm: Tidens Förlag, 1975).

trade union and SAP spokespersons have drafted successive blueprints for the implementation of a compulsory system of collective savings. The system, according to a joint SAF-LO 1981 plan, would provide Swedish industry with much-needed additional sources of investment capital while simultaneously —through the collective ownership of the funds—according workers greater indirect influence in relation to private capital. Private firms would transfer a percentage of their excess profits each year to employee funds. The funds would be used to purchase company stocks on the open market, with dividend income to be paid into the national ATP system for indirect individual disbursement as supplementary pension benefits.

How the DGB's quest for full parity in labor-management relations and the LO's concept of a new system of employee funds will affect future economic trends in the two countries remains problematic. Logically, both sets of reforms could increase economic effectiveness by decreasing worker alienation and institutionalizing postwar precedents of long-term labor peace on a firmer foundation—at least in the eyes of organized labor. Yet opposition by business groups to existing and proposed forms of industrial/economic democracy could significantly exacerbate conflict between the unions and the employer associations.

SYSTEM PERFORMANCE AND DIVERGENCE: SOME THEORETICAL IMPLICATIONS

The preceding analysis has sought to demonstrate the intricate balance between political and economic factors in accounting for postwar patterns of system performance in Sweden and the Federal Republic of Germany. Economic factors alone would seem to account for some of the outcomes. For example, the transfer of American Marshall aid funds clearly helped facilitate economic reconstruction in the western zones of Germany and the resumption of industrial growth in both countries during the early postwar years. Similarly, the expansion of world trade in the wake of the Korean war directly stimulated the high rates of economic development and increased per-capita income during the 1950s and early 1960s. More recently, the desultory domestic effects of substantial price increases by the oil-exporting countries and recurrent international monetary fluctuations underscore the increased significance of economic interdependence as a constraining influence on economic outcomes in all industrialized nations.

Yet economic analysis is insufficient for explaining all aspects of postwar Swedish and West German performance. Even the events and trends just cited were inextricably linked to political acts, notably the decision by the American government to provide Marshall aid in the first place, subsequent steps by public officials to liberalize international trade and currency exchange within such institutional settings as the Organization for European Economic Cooperation (OEEC) and the European Community, and the formation of the Organization of Petroleum Exporting Countries (OPEC) as a decision-making forum to establish common prices and set production quotas.

However, only political analysis can explain the initial dichotomy between the SAP choice of a more interventionist economic policy and a significantly greater national investment in public welfare, and the Christian Democratic preference for a more passive social market economic model. The shift toward a more active economic role by the federal government, which began with the formation of the grand coalition in 1966, was admittedly undertaken as a pragmatic response to the prevailing economic crisis, but from the outset it assumed distinctive institutional and administrative—hence political—forms: the close integration of important interest groups into the economic policy process and the new discretionary authority on the part of cabinet officials to fine-tune the economy through a combination of fiscal, monetary, and subventionist measures. Similarly, postwar reforms in the area of labor-management relations are attributable to political rather than economic factors: demands by union leaders in both countries to broaden the rights of workers as a means of humanizing conditions of industrial employment and achieving greater equality between labor and capital as a democratic value in its own right.

Superficially, the SPD's implementation of neo-Keynesian economic principles and recent policy responses to the persisting economic crisis indicate a broad similarity between the two countries. Both the Swedish and West German governments have sought to cope with recurrent economic contractions during the 1970s and early 1980s with similar interventionist measures, including an expansion of public subsidies to private industry, increased expenditures in the public sector, and greater outlays for unemployment benefits and/or retraining of workers. Moreover, mounting public debts in each country have compelled the nonsocialist coalition in Sweden and the SPD-FDP government in West Germany to undertake painful reductions in public services and welfare benefits in 1980 and 1981, respectively, in parallel recognition that there are discernible limits to the costs of state activism. Yet in a broader sense the two systems continue to diverge, as witnessed in macroeconomic and social terms by Sweden's greater commitment to welfare benefits, its comprehensive program of labor reform during the 1970s, and even the non-socialist government's willingness to invest more heavily in active labor market policies at the cost of a higher inflation rate than in the Federal Republic.

The more fundamental divergence between the two countries lies in the contrast between Social Democratic ideological hegemony in Sweden and West Germany's more conservative political culture. This contrast is rooted in a combination of factors: in Sweden, the SAP's 44 years in office, the party's policy successes during that time, the organized strength of the LO, the traditional fragmentation of the nonsocialist bloc, and the numerical weakness of the Swedish Right; in West Germany, the legacy of 20 years of CDU/CSU governance during the formative years of the Federal Republic, the continued strength of the Christian Democrats in opposition,[11] the considerable

11. The CDU/CSU not only retained 226 seats in the 1980-84 Bundestag, compared with a total of 271 for the SPD-FDP, but also exercised executive power in 1981 in 6 of West Germany's 10 state parliaments, plus

economic and political resources of the BDA and other employer groups, the SPD's need to rely on the more conservative FDP to retain cabinet office, and the DGB's lack of political leverage in comparison with the LO. In light of these multiple differences, the SAP-LO's proposal to enact employee funds is a realistic item on Sweden's political agenda—and may set the stage for the long-term transformation of the present mixed economy into an unprecedented form of "labor socialism."[12] In contrast, West Germany is likely to remain in a more traditional mold even if the SPD-FDP coalition manages to retain executive power until 1984 and beyond—with political elites acting in concert with private economic forces and the trade union movement to emphasize economic efficiency, sustained growth, and continued efforts to contain inflation rather than engage in comparable experiments in active system change.

The systemic and policy contrasts between Sweden and West Germany suggest important implications for the comparative study of advanced industrial societies as well as for democratic theory. A tentative conclusion is that the two countries have evolved different types of corporatism. To use Ulrich von Alemann and Rolf Heinze's classificatory distinction, Sweden appears to constitute economic corporatism, or an institutionalized government-administrative-interest-group linkage in which organized interest groups, notably the LO, have come to play a decisive role in initiating macroeconomic and social decisions, whereas the Federal Republic more closely approximates political corporatism, or a system of linkage characterized by a stronger role by the central state in such arenas.[13] Whether either of these models accurately describes the two cases remains subject to further empirical and conceptual analysis. But if new varieties of corporatism indeed characterize the emergence of post-industrial society, a significant consequence will be the increased centrality of politics in the management of economic and social change, rather than the reverse—posing anew fundamental questions concerning the participatory rights of citizens and the maintenance of effective guarantees of political accountability on the part of party, administrative, and interest-group elites.

---

the city senate of West Berlin. Thus the Christian Democrats commanded a majority of seats in the upper house (Bundesrat).

12. By labor socialism I mean union control/ownership of principal means of production as opposed to state—party—ownership. For an elaboration on this view, see M. Donald Hancock, "Sweden's Emerging Labor Socialism," in *Eurocommunism and Eurosocialism*, ed. Bernard E. Brown (New York: Cyrco Press, 1979).

13. Ulrich von Alemann and Rolf G. Heinze distinguish among these and other varieties of corporatism in the introduction to their edited volume, *Verbände und Staat. Vom Pluralismus zum Korporatismus. Analysen, Positionen, Dokumente* (Opladen: Westdeutscher Verlag, 1979). Also see Gerhard Lehmbruch's essay in the same volume.

ANNALS, *AAPSS*, **459**, January 1982

Coordination Styles and Economic Growth

By JERALD HAGE and REMI CLIGNET

ABSTRACT: Traditionally the problem of macroeconomic coordination has been discussed as being best done by either free-market competition or controlled planning. Such a formulation ignores several alternatives that societies can employ to encourage growth. Usually the argument for or against free-market competition has been fought on ideological grounds rather than by ascertaining whether it is most appropriate in some sectors of the economy rather than in others. To do this requires some way of conceptualizing economic sectors that breaks away from traditional thinking. This article suggests a four-sector model and then argues that there are four styles of coordination, each of which is most appropriate in a particular sector. It is argued that there is no single way to maximize growth in an economy and that different coordination mechanisms should be employed in different market contexts.

Jerald Hage, Ph.D., Columbia, 1963, has spent the last 20 years studying complex organizations. The insights gained from this are now being applied to the development of comparative macrosociological theory and in a variety of institutional sectors. A major theme in all of his work is the problem of change, innovation, and technology. He is presently chairman, Department of Sociology, University of Maryland, College Park, Maryland.

Remi Clignet, docteur recherches sociologiques, France, 1963, has spent the last 20 years in comparative societal research, most notably in the areas of education, family, and policies related to them. A major theme in much of his work is that of centralization and its internal contradictions, especially relative to various societal values such as equality. He is presently professor in the Department of Family and Community Development, College Park, Maryland.

NOTE: This article was originally presented at a conference sponsored by the Council for European Studies in Madison, Wisconsin, March 1981, and is one of a series of articles supported by the National Science Foundation (NSF). The opinions expressed are not necessarily those of the NSF.

GIVEN current concerns about economic growth and the decline in productivity, it seems wise to consider how society or the state might improve these economic performances. Traditionally economists, especially in the United States, have argued that coordination by free-market principles is the best way of increasing productivity because of competition. Recently economists have argued that coordination by hierarchy does have certain advantages for economic growth, because it eliminates duplication and provides for better information about how to allocate resources.[1]

Organizational sociologists have long been concerned about the problem of how best to coordinate firms.[2] They have advanced the idea that different products need different kinds of coordination mechanisms. They have, of course, ignored the free-market mechanisms because their concern has been with internal organizational coordination. But they have also seen that there is more than one kind of hierarchical mechanism for achieving productivity and growth.

The objectives of this article are to merge these two literatures and to argue that different products within the economy need different styles of coordination. Some are best coordinated by free-market principles. Some are best coordinated by hierarchical principles. Furthermore, there is more than one kind of hierarchy. This is different from the usual argument that has seen the economy best coordinated by one or the other mechanism. Our position is that most economies need a mixture of mechanisms, and more than the traditional two discussed by economists.

Another important objective of this article is to argue that the problems of productivity and economic growth are more complex than is normally perceived. Usually productivity is seen as the problem of cutting costs and finding more efficient ways of producing products. In turn, economic growth is maintained by investing in the more productive sectors of the economy. The organizational literature has been concerned with not only the problems of productivity and growth, but also those of innovation and of morale, which in very complex ways affect productivity and economic growth. Thus an economy might grow because it invests in those sectors that have the best productivity and that produce goods at the lowest cost, or it might grow because it invests in those sectors that are most innovative. Similarly, innovation and morale can influence gains in productivity, as the current interest in quality work circles demonstrates. Therefore, in discussing a coordination mechanism, it is important to analyze its impact not only on productivity and growth, but also on morale and innovation.[3]

1. Oliver Williamson, *Markets and Hierarchies, Analysis and Antitrust Implications: A Study in the Economics of International Organization* (New York: Free Press, 1975); Alfred Chandler, *The Visible Hand: The Managerial Revolution in American Business* (Cambridge, MA: Belknap Press, 1977).

2. Peter M. Blau, "A Formal Theory of Differentiation in Organizations," *American Sociological Review*, 35:210-18 (April 1970); Andrew Van de Venn et al., "Determinants of Coordination: Modes within Organizations," *American Sociological Review*, 41:322-38; H. Mintzberg, *The Structuring of Organizations: A Synthesis of Research* (Englewood Cliffs, NJ: Prentice-Hall, 1979): and Jerald Hage, *Theories of Organizations: Form, Process, and Transformation* (New York: John Wiley, 1980), pp. 350-76.

3. Gerhard Lenski and Jean Lenski, *Human Societies: An Introduction to Macrosociology*, 3rd ed. (New York: McGraw-Hill, 1978).

A TYPOLOGY OF
PRODUCT MARKETS

Economists have usually classified product markets as either in a
classical free-market context or in a
monopoly context. In the former
case there are multiple producers
and buyers, and in the latter
instance there are either a few large
producers or consumers who dominate the market.

Organizational sociologists have
emphasized a very similar variable,
namely, personnel size, but they
have also been interested in technology as a way of classifying markets.
When using concepts like uncertainty and fluidity of the market,
sociologists have been more concerned with assessing the rate of
change of products, or at least
assessing the rate of demand for
them. In a synthesis of the literature, Hage argues that product
markets can be classified in terms of
the sophistication of the technology
involved, the rate of product change,
and the size of its demand and its
stability.[4] In general, the higher the
level of technological sophistication,
the faster the rate of product
change. This leads to shorter and
shorter product lives. The larger the
demand, the more stable it tends to
be. This leads to longer product
lives. These two basic dimensions of
technology and demand size provide
a fourfold classification of market
contexts. Each of these needs to be
discussed in some detail.

The market context of low
technological sophistication
and low product demand

In situations of low demand and
low technology, we typically find
craftspersons working in tradi-

4. Hage, *Theories of Organization*, pp.
379-467.

tional organizations, as suggested
by the upper left cell of Table 1.
Variations in tastes and shifts in
fashion explain why demand for any
one product is low. Low technical
sophistication results from the slow
development of artisan knowledge
over the past several centuries. Barriers to entry in the market are also
low; it is relatively easy for a person
to start a new business. What is
needed is a small number of craftspersons and some sense of an unmet
taste in a particular area. Print
shops, contractors, restaurants, and
clothes makers are cases in point.
Some companies attempt to mass-
produce products in this area, but
they usually go out of business or
find that their market size has very
clear upper limits. This sector
responds easily to shifts in taste or
fashion because investments in
plants and equipment are light. The
skills required adapt easily to new
preferences. However, craftspersons do not adapt well to major technological changes in production
processes, usually because changes
eliminate jobs, as we have recently
seen in the printing industry. In this
instance, technological changes
imply that the product moves to
another cell in Table 1.

The combination of low technological sophistication and low
demand size and stability describes
the classical market situation and
traditional industry. There are multiple buyers and suppliers. Taste is
important, but so is price. Because
there is low technological sophistication, buyers can reasonably evaluate the products, shopping around
for the best price within their taste
preferences. Search behavior operates and helps maintain a competitive situation. The laws of
competitive economics work reasonably well here. It is perhaps worth
emphasizing that many of the pro-

TABLE 1
A TYPOLOGY OF PRODUCT MARKETS*

TECHNOLOGICAL SOPHISTI-CATION AND RATE OF PRODUCT CHANGE‡	STABILITY AND SIZE OF DEMAND†	
	LOW	HIGH
Low	Taste important: clothing, restaurants, housing, furniture, cigars, printing, silverware, jewelry	Price important: rubber, steel, shoes, cigarettes, dishes, paints, automobiles, cement, postal services, insurance, fast food places, typewriters, tanks, paper products, food, processing of grains
High	Distinctiveness important: laboratory tests, mini-computers, radioisotopes medical services, pocket calculators, robots, haute couture, specialized instruments, nuclear plants, gourmet restaurants	Quality important: synthetic textiles, machine manufacturers, electrical products, drugs, planes, computers, plastics, specialty steels, metallurgy

*The same product can be evaluated differently in different countries and thus might be mass-produced in one country but not another. Bread is mass-produced in the United States but not in France. Clothes are mass-produced in China by government policy—rather than as a result of consumer preferences—but not in the West. Similarly, some companies create niches, for example, producing quality, custom-made cars or mass-produced furniture.

†Demand is difficult to measure directly but the number and average firm size is at least an indirect indicator. The variety of different clothing styles is much greater than kinds of automobiles. And taste or fashion changes rapidly in clothing but not in cars. Taste is important in restaurants but not in fast-food chains, which provide a standardized product.

‡Rate of product change is best operationalized by the percentage of sales spent on R&D, the level of technological sophistication by the number of journals read. An indirect indicator is the proportion of members with Ph.Ds or other advanced degrees.

ducts produced do have large demand in the aggregate; but because not everyone wants the same kind of house, furniture, clothing, food, and the like, demand is broken up and divided among a variety of tastes or different kinds of consumers.

*The market context of low
 technological sophistication
 and high product demand*

In situations of low technological sophistication and slow rates of product change combined with highly stable and large demand, one finds assembly lines as the dominant technology. Capital intensity is greater than in the traditional sector. In contrast with the previous situation, the knowledge involved here is only a

century old. High costs sunk in machines imply few incentives to change the production line. This is not a problem as long as the rate of product change is low. Most of the industries described by Chandler in his book, *The Visible Hand*, fit this pattern, from textiles to automobiles.[5]

In this situation, competition is over who can produce a standardized product with moderate product differentiation at low cost. The low level of technological sophistication makes evaluation of the product relatively simple. Besides, consumer reports provide a series of criteria for determining the best buy relative to the particular product produced. One after another indus-

5. Chandler, *The Visible Hand*.

trial sector becomes dominated by one or several very large firms, as interfirm differences in managerial skills at developing hierarchical coordination drive out those companies that cannot lower their prices.

Automobiles, rubber tires, many glass products, cement, cigarettes, and the like are in this market context. Some product differentiation may occur, as in the production of cars, but the basic product is largely the same and can be continued over a very long-term cycle. Thus some production runs of cars have sometimes lasted for as many as 10 years. This allows for very large economies of scale and the opportunity to drive prices down extensively over the long term. It also explains why one tends to find concentration of the industry so great. Considerable efficiency is gained by spreading fixed costs over the largest volume of production. The fixed costs of large-scale plants provide an economic barrier to the entry of new firms. Thus the monopoly sector once created is difficult to change—unless there is either a technological change or a fundamental shift in consumer preferences.

The market context of high technological sophistication and low product demand

Once we move to markets with high levels of technological sophistication and rapid product change, we shift to very different kinds of market contexts, whose properties have not, to our knowledge, been worked through by economists. Technological sophistication refers to how much the technology is based on scientific knowledge and, especially, on theory. It can be operationalized by the number of trade journals and by the percentage of sales spent on research. When demand size is small, the objective is to produce custom-made, one-of-a-kind, or small batches of products. The skill level is high. Both basic and applied research are integrated into the production process.[6] Capital intensity is moderate but is spent on testing equipment and research rather than production equipment. The most distinctive feature is the high percentage of sales dollars spent on research. It is the key to survival, because product demand does not last and is unstable.

This market context has few suppliers, and they hardly compete with one another because they tend to produce different and unique products. Similarly, buyers are few and not necessarily replaceable. Because of changes in the nature of the educational system, each wants a product tailor-made to a specific need.[7] To call attention to the very small size of the product volume, our name for this market would be the individuated market. The laws of supply and demand operate in particular ways in this market context. There is no direct competition between suppliers or buyers in the normal sense of the term. There are no price leaders, nor is price the driving force of the market. Innovativeness is the driving force. Consumers want products of the latest technological advance, but they desire them in individuated forms, to meet specialized needs and to do specialized tasks.

6. Paul Lawrence and Jay Lorsch, *Organization and Environment: Managing Differentiation and Integration* (Cambridge: Harvard Graduate School of Business Administration, 1967).

7. Hage, *Theories of Organizations*, pp. 473-74.

*The market context of high
    technological sophistication
    and high product demand*

But technological sophistication
and rapid product change also can
be combined with relatively large
and stable demand, as in computers,
chemicals, and electrical products.
Production technology is characterized in what is called the continuous process,[8] which can be
changed quickly to deal with different batches. The most common
example is the chemical industry,
which is built on the theory of
modern chemistry. One might call
this market context the innovative
competitive monopoly sector. It has
a significant number of both large
and small firms. Relationships
between firms are less directly
competitive because the large
number of products generates
specialization even in the case of
large firms, such as Pfizer, Dow,
DuPont, Monsanto, General Electric, and Westinghouse. In contrast
to the market context of low technology and high demand, quality is
an important element in the product
evaluation.

As in the previous market context, competition requires innovativeness and being first with the new
generation of technology. Leaders
are defined in terms not of price but
of technology. At the same time,
there are so many products that
some product substitution is
possible.

This market context came into
existence in the 1920s.[9] In the previous market contexts, all the competitors are small. Here the
combination of high technological
sophistication and high, even if
unstable, demand requires both
medium- and large-size firms. More
critically, many firms have multi-
division structures corresponding to
different products and technologies
and hence differing market
contexts.

To conclude, our typology shows
that variations in technological
sophistication and in the size as well
as the stability of the demand imply
parallel variations in (1) the relative
age of the relevant market contexts,
(2) the central tendencies and the
dispersion of the distributions of
firms by size, (3) the types of investment required by these firms, and
(4) the extent and the form of interfirm competition.

It is our contention that technological sophistication fundamentally changes the nature of the
market context and thus the ways
economic laws apply. The first and
most fundamental change is that
product life is shortened. This has
profound implications for decisions
concerning differential investments
in capital and R&D. Increasingly
survival depends more on the latter
rather than the former. The second
change concerns the sheer number
of products that are capable of being
produced. Enhanced technological
sophistication enlarges product
range. In contrast to automobile or
textile industries, the industries
built on the theories of electricity,
chemistry, physics, and more
recently biology have many products. "Product proliferation" is a
more apt term than "product differentiation." Once there is a market
context where there are more products than any one company can
produce and where product lives are
short, the dynamics of competition
become very different. In this situa-

8. Robert Blauner, *Alienation and Free-
dom: The Factory Worker and His Industry*
(Chicago: University of Chicago Press, 1964);
Joan Woodward, *Industrial Organization:
Theory and Practice* (London: Oxford Univer-
sity Press, 1965).

9. Chandler, *The Visible Hand.*

tion, barriers to entry are technological rather than economic. RCA and GE had millions of dollars to spend, but could not build a good computer to compete in the market; both sustained large losses.

All advanced industrialized societies have all four types of product market contexts. Thus, insofar as they are concerned with growth and productivity, the policymakers should be concerned with a variety of coordination styles, our next topic.

THE TYPOLOGY OF COORDINATION MECHANISMS

Traditionally coordination has been differentiated in terms of free marketplace versus central planning combined with hierarchical state control. Uncontrolled capitalism versus regimented socialism might be the ideological words to describe the two extremes of the continuum. Seldom found in the real world, these extremes are still useful in explicating these dimensions.

The best way of discussing coordination mechanisms is to ask how much control and on what. The list of potential control areas includes kinds of technology, size of labor force and its training and qualifications, amount of investments in plant and equipment, levels of wages and salaries, organizational policy and strategy, production volume and growth rate, productivity levels, quality levels, and various side effects such as pollution.

Needless to say, the extent of control is how much freedom of action or how many choices are allowed in each of these areas. Control and coordination are not exactly the same. While control involves specifying what particular firms can or cannot do, coordination articulates

the do's and don'ts of various firms into some coherent plan. Thus control is only a first step toward a conscious coordination, the second step consisting in fitting the actions of each unit into a whole.

Clearly, all governments intervene to a certain extent.[10] Yet societies develop traditions about what is controllable and what is not. For instance, the United States pioneered with antitrust legislation and pollution control, but has been quite far behind in controlling location of enterprises, production volume, wages and salaries, prices, and the like. Although control is usually exerted by the central or local government, it may also be located in the private sector itself.

Although various schemes have been proposed to describe differences among economic systems, these generally ignore the dimensions that underpin coordination styles.[11] In contrast, our intent is to contribute to the problem of how to describe adequately vastly different economies. The concepts of coordination/control offer much, as they have a firm basis in the organizational theory literature,[12] and more recently they have been of interest to economists.[13]

Table 2 presents four kinds of coordination/control schemes. What distinguishes them is the extent of overall control exerted, the degree of detail of the plan, the number of

10. Allan Gruchy, *Comparative Economic Systems: Competing Ways to Stability, Growth, and Welfare* (Boston: Houghton Mifflin, 1977).

11. Ibid.

12. James March and Herbert A. Simon, *Organizations* (New York: John Wiley, 1958); Charles Perrow, *Organizational Analysis* (Belmont, CA: Wadsworth, 1967); Jerald Hage, *Communication and Organizational Control: Cybernetics in Health and Welfare Settings* (New York: John Wiley, 1974).

13. Williamson, *Markets and Hierarchies.*

TABLE 2
A TYPOLOGY OF COORDINATION/CONTROL MECHANISMS

NUMBER OF PARTIES INVOLVED AND THE EXTENT OF THEIR INVOLVEMENT	EXTENT OF CONTROL AND DETAILEDNESS OF PROGRAM	
	LOW	HIGH
Few, low	Free enterprise, market coordination/no control, let the buyer beware!	Centralized state hierarchical, coordination/tight state planning, let the manager beware!
Many, high	Coalitional network coordination/cooperative control, let all take responsibility!	Coalition hierarchical coordination/some state-economic planning around targets, let the elites take responsibility!

parties exerting control or engaged in controlling activities and the extent of their involvement. The combination of these two dimensions suggests four distinctive patterns of coordination or control.

The first pattern is the one most familiar to economists: market coordination. The laws of supply and demand operate as follows. Given a shortage of supply, prices climb, encouraging producers to make more, which creates a replenishment and a new equilibrium. The reverse works as well, as a fall in demand is matched by producers reducing their production. To do so frequently means dismissal of production workers. But what has perhaps not been stressed enough is that while market coordination assumes that buyers can shop around for the best price, they cannot always do so.

The free-market mechanism tends to break down when any of the following conditions occurs: (1) few suppliers, (2) long time delays in the production cycle, (3) high economic barriers to entry, (4) preference of buyers for products based on attributes other than taste/price, (5) inability of buyers to evaluate the product/service because of its technological sophistication, or (6) severe technological barriers to entry. The

first three problems are well known to economists, as they characterize the monopoly sector. Largely ignored, the next three are important in understanding problems in the coordination of more modern market contexts.

Allowing market coordination to occur in the monopoly sector implies that a few large firms will administer prices. High economic barriers and long production cycles will tend to lead to over- and underproduction. Large labor unions negotiate large wage increases in the monopoly sector, with the ensuing emergence of dual labor markets in a free-market economy.

Classical examples of economies where the state allows free-market coordination to prevail are, of course, the United States, Britain, Canada, Australia, and New Zealand—essentially the major English-speaking countries. Although Britain is seen as the prototypical welfare state, and although some of its industries are publicly owned, free-market principles apply to the management of the economy. The coal board, steel board, British Broadcasting Corporation, and other public corporations function independently.

Some of the problems of the free-market coordination mechanism are an overemphasis on consumption and short-term goals rather than the building of society and long-term goals. It tends to lead also to a downgrading of various welfare goals and an overemphasis on individualism.

The second pattern is centralized hierarchical coordination, usually combined with state control via a detailed plan backed by punitive sanctions. Here the central government specifies production quotas, investment priorities, location of plants, and a number of other factors in order to articulate a rational plan, which meshes or integrates the economy or a significant proportion of it. In the past, analyses of this pattern have paid too much attention to the role played by ownership but too little attention to the extent of coordination and of control and to the sanctions employed to back them up. It is the latter that is critical.

This coordination style attempts to maintain comparable wages throughout the society, thus eliminating or at least diminishing differences between the competitive and monopoly sectors. In addition it attempts to plan long-term growth. Precisely where lead-lag times are long and where capital investment is great, one needs planning, whether for the corporate level, the industrial sector level, or the entire economy. Needless to say, the long-time production needs are best appreciated at a more aggregate level than that of the single firm.

This centralized hierarchical model tends to break down where any of the following conditions occurs: (1) demand is volatile and subjected to sharp and sudden shifts in tastes; (2) product lives are short and unstable; (3) workers' and managers' motivations are critical for maintaining quality and innovativeness, as in quality work circles; (4) buyers prefer products on the basis of attributes, such as quality or distinctiveness rather than price; (5) administrators cannot choose research agendas with the highest payoffs; or (6) there are technological barriers to creating new products. The first three conditions are standard arguments against centralized planning. Uncertain markets and worker motivation are usually hailed as causes of the better performance of free-market coordination over modes of hierarchical control. The next three conditions emphasize the importance of innovation and of technological expertise. Although research is difficult to plan, it can be done when it is not entirely based either on consumer preferences or on administrators' initiatives.

Although the classical examples of the centralized hierarchical coordination approach are the Soviet Union, the Eastern European countries, and China, we forget that the United States also used this approach to a certain extent during World War II.

The three most distinctive features of this situation are the centralization and the detailedness of control exerted over the economy or at least over its capital-intensive sectors, as well as the use of negative santions—prison or forced labor—against the individuals who fail to meet the standard set by authorities. Everything is controlled and within rigid boundaries as well, despite surprising gaps, such as pollution control. The centralized hierarchy mechanism leads to an overemphasis on long-term development and on industrial goods, as opposed to consumer goods. Complete control by the state leads also to an overemphasis on military goals, as political goals become more important than economic ones.

Less familiar, the next two patterns of coalition control are equally important. Of the two, the most common is the coalitional hierarchy. This consists of the elites of various sectors of society—labor, the leading industrialists, and various government officials—setting targets and policies in which each organization works out its own destiny, as illustrated by the French term, *action concertée.*

Another important characteristic of this pattern is that the plan is much less detailed than in the case of hierarchical coordination. Usually objectives are set for a varying number of major industrial sectors but not for small firms. Wages and salaries, inflation and investment, and other factors are agreed upon but not tightly controlled. Usually this pattern implies the presence of some social contract by which labor and management agree about the rates of growth in wages, salaries, and profits. Typically labor is protected from layoffs, and in return labor does not stage anything but one-day political strikes. Unemployment is prevented at all costs, with wages and salaries treated as fixed costs. The coalitional hierarchy accommodates more to labor's interests; positive reinforcers—sharing of anticipated profits, subsidization of labor transfers, and so on—are preferred to invisible or visible constraints. This contrasts strictly with the two earlier coordination systems, since in the market approach labor is hired and fired as needed, while in the centralized state hierarchical approach, labor is forced to move to various employments as needed. Perhaps the most distinctive feature of the coalitional hierarchy is the relative absence of a dual labor market.

While the coalitional hierarchy offers much to both advanced capitalist and socialist societies, it is not without its own problems. It tends to break down when the following conditions occur: (1) demand is volatile and subjected to sharp and sudden shifts; (2) product lives are short; (3) worker and managerial motivation are critical for maintaining rapid rates of change; (4) buyers prefer distinctiveness even more than quality; (5) administrators rather than elites tend to pick the most appropriate research agendas; and (6) the absence of horizontal communication links prevents frontier research. The greatest weakness of this style is the problem of handling research and development in areas where the technology is changing rapidly, or what is called high technology in the United States.

Variations of the coalitional hierarchy that differ from the concept of mixed economy are found in France, Japan, and Brazil. The firms can be either publicly or privately owned. Further, there are variations in the processes by which the coalition is brought together, in the nature of the bond created among actors, and in how compliance is achieved. These variations may reflect the way and extent to which owners and workers are organized, the presence of elite schools, or the relative importance of government ownership in the economy. Thus variations in forms of coalitional hierarchy result from specific historical circumstances. But the result is the same, namely, a coalitional hierarchy that engages in planning, usually with positive sanctions.

Previously we suggested that different market contexts defined by product groups may have different coordination styles. Here we are classifying whole economies by one style. In fact, most societies have a dominant style that is employed across all or almost all product groups. This is somewhat less true of what are called mixed economies, although frequently this term is used to describe some mixture of public and private ownership. There one finds some sectors that are coordinated by free-market principles and some that are coordinated by either coalitional hierarchy or centralized hierarchy. The key point is that nowhere do these two coexist.

There is a fourth possibility of control. It is a coalition of middle managers and researchers across a wide variety of different firms of high technology and centers of research, whether public or private. The intent would be to share information both to speed up the rate of technological change and to control it more effectively. The absence of interorganizational links would mean a slowing down of communication and the realization of new opportunities for products, especially custom-made ones.

This form of coordination, called the coalitional network, is rare but is to be found in some public-sector areas.[14] Coordination and planning are not done by elites at the nation-state level but informally, by middle and lower managers who work with a variety of representatives of different industrial and governmental sectors and also with scientists in academia and various government research bureaus. The control is informal, and cooperation is the key.

In the United States, coordination boards have been established to achieve a better delivery of services in areas such as mental health,[15] care for the aged, and city planning. The relative success or failure of this

coalitional network in the public sector has yet to be clearly established.

To conclude, the four coordination styles vary along a series of dimensions. First, control and coordination are minimized in the market system, despite various forms of intervention in most mature capitalistic economies, but maximized in the centralized hierarchical system. Second, negative sanctions are most often used in the centralized hierarchical style, whereas positive sanctions are more common in the coalitional hierarchy. Third, planning occurs in both the centralized and the coalitional hierarchical styles, but it is not as detailed and programmed in the coalitional hierarchy. Fourth, these styles vary in terms of the social contracts involved, and such contracts are critical in the case of the coalitional hierarchy and the coalitional network. Last, coordination styles vary not only between but also within public and private sectors, and coordination may be achieved by the state as well as by conglomerates or multidivisional companies.

THE RELATIONSHIP BETWEEN MARKET CONTEXT AND COORDINATION STYLE

Each of the coordination styles has certain weaknesses that relate to our discussion of the characteristics of market contexts. If the market context has rapid technological change, a mechanism such as centralized hierarchy is not likely to be adaptive enough for this situation. Despite this observation, one finds societies emphasizing the same mechanism in most sectors of the economy. Thus the United States largely advocates a free-market approach and the USSR the centralized hierarchy. Those who prefer

14. Michael Aiken et al., *Coordinating Human Services* (San Francisco: Jossey-Bass, 1975).

15. Ibid.

TABLE 3
MARKET CONTEXTS AND COORDINATION STYLES

TECHNOLOGICAL SOPHISTICA-TION AND PRODUCT CHANGE	STABILITY AND SIZE OF DEMAND	
	LOW	HIGH
Low	Classical market: market co-ordination best	Monopoly market: centralized hierarchical coordination best
High	Individuated market: coalitional network coordination best	Innovative competitive monopoly: coalition hierarchical coordination best

the coalitional hierarchy also use this mechanism in most sectors.

As suggested in Table 3, the classical model of economics works best with products whose primary attributes are taste and price, that is, in situations in which the level of technological sophistication is low and demand is low and stable. There are neither economic nor technological barriers to entry. When demand exceeds supply, it is relatively easy for new suppliers to enter, whereas when supply exceeds demand, it is relatively easy for the less efficient to leave.

Since there are a large number of suppliers, firms are relatively small in the aggregate as well as in individual size. Market forces do regulate competition and price quite effectively in this area. One of the great American success stories in this regard is agriculture. In the operation of farms, where scale economies do not operate as strongly as elsewhere, one finds that allowing market mechanisms to work does result in greater food production. Admittedly, there has been some intervention by the central government, but it is relatively minor compared with the planning of production found in the USSR. The same can be said for other products where taste subdivides demand, and as a consequence there are a number of producers as well as customers.

The centralized hierarchical model is more efficient in market contexts where demand is quite large and stable and where price is an important attribute. Such markets tend to move toward monopolies because sunk costs are large and written off over a long time span. As O'Connor and others have argued, this move is paralleled by the development of large labor unions.[16] The detailed plan attempts to present the development of a dual labor market and maintains prices and wages in line among all sectors in the economy. More important, it aims at minimizing the extent of overproduction and at maintaining continuity of employment. Since the lead-lag times for orders for machinery and equipment are much greater in this sector, individual firms can seriously under- and overestimate their needs.

The advantages of centralized hierarchical coordination become even greater when applied across products that have the same market context. The links between manufacturers in this context—of cars, rubber, steel, oil, and the like—are clear. Their production cycles are tied very much together. Thus it becomes possible to plan effectively, because there are a few producers for each product and because the product demand can be estimated more easily since it is stable and pre-

16. James O'Connor, *The Fiscal Crisis of the State* (New York: St. Martin's Press, 1973).

dicted by the interconnections with other large firms in the market context. The coordination must be done in a detailed plan so that each company can achieve the most rapid and stable growth. In other words, this plan ensures a steady and predictable growth of this part of the economy. The plan works even better when backed by sanctions and tight control.

This particular style characterizes the economies of the USSR and a number of other socialist countries. Even if we take the gross national product (GNP) per capita rather than growth in various sectors, which would be our preferred measure, the GNP per-capita growth of the Soviet Union was 6.4 percent per annum in the period of 1962-72, twice as large as that in the United States, with a modified market economy during the same period.[17] What has gone unnoticed in much of the discussion about the Soviet Union is that hierarchical style works well only in selective sectors.[18]

But why does hierarchical coordination via a detailed plan work in one market context and not another? The monopoly sector involves standardized products. Coordinating the production of these kinds of products is relatively easy. In contrast, as the numbers of producers or suppliers increase, the task of coordination becomes more difficult, because of variations in both their location and their motivation. Detailed plans work against the motivation of both managers and workers. Where economies of scale and standardized production provide more efficiency than what might be lost due to poor motivation, it is worth it. But when

taste is operating, economies of scale are reduced. As standardization has clear upper limits, the loss of motivation becomes a critical problem.

Equally critical, the detailed state plan has not been as effective within those industrial sectors with high technological sophistication. This is because detailed plans do not work well when innovation rather than efficiency is the goal. Innovation is not effectively planned. Moreover, it depends on managements', workers', and consumers' motivations. This is especially true for the research and development side. A large literature indicates that innovation frequently depends on proper information. Centralized hierarchies are good for planned and sustained projects, such as Sputnik or the National Aeronautics and Space Administration (NASA), but not for the encouragement of ideas in a variety of different areas.

The economic growth of the Soviet Union has steadily declined during the past two decades, for as the economy has reached higher levels of development, continued growth has depended on the industries that have high technology. These sectors are currently languishing, because they do not submit as easily to a rational plan.

Coalitional hierarchy works best where the need for diffusion of information enhances the importance of the motivations of managers, workers, and consumers and where an important product attribute is quality. This is one of the distinctive features of Japan.

Why do certain countries make an easier use of coalitional hierarchies than others? France, Sweden, and Japan are countries that vary in how much industry is owned by the government, but in all cases both government and private elites meet

17. Gruchy, *Comparative Economic Systems*.
18. Tönu Parming, Personal communication, 1981.

and accept basic targets for the economy.[19] Further, even though all these countries exert a considerable degree of control over the economy, all rely on voluntary compliances. Rewards such as subsidies, tax breaks, and the like are used as inducements.

To be efficient, coalitional hierarchies require the cooperation of elites. The satisfaction of this particular requirement varies across nations. In France, this cooperation is facilitated by an informal network of graduates of a few grandes écoles. Another factor that facilitates the social bond among the elites is the ownership by the state of a number of key companies, notably of key banking and insurance concerns, since this results in considerable governmental control over investment. Indeed the French government has been responsible for considerable capital formation, which also increases state-economy cooperation.[20]

If the grandes écoles and government investment provide a basis of cooperation in France, the homogeneity of the society and the centralized owner and labor associations do the same in Norway and Sweden. They provide a degree of control over wage demands that is essential for sustained growth.

Thus an important element in all these societies is an essential social contract that tries to protect labor from unemployment and assures a continued rise in real wages. This may be accomplished by different means, but in all cases there is a strong commitment to maintaining employees and workers even during difficult times. Although the origins

of this commitment are different in each society because of a unique configuration of history and economic structure, the consequences are the same: much greater cooperation among different sectors of the society.

In short, the coalitional hierarchy explains the recent high growth rates of these countries. In the case of France it was 4.7 percent in GNP per capita during the 13-year period of 1960-72 before the energy crisis. An Organisation for Economic Cooperation and Development (OECD) study that attempted to evaluate how much of potential growth was realized placed France along with Norway and Sweden in the top category.[21] By 1973 the French GNP per capita was already 85 percent of that of the United States, and since then the gap has been closing. Norway's and Sweden's growth rate of 4.0 and 3.0 percent respectively during the period 1960-73 were slower than France's, but since 1973, Norway's per-capita GNP has surpassed that of the United States, as has Sweden's. This is perhaps the strongest argument for the advantages of coalitional hierarchy a la France, Norway, and Sweden. These countries did not lose as much growth during the energy crisis as did the United States, because their cooperative efforts enabled them to dampen the blow somewhat.[22]

The success story of Japan needs no documentation and is due to many factors, the coalitional hierarchy being only one of them. More than France, Sweden, and Norway, the Japanese have attempted to make quality an important attribute of products previously evalu-

19. Gruchy, *Comparative Economic Systems*, pp. 181-87, 255-59, 307-9.

20. Ibid.; Roger A. Peyrefitte, *Le Mal Français* (Paris: Plon, 1977).

21. Gruchy, *Comparative Economic Systems*.

22. Ibid.

ated on price only. They also benefit from the regrouping of firms that cut across industrial sectors and coordinate internally but compete externally. In one sense Japan has combined both market and coalition hierarchy principles together and has obtained the maximum sustained growth of any economy in the world.

As industrialization expands, the market contexts that have built on technological sophistication become more and more important. In this sense the coalitional hierarchy has much to offer as a coordination mechanism of the future.

To sum up, we would argue that in a complex world where there are a number of product groups, neither the free market nor hierarchical coordination by plan are likely to work across all products. In the former case, the lack of information leads to an underutilization of resources, to an ineffectual support of growing industrial sectors, and to a brutal phasing out of old ones. In the latter case, the detailed plan stifles upward communication and leads to a blocking of innovative ideas. The coalitional hierarchy is more likely to avoid both extremes.

Each coordination type works best in a particular context. The market mechanism works best when there are multiple buyers and suppliers and there are few technological or economic barriers to entry. The state merely intervenes or regulates in a few areas. The centralized hierarchy combined with a detailed plan works best when there are few suppliers and large economic barriers to entry. Here the need to provide predictability of wages, and to prevent them from experiencing extreme variations, are reasons for its rationality. The coalitional hierarchy combined with

a social contract works best when there are large technical and economic barriers to entry. Based on innovation and on the production of quality products, it is designed for ensuring long-term economic growth. It is especially helpful in controlling the rate of inflation. The coalitional network appears particularly well suited to high-technology firms that produce small batches or custom-made products.

CONCLUSION

We began by arguing that increased technological sophistication has meant the emergence of two new kinds of markets. Besides the classical and monopoly markets, there are now what we choose to call the individuated market and the competitive innovative monopoly market. In both cases, technological barriers to entry are more important than economic ones and the products are not evaluated on the basis of price alone but on other attributes as well. In those two markets, there are much greater problems than controlling wages and profits. Coordination is needed to facilitate innovation.

Further, we have suggested that besides the market and hierarchical coordination mechanisms, there are two kinds of mechanisms that are much less discussed. The coalitional hierarchy involves the consensus of elites who plan and accept various economic targets relative to wages, prices, and profits. The coalitional hierarchy involves the consensus of all.

Our central hypothesis is that there is no single way to maximize growth in an economy and that, instead, different coordination mechanisms should be employed in different market contexts. Yet one sees the tendency for each society to prefer a single solution. In the recent past, the centralized hierarchy combined with central planning tended to achieve faster growth than the market approach. However, in the future, as the level of technological sophistication increases, the coalitional hierarchy with a consensual plan should be preferred, if any single solution is selected.

This conclusion raises three problems. First, since the coalitional hierarchy as practiced in Japan, France, Norway, and Sweden reflects different cultural and historical circumstances, one can ask how difficult it would be to transfer this coalitional hierarchy to either the United States or the USSR, regardless of the benefits associated with such a structural transformation. Second, insofar as multinational companies are represented in differing market contexts, they should require different coordination mechanisms. But how likely is this in view of the tendency of all organizations to move toward greater consistency? Third, the tendency of all organizations to move toward greater consistency makes it even more difficult for governmental authorities to adopt diverse coordination mechanisms in various market contexts. Yet if we are to find new ways of controlling inflation, wages, prices, and profits, and of stimulating innovation, we must break out of our traditional modes of thinking and look for new structural arrangements.

ANNALS, *AAPSS*, 459, January 1982

Decentralization and Economic Growth

By HENRY TEUNE

ABSTRACT: This article addresses the question of whether political decentralization is compatible with economic growth. Although the so-called causes of economic growth are indeterminant, governmental centralization has clearly been associated with it for more than a century in industrialized Western democracies. Arguments have been made for the functions of government in facilitating and integrating national markets. The position of this article is that beginning in the 1960s governmental centralization began to shift its role from a contributing to a dampening factor in the processes of economic growth. In fact most of the Western democracies are attempting to reverse the long-term trend of central governmental concentration, whether or not this fosters economic growth.

Henry Teune is professor of political science at the University of Pennsylvania, where he has taught since receiving his Ph.D. from Indiana University in 1961. He is involved in research in several countries in Western and Eastern Europe and Asia, dealing in particular with local political systems. He also has been concerned with the problems of comparing political systems and with theories of social change, as exemplified in two coauthored books, The Logic of Comparative Social Inquiry *(with Przeworski, 1970) and* The Development of Logic of Social Systems *(with Mlinar, 1978). He is currently the president of the International Studies Association.*

G OVERNMENTAL centraliza-
tion in the industrialized world
has been the long-term trend since
the middle of the nineteenth century.
Although the specific institutions
through which centralization has
been achieved vary widely, the overall consequence has been concentration of political decisions in large
localities, municipalities, and the
central government.[1] Nationally,
whether or not the legal system is
formally federal or unitary, the
results have been the same.[2] Also
during the past 150 years or so, the
industrialized countries have been
characterized by per-capita economic growth with periods of
decline and, since World War II and
until the middle of the 1970s, by relatively high growth and economic
stability.

During the late 1960s and 1970s
most of the industrialized countries
considered or actually moved
toward decentralization by various
reforms of local government.[3] These
reforms were a response to approaching a limit of centralization and
were, in part, policies to expand
political participation in both the

public and the private sectors
(worker participation).[4]

For most of this century, it was
argued that governmental centralization would lead to, among other
things, an expansion of a national
market, stability of the monetary
system, and better terms of trade
internationally. More important,
however, were the organizational
imperatives of war and threats of
war. Governmental expansion of
control over the economy, of course,
must be distinguished from centralization, but in general, public
expansion of control over the economy meant central control if for no
other reason than that central
government in every industrialized
country had better access to the
more elastic industrial tax bases.
Industrial expansion led to national
and international production inputs;
consumption of space and goods
remained local, although territorial
constraints on consumption weak-
ened with the emergence of national
economies.[5]

After the relative weakening of
the economic performance of European Communist states in the 1970s,
one viable argument became that

1. Centralization, however assessed—
by budgets, employees, or laws—is redund-
antly observed for the industrial states. The
various variable-level explanations—wars,
elastic income, growth, and competition
among political parties—are matters of controversy. Also it is clear that in the twentieth
century the power of the executive has
increased relative to that of the legislature.

2. Again, it is difficult to find systematic
differences in comparing federal and nonfed-
eral political systems. Part of the problem is
the complexity of intergovernmental organizations and politics.

3. France, generally believed to be the
most centralized industrial country, had
decided to decentralize at the time this article
was being revised.

4. Worker participation in industries is
now the policy of the European Economic
Community (EEC). This is a form of deaggregating decisions. The effects of worker participation at the plant level on local and
national politics and the economy, although
researched, again are open to argument. See
G. David Garson, ed., Worker Self-
Management in Industry: The Western European Experience (New York: Praeger, 1977).

5. See Branko Horvat, The Yugoslav
Economic System: The First Labor Managed
System in the Making (White Plains, NY: M.
E. Sharpe, 1976). The highest rate of real
growth was achieved during the period of
decentralization, 1955-64, estimated at 8.2
percent per annum (social product). The
Yugoslav economy, of course, like many others, became destabilized with inflation at the
end of the 1970s.

they were overly centralized, which led to poor economic performance. The remedy offered by those within those countries as well as by external analysts was to decentralize economic decision-making, if not to destatize or desocialize them. Indeed, after massive decentralization in Yugoslavia in 1952-55 and later after 1965, Yugoslavia achieved one of the highest rates of growth in the world.[6] And the Yugoslavs were among the many recommending decentralization to other socialist countries.

What will be examined are some of the theoretical linkages between centralization and economic growth. The point of departure is that in the industrialized countries more governmental centralization is not possible for a number of reasons, including the most general one that social and economic diversity has reached a point whereby increased hierarchical control is yielding diminishing returns.[7] Also, the industrialized economies became increasingly international. Further, more expansion of the central government relative to the rest of the country cannot continue at the rate it has since the 1960s, if only for the simple reason that in any system one component cannot grow indefinitely at a rate faster than other components without creating a major system transformation. If the U.S. federal government expands as it has since 1960, relative to the expansion of the private sector, it will at some point absorb the private sector, as perhaps it has done with certain aspects of local politics.[8]

DECENTRALIZATION

Centralization and decentralization must be defined in the context of particular types of social systems, for example, a market or a territorial political system. Centralization is a property of the relationships among the components of a system. Total centralization would mean that the behavior of the components would be perfectly predictable from the behavior of one; that is, predicting the system's behavior as well as that of any component would require information about one component and no others. The formalism of treating national law as equivalent to system behavior is an example. The system would be a unity; that is, it could be treated as if it were an entity or component of another system, rather than composed of components, and, as such, would not be a system. A perfectly decentralized system would be one in which information about any one component would provide no information about the behavior of any other. That condition too would be a negation of the definition of a system, as each component would, in effect, behave randomly.

These are the logical extremes presented here to define the outer limits of centralization and decentralization, neither of which is a system that is characterized by interdependence among components with some autonomy of those

6. The breakdown of local markets was one condition of nationalizing the tax base in the United States.

7. For a more theoretical treatment of this, see Henry Teune, "Information Control and the Governability Territorial Political Units," in *Studies in Comparative and International Development*, vol. 14 (Spring 1979), pp. 77-89.

8. For a discussion of the nationalization of local politics in the United States, see Henry Teune, "Nationalization of Local Politics and the Governance of Cities in the United States," *International Political Science Review*, 1(2):280-95 (1980).

components. Thus any empirical system may be characterized on one or more centralization-decentralization dimensions. A market economy, of course, is defined by some level of decentralization of producers and consumers. There are other terms for this concept, including "concentration."

The focus of this discussion is centralization of government, which is the set of institutions that exercise authority through hierarchy and to some extent are separable from the multiple overlapping hierarchies, both national and international, in the economy and from those that constitute the society.

CENTRALIZATION AND ECONOMIC GROWTH

The most general argument for the relationship between governmental centralization and economic growth is that government can act and by its very logic will act, on the one hand, to offset the disintegrating consequences of economic growth and, on the other, to construct markets of size and scale, including assuring economic transactions through law and providing information to producers and consumers.

Whatever the specific linkages between centralized government control and the economy, there has been clear expansion of economic markets, most notably since the fifteenth century. This process of market expansion with the coordinate expansion of production led to the use of the term "economic integration" around 1952, although the concept of economic markets of size is much older.[9]

9. Probably the first to use the term in a book was Jan Tinbergen. See Fritz Machlup,

The historical evidence of the relationship between growth and central government becomes sharper with the industrialization in the West, particularly in the nineteenth century.[10] As an example, the U.S. government's growth until the Civil War (1860) was largely in the post office, used as an intelligence network and a political means for territorial expansion and in revenue collection in response to a growing economy. In addition, with inevitable international involvement and continental expansion there was some growth in the officer corps of the navy and army. Federal control of the economy, aside from the various acts to aid education, began a steady course in 1887 with the creation of the Interstate Commerce Commission followed by the Sherman Antitrust Act. Welfare programs and economic interest-group politics were until then limited, centered almost entirely on state and local governments. Individual-federal contacts began to be significant in the 1930s.

Central government intervention for various welfare functions was earmarked in the industrial period by Germany in 1884 and spread to 13 European countries by 1901.[11] With that, the central governments of industrial countries began acting as a direct economic allocator on the basis of various concepts of justice, rather than acting mostly to

A History of Thought on Economic Integration (London: Macmillan, 1977).

10. For a record of this growth in the United States, see Advisory Commission on Intergovernmental Relations, *The Federal Role in the Federal System: The Dynamics of Growth* (Washington, DC: ACIR, 1980).

11. See U.S. Department of Health, Education and Welfare, *The Social Security Yearbook* (Washington, DC: U.S. Government Printing Office, 1976).

increase political control or to offset similar proclivities of others internationally. Government as economic allocator gave rise to the political economy of pluralism in the United States and some other Western countries.

Whatever the persuasiveness of the various claims about the connections between centralization of government and long-term, stable economic growth, it is clear that there is an empirical connection in the long run, particularly beginning about the 1880s. But there is another side to the argument that government centralization leads to the expansion and integration of economic markets, which in turn stimulates economic growth.[12] Indeed, a contrary position is that at some point and under certain conditions, strong central government dampens economic growth.

A less theoretically attenuated argument concerning the negative relationship between centralization of government and economic growth involves concepts of political fragmentation, centralization, and sticky interest groups. The argument is as follows.[13] Politically fragmented systems, although not necessarily governmentally decentralized—for example, Britain —accumulate interest-group commitments over time. The interest groups and their subsidies stick, as do wages, to central governmental machinery, and as they stick they

inhibit the transfer of labor, capital, and government subsidies to more productive sectors of the economy, which arise because of either new technology or changes in the international political economy.

To the extent that this is true, there is falling productivity and lower economic growth. What can offset these tendencies are two factors: one political, however explained, and the other historical. The first is the development of encompassing political mechanisms, such as in Sweden and Norway, where the various parties can bargain about sharing the costs of dislocating the economy and shifting investments to more productive sectors for mutual gain in the long run. These mechanisms make the terms of the bargains credible over time. The second is the international or national catastrophe that dislocates sticky interest groups, allowing economic sectors to adapt to new opportunities of increasing productivity. The former is best illustrated by Sweden, at least until 1979-80, and by Norway, both characterized by encompassing labor unions. The latter is represented by Germany and Japan, whose prewar interest-group structures were not only totally destroyed during the war but also contained by external rather than domestic political administrations after the war. Also in this category, but to a lesser extent, is France, whose interest-group structure was radically altered with changes in political regimes during and after the war.

DECENTRALIZATION AND ECONOMIC GROWTH

One historical argument for the relationship between decentraliza-

---

12. There was substantial, if variable, economic growth in the United States that was tied to international trade prior to the expansion of the federal government. See, for example, Douglas C. North, *The Economic Growth of the United States 1790-1860* (New York: Norton, 1966).

13. This argument is taken from papers by Mancur Olson and will be published in a forthcoming book.

tion and economic growth is that during early stages of industrialization less central government control over the economy and greater political decentralization are positive conditions for rapid, perhaps costly, economic growth. Central government control, with its bias of stability rather than growth, was an impediment to early, rapid industrialization in the late eighteenth and nineteenth centuries. For example, why did Britain and Japan with fewer natural endowments industrialize more rapidly than France and China with greater natural resources? All countries had about equal access to the folk technology of the eighteenth- and early nineteenth-century industrial production.[14] Both England and Japan were marked by localism; France and China by an imperial bureaucracy. Add to this the example of rapid expansion of the United States, which, although more energy-intensive, surpassed the industrial output of the German principalities around 1850.[15] And there was the rapid economic growth of a previously highly fragmented system, Germany.

Of course, since the latter part of the nineteenth century there were the multiplication of political interests, their organization, and a shift of their organizational activities from the local to the national level. An emerging national market stimulated national interest-group politics, which under the label of pluralism or interest-group politics became a standard political descrip-

tion of U.S. politics early in the twentieth century, and which were used as a model for analyzing other political systems, including the Soviet Union.

ECONOMIC GROWTH AFTER 1945

The historically remarkable period of economic growth after the end of World War II is difficult to explain in long-term macrotheoretical terms. It clearly was accounted for—rather than explained—by neoclassical economists who assumed the position of the philosopher kings of this unprecedented prosperity. It probably will be seen, as it is beginning to be now, as unique historically. It has fallen victim to a variety of theoretical fantasies that change with small perturbations in data and that fixate obsessively on certain cases, such as those of Britain, Sweden, and Japan. But whatever happened during one generation of the West—1945-1975 —during the mid-1970s, the expectation of consistent stable growth was aborted. Indeed during the 1970s the unexpected happened: growth in the Third World, excluding The Organization of Petroleum Exporting Countries (OPEC), exceeded the average of the Western industrialized countries, including Japan.[16]

There are simpler interpretations of economic growth that are independent of political factors, some general and others historically specific. These must be entertained as alternative explanations to politics—public policies and economic growth-decline explanations.

14. This is the question addressed by Robert T. Holt and John E. Turner, *The Political Basis of Economic Development* (Princeton, NJ: D. Van Nostrand, 1966).

15. See North, *Economic Growth.*

16. See *The World Bank, World Development Report 1980*, (Washington, DC: World Bank, 1980).

Certainly they are factors contributing to economic performance.

First, there is demography, an age-old explanation of economic prosperity or decline. One persistent feature of economic growth is simply having more accessible labor and using it more intensely. The United States, Canada, and other nations had a baby boom that is only now working its way through the system, and once it does, employment will stabilize. England did not, for various reasons. Some countries, such as Germany and France, imported a labor force and squeezed additional labor from the countryside. Eastern European countries had a vast labor force available in the countryside, and as they shifted it to industry, they had early growth that diminished when they approached the margins of depleting the agricultural sector, such as Poland and the USSR.

Second, there is the exploitation of cheaper energy, which acts as a solvent both for economic growth and for governmental centralization through increased revenues. The declining real cost of energy until the 1970s was buttressed by cheap commodities, made accessible by the surplus resources of the United States and its policies of open trade, open sea lanes, and an international monetary system stabilized by domestic policies and foreign aid. Difficulties in sustaining economic growth were encountered with a hardening of the nonindustrialized countries to penetration.

Third, there is technological change—the water wheel, the steam engine, the generator. Unfortunately, new technology becomes a diverse thing for national comparisons because of its international accessibility. Nonetheless, there are general patterns, often argued for in self-interested ways, for relating post-World War II investment in education and research and development to some kind of time-lagged economic growth.

Fourth, there are specific historical circumstances that can explain specific patterns of high growth and industrialization. One example of this category of explanations concerns the presence of U.S. troops. Poor countries in the early 1950s, such as Japan, Korea, and Germany, experienced high demand for certain services and products, which, it can be argued, built an economic infrastructure that became a foundation for rapid industrial growth.

Whatever the explanation, on a worldwide basis the Western industrialized countries were transformed after World War II, following more than a decade of massive economic contraction. Although there were similar contractions earlier, they were more localized despite the high economic interdependence before World War I, a level of economic interdependence not yet regained. These global factors must be given considerable theoretical weight before deaggregating the economic performance of the industrial world into the politics and policies of specific countries.

GOVERNMENT EXPANSION
IN THE 1960s

Although data, and comparative data even from OECD countries, on growth, employment, and other factors are comparable largely by assumption and are difficult to interpret, the public or government sectors of all industrialized countries, with the possible exception of the highly international political economies of Japan and Switzerland, grew more rapidly than their relatively rapidly growing economies in the 1960s. Although the limit to this expansion is not known, given the nature of the international economy and its nongovernmental economic enterprises, most industrial countries suspect they are approaching a limit and since 1977 have made nonexpansionist corrections in their politics and policies, if only in response to popular resistance and unpopularity of government. Why this expansion?

Probably the best general explanation is the theoretical one that as the external environment of an organization becomes less stable and more threatening, there is increased asserted control within. This, of course, is one long-term explanation of the episodic pattern of governmental growth: expansion during the war and after-war retention of much of the governmental control apparatus. Data seem to bear this out in part for the United States, a highly fragmented system politically.[17] Another analysis of data during the 1960s shows that the relative size of the public sector is attributable to the openness of the economy to international penetration.[18]

As has been argued, economic expansion in the industrialized countries because of the nature of integrated markets will favor larger units that have more access to

elastic revenue based on large markets. This is borne out by comparison of government growth at the local, state, and national levels in the United States in the twentieth century.

DECENTRALIZATION AND
FURTHER ECONOMIC GROWTH

It has been suggested that decentralized political systems and perhaps small government may be conducive to economic growth in early stages of industrialization and that government, as either a cause or a consequence of economic growth, expands along with economic growth. A major policy question is whether today decentralization of industrialized countries—a change in the direction of growth of governmental control—is theoretically incompatible with further economic growth. The question for analysis is, What are some empirical indicators that decentralization is at least not incompatible with general economic growth? Or is economic growth decisively a national rather than an international or subnational phenomenon?

This is not a moot question, as a number of countries have either begun a process of decentralization, such as Italy and France, or have placed it high on their political agendas, such as the United States and Canada. Further, in North America recent data indicate for the first time in the twentieth century an increase in regional differences rather than a decrease.[19] It is also a difficult research question, since the units of comparison—Sweden ver-

17. The various war-governmental expansion explanations are difficult to support as causal explanations. For example, for much of the twentieth century European countries were at war, preparing for war, or paying for past wars.

18. See David E. Cameron, "The Expansion of the Public Economy: A Comparative Analysis," *American Political Science Review* 72:1243-61 (Dec. 1978).

19. Advisory Commission on Intergovernmental Relations, *Regional Growth: Historic Perspectives*, (Washington, DC: U.S. Government Printing Office, 1980).

sus Germany versus the United States, for example—have a magnitude of differences in scale and involvement in the world economy. And, of course, the analysis of growth is related to the analysis of internal national differences, as some areas and sectors grow and some to not; indeed some areas and sectors regress.

What is required methodologically are several point predictions over time concerning aspects of decentralization. The point predictions should be as close to the behavior of the system as possible. For example, we need predictions about the type of investment by region within countries, rather than correlations between general rank on decentralization and aggregate national growth across countries.

Investments

One characteristic of a decentralized system is that it may promote the development of different regional investment climates that to some extent are locally defined. Further, these alternative local investment environments will be better able to mesh with the needs of growing or new economic organizations. The general hypothesis is that the greater the decentralization and the greater the alternative local options on taxation and investment incentives, the higher the ratio of new investment that is national rather than international, at least in the long run.

Interest-group allocations

Although difficult to measure, centralized systems should be characterized by greater welfare and interest-group subsidies as a pro-

portion of total national governmental expenditures more than less centralized ones. In part this is a consequence of alternative foci for interest-group claims at the local levels. But more decentralized systems should have a larger number of active interest groups. This, in part, is a function of a larger number of entry points for political influence, and the larger the number of such points, the greater the potential of interest-group leaders to reward their members with more victories, even though those victories are less and less sustainable than if they were achieved at the national level.[20] A less attenuated relationship than the global one between centralization and economic growth is that decentralization invites more interest groups but less governmental allocation to them.

If it is true that central interest-group subsidies stick and make difficult the movement of labor and capital to the new and more productive sectors of economy, then there should be some long-term consequences for economic growth.

Invention

One ingredient of economic growth is technological innovation. A critical question is whether centralization of government and central control of the economy dampens the rate of innovation, however difficult that is to measure. During the past decade there have been historic shifts in the places of origin of new patents and inventions. If the theoretical arguments for why bureaucracies have difficulty in generating

20. For an elaboration on this, see Henry Teune, "Concepts of Evidence in Systems Analysis: Testing Macro-System Theories," *Quality and Quantity*, 15:55-70 (1981).

innovations is empirically true, then those countries with less centralization and less central control over the economy should have relatively higher rates of innovation. The relationship between inventions and economic growth, of course, is presumed but empirically controverted.

Inequalities

Decentralized systems tend to tolerate inequalities among both regions and population strata within countries. For this there are sound theoretical arguments, as well as some empirical evidence.

Decentralization, of course, serves goals other than those of economic growth and equality, such as those values purported to be facilitated by the principle of federalism: governmental innovation in local laboratories for which there is only weak evidence and the integrity of cultural and ethnic groups. Among other values is participation, which to some extent requires decentralization; this poses a dilemma for certain countries, as in the case of Yugoslavia, one of the few countries that after 1952 based its ideology on decentralization rather than centralization. If the ideology of a political system is political participation, as it is becoming in some Western European countries, the goals of economic growth and increased participation may be compatible though decentralization. But if, as seems to be the case, decentralization leads to greater inequality economically, then the notion of participation, requiring as it does some level of relative equality of the participants, is harmed by decentralization. The

tensions between growth, participation, and equality lead to political instability and much of the debate over decentralization.

CONCLUSION

For nearly a century professional political analysts have assumed the positive function of the state and in particular governmental centralization to achieve and assure abundance. This position was extremely controversial at the turn of the century in the United States. In the postwar period the association among centralization, economic growth, and economic equality was argued on theoretical grounds and given empirical documentation, but, most important, was vindicated by experience. Where there were observed failures, such as in Britain and the United States—particularly those arising in the 1970s—the remedies offered were to increase coordination and remove political fragmentation. Yet for a number of reasons growth in the 1980s will be slow and political fragmentation will continue.

Since 1975 there has been a loss of confidence in the capacity of central governments to perform, although the quality of their performance probably has never been higher. Decentralization is an alternative. The question is whether deurbanization, urban decentralization, regionalism, and the like are theoretically compatible with economic growth and some measure of economic equality—although the problem here is more than economic equality. It may turn out that decentralization does not dampen but in fact stimulates economic growth.

ANNALS, *AAPSS*, **459**, January 1982

The State's Role in Third World Economic Growth

By JAMES A. CAPORASO

ABSTRACT: The emergence of a group of newly industrializing countries has received considerable attention in the scholarly literature today. However, most of the attention has focused on the economic aspects of this phenomenon, for example, changing comparative advantages, utilization of cheap labor markets, and tariff structures. The role of the state in this process of industrial growth has been neglected. The state plays a role in economic growth in various ways: supplying infrastructural needs—transportation and communication—subsidizing development in areas of high growth potential, and entering the economy directly in the form of state enterprises. These forms of state economic activity, as well as an argument for state involvement in the economy, are examined in this article.

James A. Caporaso is Andrew W. Mellon Professor of International Studies at the Graduate School of International Studies of the University of Denver. He received his Ph.D. from the University of Pennsylvania in 1968 and taught on the faculty of the Department of Political Science of Northwestern University from 1968 to 1978. He is the author of articles that have appeared in the American Political Science Review, International Organization, International Studies Quarterly, *and* Journal of Common Market Studies.

T O put it in dramatic terms, a quiet revolution has been taking place that has substantially changed the position of many less developed countries in the global division of labor. While members of the Organization of Petroleum Exporting Countries (OPEC) have yet to demonstrate that they can convert their huge capital reserves into an industrial structure, a sizable number of less developed countries have quietly become industrial countries. This does not mean that South Korea and Brazil are now at the cutting edge of global production in high-speed computers and microelectronics. However, it would be equally inaccurate to cast all less developed countries in their traditional role of "hewers of wood and drawers of water."

Plainly, changes have taken place in the international division of labor. One can legitimately argue about the importance of these changes, the extent to which they reflect development in society as a whole, their permanence, and whether these countries are likely to have the capacity continually to transform themselves into more sophisticated industrial—and ultimately postindustrial—systems. In this article I will concentrate more on what has already taken place and the role of the state in these changes, rather than on the possibilities for growth and transformation.

PROFILE OF INDUSTRIAL GROWTH AMONG LESS DEVELOPED COUNTRIES

The changes in industrial structure can be described in both general terms—that is, in language describing the less developed world—and in terms of specific countries. At the general level, if we look at the exports of developing countries, we find that the increase of manufactures as a share of total exports—excluding fuel exports—rose from 19 percent in 1960 to 37 percent in 1970 to 42 percent in 1974.[1] Put on an annual basis, manufactured exports grew at a rate of over 12 percent a year from 1960 to 1975. This growth pattern was strong and withstood for the most part the slowdown of economic activity among countries of Western Europe and North America.[2]

It is true that these manufactured exports, and the domestic manufacturing production on which they are based, are nowhere nearly equally distributed across countries. The bulk of manufacturing production comes from a limited number of less developed countries. South Korea, Taiwan, Spain, and Hong Kong together supply close to 45 percent of total less-developed-country manufacturing exports, with Brazil, Mexico, Yugoslavia, India, and the Philippines also accounting for a substantial portion.[3]

Industrialization among the countries of the Third World seems to cut across a large number of differences in geography, culture, ideology, types of regimes, and resource endowments. Brazil is a large country, rich in natural resources, and possesses a high internal market. The possibilities for growth without reliance on external markets are great. Brazil's rapid growth has been engineered by an authoritarian regime and has

1. Kathryn Morton and Peter Tulloch, *Trade and Developing Countries* (New York: John Wiley, 1977), pp. 39-42.

2. Hollis B. Chenery and Donald B. Keesing, *The Changing Composition of Developing Country Exports*, World Bank Staff Working Paper no. 314 (Washington, DC: World Bank, 1979), p. 12.

3. Chenery and Keesing, "The Changing Composition," p. 13.

been accompanied by a large dose of internal inequalities. Mexico, with her oil discoveries and plans for industrial growth, is experiencing both increases in the standard of living and problems of pollution, congestion, and urban decay.

The Asian late developers—for example, South Korea, Hong Kong, Taiwan, and Singapore, those other Japans or Asian Hollands as some have called them—pose quite a contrast. Since these countries are small and resource-poor, their route to industrialization of necessity is tied to an export strategy. The strong card of these countries is their disciplined and low-cost labor force, skilled in areas such as textiles, apparel, and electronics. In South Korea strikes are not allowed and organized political activity on the part of labor is severely restricted. Young female workers form the backbone of the labor force in industries such as electronic assembly and clothing, where apparently their manual dexterity as well as docility are characteristics favored by factory owners.

These differences are important, and they make for important variations in the style, rate, and substance of the overall development process. But there is one feature shared by these countries. In almost all cases, perhaps with Hong Kong being the clear exception, the state entered the economy and played an aggressive role in the industrialization process. As Müller argues, these rapidly growing states "had one thing in common—a development strategy that emphasized the mobilization of finance (domestic and foreign) and the targeting of it into investments that raised productivity."[4] In this article, I explore the

4. Ronald E. Müller, *Revitalizing America: Politics for Prosperity* (New York: Simon & Schuster, 1980), p. 109.

role of the state in the process of industrial growth in less developed societies and explore the arguments for state involvement in industrializing countries today.

SOME CONCEPTUAL PRELIMINARIES

Before examining the role of the state in the process of industrial growth, a necessary preliminary question confronts the investigator: How does one conceptualize the state and its role in society in general? Although this question is distinctly important, to address it seriously would take me far afield. What follows is an abbreviated statement.

There are four ideal-type conceptions of the state, and I find parts of each relevant for my investigation. There is the liberal conception that sees the state as a provider of goods the markets will not produce—defense, roads, and public health—as well as the arbiter of the interest-group process. The state is relatively neutral in this process: it is not an interest group itself, nor does it serve the interest of any one societal group. The Marxist conception of the state provides stark contrast. The state is little more than the political expression of the dominant class in society. Still another contrast, this one in a different dimension, is provided by the state-for-itself interpretation. Very simply, the state is conceived neither as an impartial arbiter of group claims nor as a vehicle of the ruling class, but rather as a combination of individual careers and organizational interests that are primarily self-serving. Finally, the nationalist state is seen as one where state institutions mobilize societal resources exclusively for national concerns.

The interpretation pursued here is not consistent with a strong liberal view of the state, since the state both is an important group itself and shapes—builds up and destroys—other societal groups. It is also inconsistent with the strong Marxist interpretation in the sense that some, indeed quite a bit, of state autonomy is presumed.

THE STATE'S HISTORIC ROLE IN DEVELOPMENT

The modern state plays a strong role in economic development. This is generally recognized. What is not usually recognized is that the state has played an important part in economic development historically. If we leave aside the case of England, and perhaps later the United States, where economic development took place with minimum state intervention, the state played a central role in industrial development.

The domestic economic policies of states led, often unwittingly, to the conditions for industrial growth. States were not primarily interested in economic welfare and modernization during the seventeenth and eighteenth centuries. They were interested in creating what Tilly calls "the domestic sinews of war."[5] Nevertheless, many of the state's activities that led to an efficient military machine also led to the conditions for economic growth: an integrated system of roads and canals, the destruction of local sources of revenue, standardization of languages, a centralized bureaucracy with efficient mechanisms to collect taxes, and so on.

In the eighteenth century the British Parliament initiated a system of toll roads and canals. In France, Louis XIV's minister of finance, Jean Baptiste Colbert, reduced river and road tolls and substituted a national customs union.[6] Royal leaders, from Charles XII of Sweden to Peter the Great in Russia, involved the state in the economy. Royal factories were created, joint stock companies were chartered, and supplies of crucial industrial materials were assured.[7]

There are, of course, important differences between the early industrializers and those countries seeking to go down that road today. Purely at the psychological level, important differences are to be expected. The people of the world today are confronted with the existence of rich countries and, within their own boundaries, wealthy classes of people. Their awareness of what is possible has been expanded and their hopes have been excited. Thus they expect more and they place pressure on governments to deliver.

Second, the less developed countries of the world today have a greater capacity to mobilize resources. Although the problems of governing their own societies should not be underestimated, the ability to establish centralized institutions, to penetrate the society, to collect taxes, and to wield the tools of economic policy are probably greater today. State institutions during the seventeenth and eighteenth centuries were trying to make peasants aware of their mere existence, to secure food supplies from country to city, to extract a steady flow of revenue from outside the narrow regions they controlled. Today's obstacles to state development are

5. Charles Tilly, "Reflections on the History of European State-Making," in *The Formation of National States in Western Europe*, ed. Charles Tilly (Princeton, NJ: Princeton University Press, 1975), pp. 3-83.

6. W. W. Rostow, *How It All Began: Origins of the Modern Economy* (New York: McGraw-Hill, 1975), p. 47.

7. Rostow, *How It All Began*, pp. 39-60.

real, but they do not measure up to the obstacles present in earlier times.

A third difference is perhaps the most relevant one for current developing countries. I am speaking of differences in the context or environment of industrialization. Briefly, countries wishing to industrialize today have more competitors, and these competitors occupy a more differentiated industrial terrain than previously. This means that the available niches, or slots, in the international system are more limited. For today's industrializers, therefore, the process of industrialization cannot be a haphazard affair, nor can the pace, content, and direction be left solely to market forces. This leads us directly to the position that the state will play a large role in planning and guiding the industrial process, a theme I will take up in the next section.

CONTEMPORARY ROLE OF THE STATE IN ECONOMIC DEVELOPMENT

The state plays an important and increasingly varied role in economic development today. The state's presence in the economy ranges from simply providing the infrastructure for development—roads, communications, and electricity—to reorganizing the productive enterprise.[8] In between, the state may encourage industrial activity by subsidizing the export sector, fostering liberal trade and payment regimes, providing fiscal incentives for the industrial sector, allowing accelerated depreciation allowances for industrial machinery, and encouraging cheap input for industrial goods.

8. Behrouz Zare, "The State and Economic Development in Non-Socialist Developing Countries," mimeographed (Denver: University of Denver, June 1980), p. 2

In South Korea the state is heavily involved in the private sector, where it has tried to follow the Japanese example in fostering zaibatsu-like conglomerates to compete in today's environment. In 1979 the South Korean government promulgated a law aimed at modernizing its already aging textile industry and established new goals for annual textile exports.[9] The following year, South Korea demonstrated its capacity in steel-making by completing its first integrated steel mill, the state-owned Pohang Iron and Steel Company (POSCO). South Korea supplies her domestic market with steel costing $50 to $100 per ton less than steel produced in the United States and Japan.[10]

Individual policies vary widely, but it is in the ownership of firms—that is, state firms—that one can most clearly see the state's ascendant role. In Mexico, the government's share of capital investment rose from 33 percent in 1970 to 50 percent in 1976, and President Portillo has pledged himself to state-backed production quotas, backing these pledges up by a system of fiscal incentives and efforts to clear away bureaucratic obstacles.[11] Mexico is no exception when it comes to state-owned enterprises. These enterprises have increased in countries as diverse as Brazil, South Korea, Indonesia, Bolivia, and the Philippines. Gillies reports that the share of state-owned enterprises in gross investment outside agriculture is around 75 percent in Bolivia, Ban-

9. "South Korea's Mills Are Aging," *World Business Weekly* 4(9):12 (Mar. 9, 1981).
10. "South Korea's Steel Plans Come to Fruition," *World Business Weekly*, 4(12):11 (30 Mar. 1981).
11. "Mexico's Reluctant Oil Boom: A Tight Rein on Development to Promote Balanced Growth," *Business Week*, 2568-68 (15 Jan. 1979).

gladesh, and Mexico, 50 percent in India and Turkey, and between 25 and 33 percent in South Korea and Brazil.[12] The state as entrepreneur, acting to achieve industrial growth, has clearly arrived.

UNDERSTANDING THE ROLE OF THE STATE IN DEVELOPING ECONOMIES

One could multiply examples of the role of the state in developing economies indefinitely, but this would not serve a clear purpose. In this section I put forth some arguments, based on the economic development literature, for state participation in economic development. I present four such arguments, all of them related, and all point, I think, to a continued role for the state, at least during the early stages of economic development.

The first argument concerns the large, lump-sum capital requirements needed to enter particular industries. According to this view, the entrance requirements in terms of financial capital and capital equipment are very large in certain industries, and the size of these obstacles will serve as barriers to entry on the part of private investors. One can imagine that these obstacles are imposing in industries such as steel production, automobiles, electronics, and perhaps even parts of the textile industry. In addition, there are what Myint calls "technical indivisibilities in social overhead capital."[13] Public utilities, transport, and communications facilities must be in place before industrial development can occur,

and they do not lend themselves to small-scale improvements.

The implication of this position is that a minimum critical mass is required for certain inputs into the productive process. Gerschenkron speaks of "minimum capital needs of an industrializing economy" or the "minimum size of the individual industrial firm and the availability of technologically required inputs."[14] These words, written with the late nineteenth and early twentieth centuries in mind, seem all the more insightful and relevant in the context of our more internationalized world today.

A related argument centers on the demand side of the economy. This economy is seen as fragmented, disconnected, and incapable of using inputs from other parts of the economy. Consequently, economic activity in one part of the economy does not generate the dynamism in other sectors that is expected in more cohesive economies. This results in important economic losses. As Behrouz Zare points out, "Because of the low interconnectedness between sectors, and the lack of sufficient diversified investment, these countries are not able to capture or exploit external economies."[15] By external economies he means such things as infrastructure and cheaper intermediate inputs.

This argument goes beyond the need for minimum capital inputs for industrial development. It argues that the process of industrialization necessarily involves many different sectors, that it will be stunted if confined to a few sectors and that, if industrialization is to occur at all, it

12. Malcolm Gillies, "The Role of State Enterprises in Economic Development," *Social Research*, 47(2):224-55 (Summer 1980).

13. Hla Myint, *The Economics of the Developing Countries* (New York: Praeger, 1964), p. 116.

14. Alexander Gerschenkron, *Economic Backwardness in Historical Perspective* (Cambridge, MA: Belknap Press, 1962), p. 35.

15. Zare, "The State and Economic Development," p. 27.

must occur along a broad front. Economic enterprises will thrive best in an environment in which they draw on inputs from related economic sectors and, in turn, release their own goods for industrial utilization within their own economies.

A third argument concerns the low-level equilibrium trap in which less developed countries find themselves.[16] The argument is as follows. At subsistence levels, societies are in equilibrium in the sense that they consume exactly what they produce. There is no remaining surplus for reinvestment. As per-capita income rises, however, the additional income will not be used for savings and investment. Instead, it will have the effect of increasing the population that will eat up the surplus and force the society to its former subsistence position. Population increase, opportunistically working in conjunction with a rise in per-capita income, locks people into a vicious cycle of poverty.

The traditional view of the vicious circle as going from low productivity to low savings and investment to low productivity somewhat understates the problem. It does not take into account the perverse forces working against incremental advances in productivity, forces that pull Sisyphus and his rock inexorably back to the bottom of the hill.

The bright point for advocates of economic development, if not for Sisyphus, is that there is a plateau at the top of the hill. Once reached, this plateau provides a kinder environment for economic development. At a less metaphorical level, what I am saying is this: population does increase along with increases in income, but it does not do so indefi-

nitely. After a certain point, the rate of population growth will decrease and perhaps even reach zero. When this happens, economic growth will intersect with and eventually outstrip population growth.

The policy conclusions of all three arguments are the same, though the reason varies in each case. The minimum capital needs for a firm, the need for diversified growth, and the failure of incremental increases of output in overcoming population increases all argue for state intervention in the economy. The private sector will not be able to provide the large doses of capital, the simultaneous growth across sectors, and the one-shot large dose of capital to push economic growth beyond those levels where population increases eat up the incremental advances.

The final argument to be considered concerns the relationship between delayed development and the state. Let us start with the general hypothesis advanced by Gerschenkron. Gerschenkron argued on general theoretical grounds and with reference to case studies that the later the process of industrial development occurs and the more backward the country on the eve of industrialization, the more likely will it be that it proceeds under strong organized auspices, for example, banks and the state.[17] Why is this so? To the previous arguments about the minimum capital requirements of an industrializing economy, the vicious circle, and the need for diversified investments, we now add the increasingly competitive global economic environment in which less developed countries must now pursue their goal of industrial growth.

16. For a lucid account of the low-level equilibrium trap, see Myint, *Economics of Developing Countries*, ch. 7.

17. Gerschenkron, *Economic Backwardness*, p. 44.

This argument must be prefaced by an answer to the question of why a developing country would want to enter the global economy at all. Why not just produce for the local market, as advocated by some proponents of self-reliance? While this has some attractions, the case for trade is a compelling one. The small size of most less-developed-country markets and the limited ability of less developed countries to fulfill their needs solely through development of their own resources makes this strategy a difficult one. The expansive foreign markets, finished goods, and importable technologies make some division of labor almost necessary.

When the first countries industrialized, they had no superior, established, industrial competitors in front of them. They were in effect the cutting edge of industrial growth. This front-line position had associated advantages and disadvantages. On the positive side, there were no superiors to overtake, no established producers with historical market shares with which to deal. It also meant, however, there was no one to imitate, to take out loans from, or from whom they could import technology.

As more and more countries industrialized, the international system became a more competitive place. True, the technical possibilities for imitating the success of others and borrowing from their storehouse of recipes for industrial growth were advanced by each new entrant. But the number of positions available could not be expanded indefinitely and competition became very stiff.

From the standpoint of an industrializing country today, the competition faces them at many levels. They are faced with the advanced capitalistic countries who have large, efficient firms, various forms of state support of the private sector, superb marketing strategies, and the organizational know-how necessary for holding onto their historical market shares in domestic and foreign markets. Given the slowdown of economic activity in Western Europe and North America during the 1970s, the dramatic successes of Japan in taking over some of their markets, and the oil price increases, the countries in the North Atlantic world are more rather than less motivated not to let their market positions deteriorate further.

There are other levels of competition in addition to that of the advanced, industrial countries. For the newly industrializing countries, there is also the threat of competition from below. South Korea has Sri Lanka, Thailand, and China to worry about. Given the availability of machinery and capital equipment in low-technology areas such as clothing and footwear, other countries could acquire it. South Korea's asset, a cheap and industrious labor force, is by no means unique, and her political and industrial leaders are well aware of this. If labor is cheap in South Korea, it is even more so in Sri Lanka.

In addition to the increased number of countries already placed in the industrial ranks, the global economy has become increasingly competitive in a different way in terms of the internationalization of the world economy. The share of trade in total domestic economic activity has increased, as has the spread of capital and technology across national borders. With the opening up of these borders, it has become very difficult to produce for domestic markets. With the flow of technology and the diminishing of barriers to trade, the cost requirements for producing competitively in the domestic and the international environments have become increasingly synchronized.

International competition has forced governments in developing societies to identify their strong card and to pursue it vigorously. This strong card has generally been identified as some combination of cheap labor, operating in labor-intensive, low, and intermediate technologies, in an overall business environment that is considered safe by foreign investors. Sometimes this combination is given full expression by the establishment of free production zones, where low taxes, generous credit, cheap labor, and incentives to export are brought together to entice foreign investment into a country.

CONCLUSION

The state has played a strong role in economic growth historically and plays an even stronger role today. Part of the reason for a strong state presence is to be found in traditional economic arguments about balanced growth and critical minimum inputs of capital and technology to overcome the vicious circle. Part of the reason is new and relates specifically to the competitive international environment in which modern countries and firms must operate.

Perhaps the strong role of the state is a temporary one and will not outlive the period during which a country seeks to overcome the initial obstacles to its industrialization. Once it has overcome its initial barriers to development, the state might see its mission fulfilled and hand back the running of the economy to the private sector. On the other hand, industrial development is an ongoing process with new challenges constantly posing themselves. The years ahead are likely to see new and more intense forms of political intervention in the economy.

ANNALS, *AAPSS*, **459**, January 1982

Government Regulations and Their Impact on the Economy

By GREGORY B. CHRISTAINSEN and ROBERT H. HAVEMAN

ABSTRACT: The performance of the American economy during the 1970s was distinctly inferior to the record of the previous decade. A prominent hypothesis is that oppressive government regulation was largely responsible for the poor performance of the 1970s. This article examines that hypothesis with respect to a key marcoeconomic indicator: the rate of productivity growth.

Gregory B. Christainsen is an assistant professor of economics at Colby College in Waterville, Maine. He received a B.A. in economics and philosophy at the University of Wisconsin, Madison, in 1974 and has since received an M.A. and a Ph.D. in economics from that institution. He has served as a consultant to the U.S. Office of Technology Assessment and Resources for the Future and has written widely on the impact of government regulation on employment and productivity.

Robert H. Haveman is professor of economics and Fellow, Institute for Research on Poverty, University of Wisconsin, Madison. From 1970 to 1975 he was director of the Institute for Research on Poverty. He has served as senior economist on the Joint Economic Committee of the U.S. Congress, research professor at the Brookings Institution, and Fellow of the Netherlands Institute for Advanced Study. He has written widely in the areas of benefit-cost analysis, and economics of poverty and inequality, regional economics, and the economic effects of government regulation.

DURING the decade of the 1970s the performance of the U.S. economy in terms of its key macroeconomic indicators was extremely disappointing. Statistics on the growth rate of output, unemployment, capital formation, productivity growth, and inflation combined to paint a gloomy picture.

During the previous decade there was no year in which real gross national product (GNP) declined, and the average annual growth rate was 4.12 percent.[1] In the 1970s, however, real GNP showed a decline in three years—1970, 1974, and 1975—and the average annual rate of real GNP growth was only 2.87 percent.

As one might expect, the growth in output during the 1960s was accompanied by lower rates of unemployment. From 1960 to 1969 the nation's unemployment rate averaged 4.78 percent. The corresponding figure for 1970-79 was 6.19 percent. The rate of inflation was also lower during the 1960s, with the Consumer Price Index rising at an average annual rate of 2.33 percent. The average inflation rate for the 1970s was 7.11 percent.

A declining rate of capital formation has been another source of concern. Real gross private domestic investment advanced at an annual rate of 4.78 percent during the 1960s, but increased at a rate of only 2.49 percent during the 1970s.

The gloomy economic experience of this decade was accompanied by rising popular concern that government regulations were impeding economic performance and thereby contributing to inflation and unemployment. In this article, we will discuss the potential role of these regulations in adversely affecting a most basic economic variable: the rate of growth of productivity. If regulations can be blamed for bad economic performance, it is through their effect on this engine of economic growth.[2]

THE IMPORTANCE OF PRODUCTIVITY GROWTH

Statistics can be misleading, and some observers question the relevance of oft-cited macroeconomic variables as indicators of an economy's performance. Almost all of these variables refer to output or inputs, but not to both at the same time. The efficiency with which an economy performs, however, is reflected in its output per unit of input—both output and inputs must be considered. Thus measures of the rate of growth of productivity—output per unit of input—are crucial in explaining an economy's performance.

In concept, a nation's productivity can be defined simply as its aggregate final output per unit of input. However, because of difficulties in aggregating the diverse outputs and inputs of a modern economy, the measurement of productivity performance is not a straightforward matter. The most common procedure has been to measure productivity by obtaining an estimate of final aggregate private-sector output divided by the number of person-hours of labor input used in producing this output. This concept could be called a single-factor productiv-

---

1. See the *Economic Report of the President, 1980* (Washington, DC: U.S. Government Printing Office, 1980).

2. Of course, regulations are not the only means by which the state may affect economic efficiency. Tax policies, monetary and financial policies, and the impact of official statements on public attitudes toward work and risk-taking are also important.

ity measure, and because it does not reflect in its denominator the full set of inputs, it has clear weaknesses. It is, however, the official way in which productivity growth is measured.

DOCUMENTING THE PRODUCTIVITY DECLINE

By this measure—or any fuller measure developed by economists—productivity growth in the United States has undergone a sharp decline since the mid-1960s. From 1947 to 1966, output per person-hour in the private sector grew at an average annual rate of 3.44 percent.[3] During this period there were cyclical deviations from the trend rate of growth, but otherwise the series is a relatively smooth one. Then, beginning in 1966 or 1967, there appears to have been a break in the time trend. From 1966 to 1973, private-sector output per person-hour grew at an average annual rate of 2.15 percent, a decline of almost 1.3 percentage points from the earlier period. In 1973, a further break seems to have occurred, and from 1973 to 1978 an annual rate of only 1.15 percent was registered—only one-third of the recorded rate for the immediate war period and a further decline of a full percentage point from the period 1966-73. Since 1978, productivity growth has been effectively zero—indeed, negative in some quarters. If the growth trend from 1945 to 1965 had persisted until 1980, labor productivity in the United States would have been

about 15 percent greater than it actually was.

This poor productivity growth performance has not been uniformly spread over the economy. The manufacturing sector, for example, has had only a slight deterioration in its productivity growth, even though the brunt of government regulations has fallen on it. The most dramatic slowdown in productivity growth has occurred in the nonmanufacturing industries of mining, construction, and utilities.

One final note: while the productivity growth trend in the United States does not compare favorably with those in other countries, output per person-hour is still higher in the United States than in any other country. The gap is closing, but it still exists.

INFLATION AND PRODUCTIVITY GROWTH

Declining productivity growth reflects a fundamental problem in macroeconomic performance and underlies other symptoms of economic malfunction. The problems of inflation and the productivity slowdown are related in a number of ways. For example, the dislocations caused by accelerating rates of inflation may well generate inefficiencies that contribute to the decline in productivity growth. Conversely, to the extent that inflationary pressures exist, low rates of productivity growth will contribute to these pressures.

There is a simple but very important statistical relationship among labor productivity, wages, and inflation: to the extent that wages go up at a faster rate than productivity, the balance must come out in the form of higher prices. Stated alternatively, wages can increase at a

3. See J. Mark, Testimony Before the Congressional Joint Economic Committee, in *Special Study on Economic Change: Hearings Before the Joint Economic Committee*, part 2 (Washington, DC: U.S. Government Printing Office, 1978), pp. 476-486.

rate equal to that of productivity, without increasing production costs and prices. If productivity growth is zero, wage demands of, say, 6 percent necessarily imply cost and price increases of 6 percent. Only if productivity growth increases can these wage demands be met without such large inflation consequences. During the 1960-64 period, for example, wages went up at an annual rate of 4.5 percent. Because productivity increased at a 3.5 percent clip, inflation was only one percent a year as measured by the Consumer Price Index. The 3.5 percentage point difference in the growth rate of wages and prices represented a significant improvement in living standards during this period.

In 1974, on the other hand, wages increased at a 9 percent rate, twice the pace of the 1960-64 period. But the inflation rate of 12 percent meant a decline in living standards —productivity growth fell by 3 percent during that year.

REGULATIONS AND
PRODUCTIVITY GROWTH:
THE CHANNELS OF IMPACT

Over the past few years, government regulations have required that an increasing proportion of the labor and capital employed by business be devoted to activities meeting the objectives of the regulations. Pollution abatement is a primary example. While such regulations may involve substantial benefits, their contribution to measured output—the marketed goods and services produced—is minimal. Capital spending as a percentage of GNP, which has fallen to 9.5 percent from a peak of 11 percent in the mid-1960s, drops to 8.7 percent if one considers the investments mandated by these pollution-control regulations to be nonproductive.[4]

The 1960s and 1970s have seen a virtual explosion in the volume of regulations that have been imposed to achieve social goals—environmental, health, safety, and land use goals. The extent of the recent increases in the number of regulations and their complexity is suggested by the ever-growing size of the Federal Register. Regulatory agencies have been required to publish their regulations in the register since 1937. From a size of 3450 pages in that year, it increased to 35,591 pages in 1973, to 60,221 pages in 1975, and to 77,498 pages in 1979. It has been speculated that this explosion is responsible for the slowdown in productivity growth and, hence, inflation and poor economic performance. Consider, for example, the various arguments that have been made with respect to the impact of environmental regulations. In every case, it has been suggested that because of regulation, labor input goes up, but output does not, or that output goes down with no offsetting decrease in inputs.

1. Pollution-control regulations, it is noted, require abatement investments, which compete with normal investments in production plan and equipment, crowding out the latter to some unknown extent. Hence, labor has less conventional capital with which to work than it would otherwise have, and as a result its output may be reduced.

2. Pollution-control regulations, it is argued, subject new sources of

4. See M. Evans, Testimony Before the Congressional Joint Economic Committee, in *Special Study on Economic Change: Hearings Before the Joint Economic Committee*, part 2. (Washington, DC: U.S. Government Printing Office, 1978), pp. 596-615.

pollution to much more stringent standards than existing sources. This uneven treatment encourages business to use existing—and lower-productivity—plants and equipment longer than otherwise and to delay the introduction of new capital with more advanced technology.

3. Pollution-control equipment, once installed, requires manpower for its operation and maintenance. This manpower adds to labor input with no addition to salable output.

4. For business to conform to environmental regulations, it must secure information regarding them, obtain information regarding options to meet them, and take legal and administrative activities to avoid, delay, or change them. These activities require labor services that yield no salable output.

5. Uncertainty regarding (1) future regulatory requirements, (2) interpretation of current regulations, and (3) security of proprietary information demanded by regulators tends to inhibit investment.

OTHER CAUSES OF THE
PRODUCTIVITY SLOWDOWN

In addition to government regulations—especially environmental regulations—there is a wide range of other factors that have also been cited as causing the productivity slowdown. Consider the following:

1. The shift of labor from lower-productivity farming to higher-productivity manufacturing in the 1950s and 1960s fueled productivity growth during that period. This shift has been nonexistent in the late 1960s and 1970s.

2. The late 1960s and 1970s witnessed a shift from manufacturing to service outputs. This shift, from a

high- to a low-productivity sector, did not affect the economy much in the early postwar period, but has worked against productivity growth since the 1960s.

3. A major contributing factor to past advances in knowledge has been substantial and growing R&D outlays. In recent years, the pace of such spending has not been as rapid as in the past, and as a percent of GNP, R&D spending has decreased from a high of three percent in the mid-1960s to about two percent in the 1970s.

4. During the post-1966 period there have been sharp increases in the labor force and in labor force participation rates, and the age-sex composition of these increases has been heavily weighted toward women and teenagers. Because they lack work experience and have average education levels below the prime-age working groups, new entrants into the labor force are typically less productive than their more experienced counterparts.

5. While changes in relative prices may occur daily without tremendous strain on the economy, the fivefold increase in energy prices since 1973 has been a serious blow. This sharp hike increased the obsolescence of a good deal of capital already invested. Moreover, there were adjustment costs as business had to employ resources, first, to learn how to operate in the new energy environment, and second, actually to make the necessary adjustments in the structure of production.

6. At the same time that the labor force in the United States has experienced an increase in its growth rate, the country's capital stock has grown at a somewhat reduced rate. From 1947 to 1973, the capital stock

grew at an average annual rate of 4.0 percent. Since 1973, however, this average has been 1.5 percentage points lower. Because new technologies are introduced through the installation of new plants and equipment, this investment slowdown may be an important contributor to the slowdown in productivity growth.

7. It has been argued that high and unpredictable rates of inflation have contributed greatly to the decline in productivity growth. In an inflationary environment it is difficult to determine the profitability of investments, especially those with long lead times. This factor will tend to reduce investment generally and, moreover, will tend to bias investment away from long-term, high-risk projects that might have salutory impacts on productivity.

DETERMINANTS OF THE PRODUCTIVITY SLOWDOWN: AN OVERVIEW

During the past several years, numerous researchers have attempted to sort out the contribution of various factors to the decline in productivity growth. Some of these studies have been global, or comprehensive, in nature: they have sought to allocate the decline in productivity growth among the large number of factors thought to affect it. Others of them have been more specific and have focused directly on the contribution of environmental and health-safety regulations to the slowdown. We have assembled all of the relevant studies of these types in an effort to reach some conclusion about the role played by these newer forms of regulation.

Table 1 summarizes the results of these studies. Each of them seeks to account for the difference in produc-

tivity growth from a pre-1970s period to a 1970s period. The varying periods of comparison and the varying definitions of productivity account for differences in the decrease in productivity growth—measured in percentage points—that is being studied. The top line of the table shows the decrease in growth that is at issue in each study. The contributions of each source to this decrease in growth are shown, as percentages, in the parentheses. Across all of the studies, 25 separate determinants of productivity growth are identified.

This survey produces no real consensus on the relative magnitudes of the contribution of the factors studied. The changing demographic composition of the labor force and hours worked, together with sectoral shifts in the composition of output, seem to receive substantial weight in most estimates, accounting for between 20 and 30 percent of the observed slowdown. The slowdown in the rate of capital investment is also assigned a major role. It results in both a declining rate of increase in the economy's capital-labor ratio and a capital stock embodying a technology that increasingly deviates from what is possible. Considering both microeconomic studies and the studies reviewed here, it seems reasonable to attribute from 25 to 35 or 40 percent of the slowdown to this factor. The third important factor appears to be cyclical: during much of the period from the later 1960s through the 1970s the economy has shown many characteristics of a quasi-permanent recession, with persistent high unemployment and low utilization of the capital stock. These factors, together with weather and work stoppages, account for another

TABLE 1

FACTORS ACCOUNTING FOR THE RECENT DECLINE IN PRODUCTIVITY GROWTH: VARIOUS ESTIMATES (in percentages)

FACTOR	DENISON*	DENISON†	KENDRICK‡	SIEGEL§	KUTSCHER et al.||	MARK||	EVANS#	CLARK**	NORSWORTHY et al.††	THUROW‡‡
Estimated decline explained (= 100 percent)	3.1§§	1.1	1.5	1.8	1.2	1.5	1.5	1.9	2.1	2.1
Percentage of decline explained by:										
Labor market tightness	—	—	40 }	−11	—	—	—	—	—	—
Cyclical and work stoppage effects	−7	40	}	22	—	—	—	11	—	14
Shifts										
From manufg. to service	—	—	7 }	0	0/8	−7/7	—	—	—	5
From farm to nonfarm	13 }	30 }	7	—	25	20	—	—	10	14
Out of self-employment	}	}	7	—	—	—	—	—	—	—
Labor force										
Hours worked	10	10	— }	—			33			
Composition	3	0	20	−11 }	−17/25||| }	13/20 }	33 }	−5 }	0 }	5 }
Education	−13	−20	−13	−11	}	}	}	}	}	}
Nonlabor inputs										
Nonresidential structures and equipment	3 }	10 }	— }	33 }	0/8 }	13 }	33 }	16/63 }	33 }	20 }
Inventories	3	0	—	}	}	}	}	}	}	}
Other capital	0	10	7	}	}	}	}	}	}	}
Land	7	0	—	}	}	}	}	}	}	}
Economies of scale	—	—	13	—	—	—	20	—	—	—
Energy prices	13 }	—	—	39	—	—	—	—	—	10/14 }
Government policies										
Pollution abatement	13 }	20 }	7 }	0	8/17	—	—	—	5	}
Other regulations	}	}	7	—	—	—	—	—	—	—
Government services	—	—	7	—	—	—	—	—	—	—
Expectations	—	—	—	22	—	—	—	—	—	—
Knowledge										
Formal advances	68 }	−20 }	10	—	—	—	13	—	10	0
Informal advances	}	}	0	—	—	—	—	—	—	—
Diffusion	}	}	10	—	—	—	—	—	—	8/12
Residual factors ##	—	—	−7	—	17/50	40/60	—	32/84	43	—

Notes for Table 1:

NOTE: Components may not always add to 100 because of rounding errors. Positive (negative) numbers represent contributions (offsets) to productivity decline.

*Compares nonresidential business income per employed person in 1973-76 to 1948-69. See E. Denison, "Explanations of Declining Productivity Growth," *Survey of Current Business*, 59 (27): 1-24 (August 1979).

†Compares nonresidential business income per employed person in 1968-73 to 1948-69. See Denison, pp. 1.24.

‡Compares private-sector output per total factor input in 1966-78 to 1948-66. See J. Kendrick. Testimony before the Congressional Joint Economic Committee, in *Special Study on Economic Change: Hearings before the Joint Economic Committee*, Part 2 (Washington, DC: U.S. Government Printing Office, 1978), pp. 616-36. Kendrick also considered "health and vitality" and found it to have no effect.

§Compares private nonfarm output per person-hour in 1973-78 to 1955-65. See R. Siegel, "Why Has Productivity Slowed Down?" *Data Resources U.S. Review* (March 1979), pp. 1.59-1.65. Siegel also considered "taxes" and found them to have no effect.

|| Compares private output per person-hour in 1966-77 to 1947-66. See R. Kutscher, J. Mark, and J. R. Norsworthy, "The Productivity Slowdown and the Outlook to 1985," *Monthly Labor Review*, 100: 3-8 (May 1977); and J. Mark, Testimony before the Congressional Joint Economic Committee, in *Special Study on Economic Change: Hearings before the Joint Economic Committee*, Part 2 (Washington, DC: U.S. Government Printing Office, 1978), pp. 476-86.

#Compares private nonfarm output per person-hour in 1968-77 to 1947-68. See M. Evans, Testimony before Congressional Joint Economic Committee, in *Special Study on Economic Change: Hearings before the Joint Economic Committee*, Part 2 (Washington, DC: U.S. Government Printing Office, 1978), pp. 596-615.

** Compares private nonfarm output per person-hour in 1973: II-1976: IV to 1955: IV-1965: IV. See P. Clark, "Capital Formation and the Recent Productivity Slowdown," *Journal of Finance,* 33: 965-75 (June 1978).

††Compares private output per person-hour in 1973-78 to 1948-65. See J. R. Norsworthy, M. Harper, and K. Kunze, "The Slowdown in Productivity Growth: Analysis of Some Contributing Factors," *Brookings Papers on Economic Activity*, 2: 387-421 (1979).

‡‡Compares private output per person-hour in 1973-78 to 1948-65. See L. Thurow, "The Productivity Problem," *Technology Review* (1980).

§§Productivity growth rate over recent time spans minus the productivity growth rate over earlier time spans, as indicated in notes* through now.

|| ||Numbers separated by a slash represent estimated ranges.

##The portion of the decline in productivity growth not accounted by the authors was assigned in the "residual factors" category. In the case of Thurow, most of the residual is explained by declining productivity growth in the construction industry.

10 to 20 percent of the productivity slowdown.

If this characterization is correct, between 10 and 40 to 45 percent of the slowdown is to be allocated to the large number of other determinants, of which government regulations are one. The bulk of the existing research on the impact of government regulations has been limited to an assessment of those in the environmental sphere, with most estimates attributing about 5 to 15 percent of the productivity slowdown to their influence. After considering the various biases inherent in these estimates, we have concluded that a reasonable assessment of the impact of environmental regulations would leave them responsible for 8 to 12 percent of the slowdown.

GOVERNMENT REGULATIONS AND THE PRODUCTIVITY SLOWDOWN

Given the large unexplained portion of the productivity slowdown, it would seem important to try to narrow down the role that may have been played by the full set of government regulations. In a recent study we attempted to do this by analyzing time-series data for the manufacturing sector—that sector expected to bear the primary impact of government regulations.

This analysis was undertaken though the use of a straightforward regression model. First, it was assumed that the total amount of output produced in this sector is directly related to the quantity of inputs employed. The average amount of output produced by each input—total factor productivity— was then hypothesized to depend on three primary factors: the extent to which the sector is in a boom period as opposed to a recession period, the technical know-how possessed by management, and a variable we refer to as regulatory intensity.

The first factor is important in that, during recession periods, businesses tend to refrain from dismissing skilled laborers in proportion to the decline in the demand for their output, due to the costs of hiring and training new workers when conditions improve. Thus output per unit of input tends to suffer during recession periods.

With respect to the second factor, it was assumed that technical know-how is a function of time. That is, it is hypothesized that there occurs a general growth in knowledge that enables managers to produce more output per unit of input in the pres-

ent than would have been possible in years past.

Regulatory intensity is a difficult concept to define, let alone qualify. Our definition of this concept is based on the view that regulatory agencies distort private-sector decisions that would, in general, maximize the measured rate of productivity gorwth. Three alternative measures of regulatory intensity were constructed and used for the analysis. The first is based on an estimate of the cumulative number of major pieces of regulatory legislation in effect during any of the years in question.[5] The second and third measures are based on the volume of real federal expenditures on regulatory activities for the years in question and the number of full-time federal personnel engaged in regulatory activities.[6] Though crude proxies for regulatory intensity, these measures do provide a reasonable characterization of postwar trends in the regulation of the manufacturing sector.

Estimates of the importance of each factor in explaining productivity growth from 1958 to 1977 were obtained by using unpublished data on output and inputs in the manufacturing sector, compiled by the U.S. Department of Labor.[7] Regula-

5. Basic data on the number of major pieces of regulatory legislation are found in *Directory of Federal Agencies*, Center for the Study of American Business, Formal Publication no. 31 (St. Louis, 1980). Our measure is calculated from these data.

6. The second and third measures are derived from agency data published in the *Budget of the United States Government*.

7. The equation estimated is as follows:

$$\ln(\text{TFP}) = \ln A + \alpha R + \beta T + \gamma \ln (Q/Q^*) + \delta \ln(Q/Q^*)_{-1} + u$$

tory intensity was estimated to be responsible for anywhere from 12 to 21 percent of the slowdown in the growth of labor productivity during 1973-77 as compared with 1958-65, depending on the regulatory measure employed.[8]

CONCLUSION

On the basis of the limited amount of research that has been done to date, we therefore conclude that anywhere from one-eighth to one-fifth of the slowdown in the growth of labor productivity in recent years has been due to government regulation. Perhaps 60 percent or more of the regulatory impact is accounted for by measures taken in the environmental sphere, with the remainder attributable to regulation in the area of worker health and safety, and consumer protection.

It should be emphasized that a great deal of uncertainty surrounds these estimates. The unexplained portion of the productivity slow-

down is substantial in every study we have seen, including our own. It is quite possible that studies that were able to account for the impact of such difficult-to-measure factors as worker motivation or the quality of management would reduce the estimated effects of regulation. The uncertainties and operating adjustments required by periods of double-digit inflation are additional factors for which existing research does not adequately account.

Our bottom-line estimate, we would note, accounts for both the direct and the indirect effects of regulation. As a result, whatever effects regulation has had on capital investment and the ratio of capital to labor have been accounted for. In this vein, the evidence on the adverse impact of regulation on the capital stock and its productivity appears weak.[9] The dramatic impact regulation may have had on specific industries, for example, copper, apparently paints an exaggerated picture of its overall effects.

One basic and overriding point should be made with respect to government regulations. The contributions to economic welfare that they are intended to make are, by and large, not reflected in marketed or measured output. These effects include improved heath, greater enjoyment of recreation opportuni-

---

where α, β, γ, and δ are parameters, TFP is total factor productivity (a measure that differs from labor productivity by a factor reflecting the ratio of nonlabor to labor inputs, K/L); R is regulatory intensity (which enters the equation in lagged form); T is an annual time variable; Q is actual manufacturing output; Q^* is a measure of the level of output that would have been produced in the absence of cyclical influences; u is a random error term; and $(Q/Q^*)_{-1}$ refers to (Q/Q^*) lagged one year. For details of the estimation procedure, see G. Christainsen and R. Haveman, "Public Regulations and the Slowdown in Productivity Growth," *American Economic Review*, 71:320-25 (May 1981).

8. Reduced growth in the ratio of nonlabor to labor inputs was estimated to be responsible for about 15 percent of the slowdown. Cyclical influences could account for anywhere from 0 to 15 percent of the decline.

9. See G. Christainsen, F. Gollop, and R. Haveman, "Environmental and Health-Safety Regulations, Productivity Growth, and Economic Performance: An Assessment," Joint Economic Committee, U.S. Congress, 1980. We also tested this assertion by estimating an equation for the level of labor productivity that included a term for the interaction of R and K/L. The regression coefficient for the term was not statistically significant.

ties, and improved safety. Were the standard productivity measures effective indicators of economic welfare, these outputs would be included in the numerator of the measure. Although they are difficult to quantify, let alone value, numerous studies have indicated marked increases in these outputs from government regulations. The task for future investigators is to identify more precisely those regulations whose benefits exceed the value of the conventional output that is lost when they are promulgated.

ANNALS, *AAPSS*, 459, January 1982

Taxation and Economic Management in the Western Nations

By ROBERT A. HANNEMAN

ABSTRACT: Trends in the tax revenues of five Western nations from 1900 to 1978 are examined. As tax revenues have increased from 10 to 40 percent of gross national product (GNP), indirect taxes have proportionately declined, displaced by social insurance and direct taxes. More of the tax burden is being paid by employers; sales and value-added taxes have become more important among indirect taxes; income taxes have displaced wealth taxes among the direct tax forms. Changes in tax administration, economic impact, and the politics of taxation are examined as possible limitations on the further growth of taxation and economic management by taxation. It is argued that the marked increase in the tax/GNP ratio cannot be regarded as having a proportionate impact on the ability of governments to manage economic performance by taxes.

Robert A. Hanneman is an assistant professor of sociology at the University of California, Riverside. His main research interests are in comparative and historical analyses of social inequality and formal organization in the Western nations. His current work includes analyses of trends in centralization in medical and educational delivery systems in the United States and Great Britain; changes in income distribution in Britain, France, and Germany since 1850; the origins and development of welfare states in Britain, France, Germany, and Italy; and the performance of medical care systems in Sweden, the United States, France, and Britain.

GOVERNMENTS engage in a wide variety of strategies to attempt to control change in both the performance and the structure of their economies. While taxation has been used for centuries as an economic management tool, only in the last 80 or so years has the impact of governmental finance on economic performance become so obvious, as the share of gross national product (GNP) passing through the budgets of most Western governments has roughly tripled. As a consequence of this growth, the fiscal power of states seems to have increased dramatically. Manipulation of the rates and forms of taxation by governments, however, has proven to be a rather blunt instrument for controlling economic performance.

Particularly in this century, pressure on government to increase public expenditure has driven up taxation levels dramatically. To finance the growth of public expenditure, governments have taxed more heavily a much wider variety of economic flows than ever before. The new types of taxation developed to meet these needs have given governments unprecedented capacities to control economic performance. However, the proliferation of forms of taxation and the greater intensity of taxation have set off a series of economic and political consequences that tend to place substantial limits on the further growth of government. Equally important, these political constraints have increasingly limited the flexibility of taxation as a policy tool.

In the following section we will first trace some of the major trends in taxation in several Western nations from 1900 to 1978, with particular emphasis on recent developments. This exercise reveals that very

marked changes have occurred in governmental finance that are consistent across several Western nations. A second section examines these changes with regard to their implications for the further growth of taxation and the flexibility of taxation as an economic management strategy.

TRENDS IN THE FINANCE OF WESTERN GOVERNMENTS

From 1900 to 1980 the size of the public sector increased dramatically in the Western nations. In 1900-1901, total governmental revenues—central government, local government, and social insurance system revenues from all sources—stood at roughly 10 percent of GNP in most nations. By 1978-79, the equivalent figure had risen to roughly 40 percent. This fairly rapid and general expansion of the public sector was made possible by some equally dramatic changes in the manner that governments finance themselves. In Table 1 some general indicators of these changes are presented as equally weighted averages of five major Western nations: Italy, United Kingdom, Sweden, Germany, and the United States.[1]

1. Data on all five nations in the period 1955 to 1978 are drawn from the Organisation for Economic Cooperation and Development (OECD), *Revenue Statistics of O.E.C.D. Countries 1965-1979* (Paris: OECD, 1980). For the period 1900 to 1940, data on the United States are taken from U.S. Department of Commerce, *Historical Statistics of the United States from Colonial Times to 1957* (Washington, DC: U.S. Government Printing Office, 1960). Data on Britain, Sweden, Germany, and Italy from 1900 to 1940 are adapted from Kurt Seebohm, "Die Entwicklung der steuerstruktur im Prozess der Modernisierung: Eine vergleichend-historische Analyse Westeuropaischer Staaten" (Diplomarbeit, University of Mannheim, 1976).

TABLE 1
TRENDS IN GOVERNMENT FINANCE, 1900-1978
(five-nation averages)

		AS PERCENTAGE OF ALL TAXES		
	ALL TAXES AS PER- CENTAGE OF GNP	SOCIAL SECURITY TAXES	DIRECT TAXES	INDIRECT TAXES
1900	9.5	NA*	46.3	53.7
1910	9.4	NA	54.1	45.9
1920	14.4	NA	54.4	45.6
1930	17.1	NA	54.4	45.6
1940	18.0	NA	49.4	50.6
1955	27.3	15.8	48.8	35.4
1960	29.3	18.4	47.9	33.7
1965	30.3	21.1	47.2	31.7
1971	33.3	23.9	46.1	30.0
1976	36.7	29.6	46.0	24.4
1978	37.6	28.9	47.2	23.9

NOTE: Data are taken from sources listed in footnote one. All levels of government are included except social insurance from 1900 to 1940. Direct taxes include property, inheritance, corporate income, and personal income taxes. Indirect taxes include customs, excise, monopoly, employer's, sales, and value-added taxes, as well as miscellaneous user's fees and special taxes.
*NA = not available.

Governments have available to them a variety of financial mechanisms: taxation, profits from public enterprises, contributions to public insurance systems, and manipulations of money supply, usually through debt financing. While our interest here focuses primarily on taxation, some general comments on the development of alternative mechanisms are appropriate to place taxation in perspective. While income from governmental properties has historically been an important source of state finance, this source of revenue has been largely irrelevant in the twentieth century. Financing government through increased indebtedness appears to have become rather more important during this century in most of the Western nations. This phenomenon is significant enough to deserve separate analysis, though it will not be treated here.

The most striking general feature of the evolution of governmental revenue structure in the twentieth century has been the creation of public and quasi-public enterprises, most notably social insurance systems. While total governmental revenues increased from about 10 percent of national product to about 40 percent since 1900, when social insurance taxes are excluded the increase is only from about 10 percent to about 27 percent. In fact, since 1955 nonsocial insurance tax revenues as a share of GNP have increased by only 16 percent—from 23 percent to 27 percent of GNP—while social insurance taxes have increased by 152 percent—from 5 percent to 11 percent of GNP.

While social insurance contributions and debt financing have increased even more rapidly, conventional taxation in ratio to GNP has nearly tripled since the turn of the century. Of the increase in taxation relative to GNP since 1900, 55 percent has occurred in the decades of the world wars, with much slower growth in taxation relative to GNP occurring in nonwar periods.

The single most dramatic change in public finance in the Western nations in this century has been in the development of social insurance systems. This change deserves a somewhat closer look, as do quite dramatic changes in the composition of nonsocial insurance shares of public revenues.

Social insurance

The large public social insurance systems that currently exist in the nations examined here are of fairly recent origin. While the German system was substantial in both size and coverage as early as the mid-1880s, large public social insurance systems have been slower to develop in the other nations. While social insurance taxes were of some importance as a source of government revenue in some countries prior to 1940, the most interesting and dramatic changes have occurred since that time.

Since 1955, social insurance taxes have more than doubled in ratio to GNP and, on average, have risen from 16 to 29 percent of total government tax revenues in the five nations. This upward trend has slackened in the late 1970s because of declines in employee contributions. In fact, the general tendency over the period has been for much more rapid growth in taxes on employers than in taxes on employees and the self-employed. In several nations the expenditures of social insurance systems have grown more rapidly than receipts from social insurance taxes, placing

part of the burden of funding on debt financing or the general government budget.

Direct taxation

Since the turn of the century there have been some marked changes in terms of what is taxed and who pays taxes. When social security taxes are counted as direct taxes, the share of total revenues derived from direct assessments of individuals and corporate entities has risen dramatically since the turn of the century. Virtually all of the increase in this direct tax share in total taxation, however, is due to social insurance. The proportion of total tax revenues derived from individual and corporate taxation has remained nearly constant in this century.

The locus of the burden of nonsocial insurance direct taxes has shifted markedly away from taxation on wealth and toward taxation on income. In 1900 fully three-fourths of all nonsocial insurance direct tax revenues were from property and inheritance; by 1978 less than one-seventh of all nonsocial insurance direct taxes were derived from levees of this type. Another interesting change has occurred in terms of who pays direct taxes. Adding social insurance back in, in 1900 95 percent of all direct taxes consisted of assessment primarily on individuals—income, property, and inheritance. By 1978, only 63 percent of the direct tax burden was individuals; the remainder was paid by employers—contributions to social insurance, corporate income taxes, payroll taxes.

Indirect taxation

As the social insurance tax share has increased and the direct tax share has remained roughly constant over the period from 1900 to 1978, the share of all tax revenue derived from indirect taxes has declined. There have been some notable innovations, however, in how indirect taxes are extracted.

The traditional forms of indirect taxation—customs, excises, and monopoly taxes—have not kept pace with the growth of other forms of taxation. These levees, normally paid by producers and passed on in the form of higher prices, have been partially replaced by two innovative indirect forms: general sales and value-added taxes (VATs). General sales taxation became increasingly common in most nations in the post-World War II years, but has declined dramatically in recent years. In its place, four of the five nations—the United States being the exception—have adopted value-added taxation. VATs tap an even wider variety of transactions than do sales taxes and have their first incidence primarily on producers, rather than on consumers. Germany was an early pioneer in utilizing this form of tax originating in the Weimar period. During the 1970s Britain, Sweden, and Italy all found it an alternative to further increases in general sales taxation.

At the turn of the century, customs, excise, and monopoly taxes composed a major share of all governmental revenues. By 1978 these forms of taxation had become far less important as a source of government finance. It is not the repeal of such taxes that explains their relative decline—with the exception of some customs revenues, particularly in EEC nations—but rather their slower growth relative to social insurance and some forms of direct taxes. The economic flows tapped by such taxes on specific goods and services have generally not grown as fast as the remainder of the Western economies, and general rather than specific forms of taxation have been more extensively utilized in this century.

Summary

In the last 80 years the share of GNP that passes through government budgets has roughly tripled in the Western nations. This has necessitated major changes in the ways that governments acquire revenues. A substantial portion of the new revenues have been derived by taxing previously untaxed economic flows and by taxing some income streams far more heavily than at the turn of the century. The share of all government revenues derived from social insurance taxes has grown from virtually none to almost one-third of total income. Direct taxes on income, wealth, and corporations have remained at roughly half of government tax revenues, while indirect taxes have declined markedly.

Within these overall trends, some other changes of considerable interest have occurred. The employer-paid share of social insurance taxes has increased more rapidly than the employee-paid share. Income taxation has grown far more rapidly than wealth taxation. When social insurance contributions are also considered as a form of direct taxation, the burden of direct taxes has fallen increasingly on employers rather than on employees.

The share of governmental revenue derived from indirect taxes has declined substantially, and the nature of indirect taxation has changed. In 1900, virtually all indirect tax revenues were derived from levees on specific goods and services, mostly paid directly by producers. After serious flirtation with general sales taxation, most nations are moving toward VATs. These taxes are again borne directly by producers, but tap a far wider range of economic activities than earlier tax forms.

THE LIMITS OF MANAGEMENT BY TAXATION

The large share of GNP that passes through various governmental budgets yearly in the Western nations would seem to provide these governments with a very powerful tool for managing economic performance through incentives built into both taxation and expenditure policies. Indeed, the rhetoric of tax reform in all of these nations routinely argues for modification of tax law as a means of altering economic performance.

There are, however, substantial limits on the efficacy of taxation as an economic management tool. In good part, the same forces that have enabled the tax share of GNP to increase so dramatically have generated limits on both the further growth of the tax share and the flexibility with which it can be applied as a management tool. In this section several of these forces will be examined, in a speculative fashion, in an effort to form a clearer view of the limits of economic management by tax policy.

Technology

By far the largest portion of the increase in taxation levels since the turn of the century is accounted for by social insurance, individual income, and sales and value-added taxes. Social insurance taxes and substantial levels of personal income taxes would probably not have been possible without the remarkable innovation of stoppage at source—or payroll deduction—as a means of administration. Value-added and sales taxes have similarly required substantial administrative innovations to be effective.

While both the size and the technological sophistication of tax administrations have increased markedly with these innovations, an increasing reliance has been placed on the cooperation of nongovernmental actors in contemporary tax administration. Increasingly employers, and not government agents, are the mainstay of tax administration.[2]

One virtue of this system of tax administration, from the point of view of government, is that private intermediaries act as buffers between the state and the general population, thus somewhat diffusing popular resentment. On the other hand, as levels of taxation rise and the complexity of administration increases, rising costs are imposed on employers. In the case of small business, these costs may prove exceedingly burdensome, leading to both increased avoidance —as in the case of the growth of

2. This particular form of administration is not unique to taxation. For an interesting discussion of the evolution and limitations of such arrangements, see Harold Wilensky, *The "New Corporatism": Centralization and the Welfare State* (Beverly Hills, CA: Sage Publications, 1976). Similar developments may be noted in particular delivery systems for social services. Robert Hanneman and J. Rogers Hollingsworth, in "The Problems of Centralization: Health and Education Policies in Great Britain and the United States" (Paper delivered at the American Political Science Association meetings, New York, 1979), examine the changing structure of administration in two such systems.

underground economies—and political mobilization of employers.

Without substantial revision in the mechanical and human technology of tax administration that allows for both more direct monitoring and more rigorous enforcement of taxation, continued increases in levels and complexity of taxation would seem to be limited. The technological capacity of governments to extract taxes effectively, however, may not be as important as other constraints.

Economics

The consequences for economic structure and performance are seldom the only factors considered when tax reforms are proposed. Indeed, most major tax reforms in the Western nations in this century have been associated with either war-financing or changes in the support for political parties.[3] Taxes, of course, do have substantial impacts on the structure and performance of

3. A. T. Peacock and J. Wiseman argue that wars are critical events in British fiscal history, allowing the state to increase levels of taxation without encountering mass rebellion; see *The Growth of Public Expenditures in the United Kingdom* (Princeton, NJ: Princeton University Press, 1961). A similar case is made for Germany by S. Andic and J. Veverka in "The Growth of Public Expenditure in Germany Since the Unification" (*Finanz Archiv*, vol. 23, 1964), pp. 169-277. Several writers have noted the close connection between support for leftist political parties and the progressivity of taxation: D. R. Cameron, "Inequality and the State: A Political-Economic Comparison" (Paper delivered at the American Political Science Association meetings, Chicago, 1976); L. Bjorn, *Labor Parties and the Redistribution of Income in Capitalist Democracies* (Ph.D. diss., University of North Carolina, 1976); R. Hanneman, *Inequality and Development in Britain, France, and Germany from 1850 to 1970* (Ph.D. diss., University of Wisconsin, 1979).

economies, though these impacts are only partially understood and partially intended. At both the macroeconomic and the microeconomic levels, these consequences may limit the further expansion of taxation and the flexibility of tax policy.

While substantial debate exists among economists about the specific impacts of various taxes on economic performance, two widely held beliefs, whether or not they are correct, act as substantial political constraints on tax expansion or reform. The first is the belief that taxation at high levels disrupts the efficiencies of markets in allocating resources. Various forms of taxes on producers—for example, excises, VATs, payroll taxes, and social insurance contributions—are often seen, particularly by producers, as imposing unequal burdens on them that damage their competitive position. One particular and probably largely unintended consequence of sales taxation is to impose a disproportionate administrative burden on small business, which leads to greater concentration at the retail level. Particularly for export-oriented firms, producers' taxes may impose costs that cannot be passed on to the consumer in the form of higher prices. All such impacts are seen as lessening the efficiency of economic production and consequently limiting and distorting growth.

The second widely held view on the economic impacts of taxation is at the more macroeconomic level. While also of dubious economic validity, it is believed, particularly by supply-side economists, that high levels of taxation result in lower levels of capital investment and entrepreneurial activity. The argument holds that taxation, particularly of the progressive variety, lessens incentives to invest. It is also believed that governmental expenditure, oriented heavily toward consumption rather than investment, distorts the macroeconomy, resulting in price inflation and lower levels of investment—and hence in lower levels of productivity and growth.

The actual economic impacts of various levels and types of taxation are the subject of lively debate among highly sophisticated researchers, and the results of these explorations do not always conform to popular beliefs. Nonetheless, the beliefs that are held about the economic impacts of taxation represent a substantial political constraint on both the level of taxation and the flexibility in manipulating tax law to manage economic performance. While revolts by groups affected by specific taxes have a long history in the Western nations, in recent years political mobilization around both specific and general taxes has become more common. It is in the area of politics, rather than in technology or economics, that the constraints on tax policy become most apparent.

Politics

Because the creation, modification, and administration of taxation are governmental acts, the previously discussed constraints are filtered through the political system. Over the past 80 years changes in both systems of taxation and in the nature of political systems have interacted to create a situation of substantial inflexibility in tax policy. Tax revolts in Western nations are only one manifestation of this development.

While tax revolts are not a new phenomenon in the Western nations,

some scholars have argued that the increasing visibility of taxation in recent years has contributed substantially to their widening and deepening intensity.[4] Since the turn of the century, however, the changes in levels and forms of taxation have increasingly mobilized larger segments of the population continuously and actively to resist increases or changes in tax policy. In Table 2 several indices are shown that throw some light on this pattern of increasing popular resistance.

Table 2 presents three indices of taxation visibility. Generally, the index varies from near zero, representing a condition of both low tax rates and hidden tax forms, to near unity, representing a condition of high tax rates and direct forms. In the first column of the table, the actual index values for the five nation averages are shown. This series shows a fairly steady increase in the visibility of taxation since the turn of the century. In the second column the index has been recomputed under the assumption of no change in the proportion of revenues derived from various kinds of taxes since 1900; in the third column the index is calculated under the assumption of no change in the level of taxation—relative to GNP—since 1900.

The most important conclusion to be drawn from these index numbers is that, without changes in the kinds of taxation used, tax visibility would be markedly higher in 1978 than was actually the case. This may be

4. The connection between tax visibility and tax revolt is examined most closely by Harold Wilensky (see note 2). Wilensky argues that the visibility-revolt connection is decreased by centralization. I regard it plausible that centralization may deepen the crisis by mobilizing conflict at the national level in more centralized systems.

TABLE 2
TAX VISIBILITY UNDER ALTERNATIVE ASSUMPTIONS

	VISIBILITY (Actual)	VISIBILITY (Constant form)	VISIBILITY (Constant rates)	CENTRAL TAXES AS PERCENTAGE OF ALL TAXES
1900	.039	.039	.039	62.0
1910	.041	.038	.041	58.8
1920	.044	.059	.029	60.2
1930	.075	.070	.042	58.1
1940	.066	.073	.035	62.5
1955	.080	.111	.028	80.0
1960	.091	.120	.029	79.3
1965	.102	.124	.032	79.8
1971	.109	.136	.031	77.6
1976	.115	.150	.030	79.3
1978	.115	.154	.029	NA*

NOTE: Tax visibility indices are calculated by weighing the proportions of all tax revenues from various sources as follows: wealth taxes = 3; income taxes = 2; employee social insurance contributions and sales taxes = 1; and all other tax forms = 0. The resulting weighted sum is then multiplied by the ratio of all tax revenues to GNP and rescaled by linear transformation to vary between zero—low visibility—and one—high visibility. The constant form visibility index holds constant the proportions of all tax revenues derived from various sources at their 1900 values and allows the ratio of tax revenues to GNP to vary as observed; constant rates holds the ratio of all tax revenues from GNP constant at its 1900 level and allows the weighted proportions of all tax revenues from various sources to vary as observed. Central taxes as percentage of all taxes allocates central government and (from 1955 on) social insurance tax revenues to central government. These figures refer to the level of government at which taxes were actually collected, regardless of revenue sharing and other such schemes.
*NA = not available.

seen particularly in the third column, which shows that overall visibility of taxation would have declined somewhat, because of changing forms of taxes, had overall tax rates remained constant. The real increase in taxation visibility over the time period, then, is due to increasing levels of taxation and is only partially offset by decreased directness of tax forms.

Two other trends in taxation must also be taken into account. The first is that, while taxes have become somewhat less direct in administration, far larger proportions of the population were subject to visible taxation in 1978 than in 1900. Despite the varying degrees of hiding these taxes—by means of payroll deductions, for example—their burden is quite apparent to almost all people. Second, as the last column of Table 2 shows, taxation

has increasingly concentrated in central government. Before World War I, roughly 60 percent of all taxes were imposed by central authorities. In the interwar period, if social insurance taxes were included, roughly 70 percent of all taxes were paid to central authorities. In the post World War II period, almost 80 percent of taxes flowed into central authority budgets.[5]

These are some of the factors underlying the current popular discontent with taxation. Taxation has become more obvious to far larger segments of the population, despite

5. Although social insurance data for the pre-World War II period are not included in the tables in this article, such taxes constituted five percent or less of all tax revenues in the 1900-1910 period in most nations, and generally constituted about 10 percent of all tax governments in the interwar period.

changes in types of taxes that somewhat offset the trend. Taxation rates have increased substantially, and a larger share of all taxes are collected by central authorities. Taken together, these forces have made the politics of taxation far more salient to large portions of the population and consequently have placed substantial limits on the freedom of government action in utilizing taxes to manage economic performance.

The changing nature of the political systems in the Western nations has interacted with changes in taxation to produce a particularly intractable situation. Throughout much of this century taxation rates have risen primarily during wars and primarily at the central government level. While narrow special interests have always been involved in tax politics at the central government level, in recent years new and intensive political pressures from widely based groups have been brought to bear on central government tax policy. The movement of taxation from the local to the central government level in the early part of this century provided a possibility of tax increases at the central level, where mass organization around tax issues was weaker. This freedom of action of central government has now largely been lost, as mass-based interests have become effectively involved in national-level tax politics.

In addition to increasing the political constraints on the general level of taxation, the more active tax politics of recent years have also made taxation less flexible as a management tool. It would not be correct to suggest that governments are no longer able to affect economic performance by manipulating tax law. However, the complexity of compromises, the political efficacy of the parties involved in tax policy forma-

tion, and the length of time involved in decision-making all appear to be growing larger. As a result, tax law provisions have acquired a considerable political inertia and have become less immediately useful as a short-run management tool.

CONCLUSION

This article has sought to summarize very briefly recent tendencies in the ways that contemporary Western governments are financed and to explore some of the constraints on revenue policy as a tool for managing economic performance and structure. By and large, this analysis has suggested that technological, economic, and political constraints on revenue policy are substantial and increasing.

Constraints on the use of revenue policy as an economic management tool arise from many sources. All else being equal, governments might be expected to tax most heavily those aspects of economic activity that are administratively easiest and least costly to monitor. However, the level of finance required by governments appears to have far exceeded the capacity of simple and easy taxes to extract it. Governments have been forced into extracting revenues from ever wider segments of the population and from a wider range of economic flows. As a result, even with dramatic improvements in technology, taxation has become both more visible and more vulnerable in its administration.

The power to impose differential levees on certain products, firms, and economic sectors has traditionally been used by governments to promote and retard growth, control concentration, and guide investment into desired areas. Such guidance by taxation continues to be important in government revenue policy. However, as the political system has expanded and needs for revenues have increased, most taxation has become general taxation, not well suited to detailed manipulation of economic structure and performance. Particularism and special treatment in taxation is a useful policy tool, but is difficult to legitimize in governments based on working-class and middle-class support. As the political systems of the Western nations have been transformed, detailed regulation by differential taxation has become less viable as a management strategy.

The twentieth century has seen numerous and important innovations in both forms of taxation and means of administration. Income, sales, corporate, and value-added taxes have all become important bases of government finance, and a variety of indirect or hidden means of administration have been developed. These innovations are one facilitating factor in the rapid growth of government in this century. However, as the earlier discussion has suggested, the expansion of government has created both economic and political constraints. It is widely believed that government budgets cannot grow much further in relation to GNP unless either investment is nationalized or fiscal policy acts to redistribute income to private investors. Utilization of government budgets for the purposes of economic management is seriously constrained by the political power of large and well-organized interest groups as well, making substantial change in who benefits or rapid change of any sort far more difficult now than in the past.

It has become rather commonplace to assert that there exists a fiscal crisis of the state in Western capitalist nations, one that has been created by the convergence of increasing demands for governmental services and limits on governmental revenues. Fiscal crises of governments, like taxes and tax revolts, have been commonplace in the histories of the nations examined here and have often played important roles in rearranging the relationships between governments and their societies. The forces that have brought about the current financial difficulties of governments in the Western nations examined here suggest that the current situation is one that may require significant rearrangements in the ways that governments attempt to manage economic performance.

ANNALS, *AAPSS*, 459, January 1982

French Urban Housing and the Mixed Economy: The Privatization of the Public Sector

By PETER K. EISINGER

ABSTRACT: This examination of the French experience with public-private or mixed-economy corporations in the area of urban renewal and housing explores the advantages and disadvantages of involving private capital on a for-profit basis in the financing and implementation of certain types of public service. Although urban mixed-economy corporations initially helped the French to address their postwar housing crisis, the private partners to such arrangements have increasingly turned from low-income housing to more profitable ventures. The French case suggests the difficulty of sustaining a social housing program underwritten by private capital.

Peter K. Eisinger is professor of political science at the University of Wisconsin, Madison. He is the author of several books, including, most recently, a study of politics in Detroit and Atlanta under black mayors, The Politics of Displacement, and a number of articles on various aspects of urban politics.

ENGAGING the private sector to one degree or another in the performance of public-interest tasks and obligations has long been a strategy of governments in Western nations.[1] The specific forms such arrangements take vary widely. Government contracting with private-sector firms, public subsidies of private entrepreneurs, franchising monopolies, and the creation of public/private corporations are common examples of the ways governments enlist private capital, managerial techniques, and personnel to perform functions that are deemed to fall within the domain of public-sector responsibility. Growing reports of the greater efficiency of such arrangements vis-à-vis the purely public or in-house production of services,[2] coupled with deepening fiscal crises in local governments across Europe and the United States, have increased the attractiveness of these public-private partnerships, particularly among municipal officials. Yet recent critical examinations of experiences in this quasi-public sector, enumerating costs as well as benefits, are few in number.

There are two basic sources of private involvement in the provision of public goods and services: the nonprofit sector and the for-profit sector. Nonprofit involvement reflects the ancient tradition of philanthropy. As the "institutional expression of the gift relationship,"[3]

nonprofit involvement raises none of the issues associated particularly with profit-seeking behavior. But several of these issues—notably the need to satisfy investors and the ability to exit from unprofitable markets—can become problematic when the for-profit private sector becomes involved, either alone or in partnership with government, in the provision of public goods. French public-private or mixed-economy corporations in the area of urban housing, which have a long history and a singular degree of complexity, offer a particularly instructive focus for exploring some of the implications of such private-sector activity.

Begun as a broad-gauged postwar device to renew the bulk of the housing stock of the nation, these mixed-economy arrangements in France were nevertheless infused with a strong social ethic that placed a high priority on the provision of housing for the working class. The great strength of these arrangements lay in the administrative flexibility achieved by operating outside the rigid structure of French local government. Yet the social costs of involving private capital in housing policies aimed at the lower-income strata have been substantial. In the French case, the profit requirements of private capital eventually led to a shift away from housing policies designed to serve those who could not pay their way toward a middle-income housing strategy. In sanctioning this shift, French local governments, as partners with private capital, allowed the latter to redefine the nature of public-sector involvement in mass housing. As a result, public-sector responsibilities to the poorest strata in French society were allowed to deteriorate

1. Ira Sharkansky, *Wither the State?* Chatham, NJ: Chatham House, 1979.

2. R. Ahlbrandt, *Municipal Fire Protection Services: Comparison of Alternative Organization Forms.* Beverly Hills, CA: Sage Publications, 1973; E. Savas, "Municipal monopolies versus competition," in *Improving the Quality of Urban Management*, ed. W. Hawley and D. Rogers (Beverly Hills, CA: Sage Publications, 1974).

3. Jacquelyn Hochban, "Serving Public Needs Through Nonprofit Organizations,"

as private capital directed the partnership in quest of profit.

The case suggests, on a more general level, that public/private partnerships are likely in the end to be dominated by the needs of the private partner. Certain goals of public-sector policy—principally social justice aims as they are defined in a welfare-state context—cannot be or will not be sustained.

THE FRENCH HOUSING CRISIS AND THE MIXED-ECONOMY RESPONSE

In the 20 years after World War II, France experienced a rate of urbanization that nearly matched the size of its urban growth in the entire century before the war. By the beginning of the 1970s, nearly seven of ten Frenchmen lived in cities, compared with fewer than one-third in 1940. In raw population terms, by 1968 urban areas had grown by 11 million people in the postwar period in a nation of slightly under 50 million. French cities were ill prepared to accommodate this rapid demographic change, the most intense population shift in the nation's history.

Although the French urban crisis in these two postwar decades had a variety of aspects, the most dramatic need lay in the area of housing. Most housing was more than a century old, dilapidated, and overcrowded, and the state of French plumbing, a not-insignificant indicator of housing quality, was thoroughly dismal. The census of 1954 revealed, for example, that only 26 percent of nation's housing units had private interior sanitary facilities.[4]

Even in Paris, only 48 percent of all units were equipped with interior toilets, and fewer than one-quarter had bathtubs.[5] Matters had improved only slightly by the 1960s. By 1963 a national survey of housing found that only approximately 35 percent of all housing units now had interior toilet and washing facilities.[6] In the Île-de-France, the heavily urbanized region that includes Paris at its core, 43 percent of all housing units still relied in 1960 upon exterior sanitary facilities and 54 percent had no bathtub.[7] Of the housing stock in that region, 83 percent had been built before 1848.

In the late 1940s, housing had not ranked among the top national priorities in the effort to recover from the war, but by the early 1960s France was ready to address the problem. The path to a workable housing policy, however, was constrained by a still grave national economic situation, by antiquated municipal government structures and capabilities, and by a state bureaucracy far too centralized to implement programs responsively at the local level. In addition, any solution to the housing crisis had to take into account a basic French preference for a capitalist economic order, tempered by a growing national experience with state *dirigisme* in certain vital economic sectors. Given these various constraints,

4. Institut national de la statistique et des études économiques, *Recensement géneral de la population de mai 1954: Résultats du sondage au 1/20ème—ménages et logements* (Paris: Centre de recherche et de documentation sur la consommation, 1957), p. 207.

5. Institut international de la statistique, *Statistiques de logement et de la construction, 1946-1953* (The Hague, 1956), p. 13.

6. Institut national de la statistique et des études économiques, *Aspects du logement en France en 1963* (Paris: Centre de recherche et de documentation sur la consommation, 1963), p. 127.

7. M. Gérard, "Evolution du milieu urbain et du plan d'aménagement dans la region d'Île-de-France depuis 1960" (Paper delivered at Deux Villes Mondiales: Paris et New York, conference sponsored by Fondation Franco-Americaine, Paris, May 1978), p. 2.

then, the problem the French faced was how to mobilize the capital and expertise within a flexible administrative framework to house and rehouse the greater part of her population.

One device the French adapted to help meet their housing and urban renewal requirements was the *société d'économie mixte* (SEM), or the mixed-economy corporation. An SEM may be defined as an arrangement in which public and private capital, public authority, and private managerial methods are combined in a corporate partnership to perform a specific set of tasks deemed to involve the public interest.[8] Mixed-economy enterprises are relatively common in French society, including, technically, the French railroad system, Air France, various utilities, mines, and certain banking and credit institutions. Although such devices are to be found in other countries, the profusion of mixed-economy corporations in France, as well as their particular form and level of development, are unmatched among Western European nations. In urban affairs in particular, mixed-economy arrangements are employed not only for housing and urban renovation, our special focus, but also for the construction and maintenance of industrial parks, central markets, parking facilities, pedestrian malls, shopping centers, and urban land management.[9]

The French decision to encourage the adaptation of mixed-economy corporations after World War II to help rebuild the country's housing stock was a product in the first instance of historical familiarity with the form of such arrangements. Mixed-economy corporations, devoted primarily to the distribution of water, gas, electricity, and milk on a regional basis, first appeared on French soil in German-ruled Alsace-Lorraine around the turn of the century. The French Parliament, however, refused to endorse such arrangements in its own domain, fearing that the management of public utilities "ceased to be sufficiently commercial when it was done for the State's account."[10] Utility functions continued to be handled in France until the 1920s entirely by private firms operating on a concession basis. When concessionaire profits began to decline sharply after World War I, the French Parliament in 1926 cautiously authorized local governments to become minority partners in mixed-economy enterprises in order to share the financial risk.[11] Local governments were permitted by the Law of 1926 to hold up to 40 percent of the corporation's shares. Although the legislation specifically permitted local SEMs to carry out public housing projects, their major impact was felt in the management of utilities.

In 1935, however, the Parliament reinforced the provisions of the 1926 act and further encouraged the establishment of mixed-economy arrangements to build housing. The economic depression had by this

8. Colloques de Marly, *Les sociétés d'économie mixte d'aménagement et d'équipment* (Paris: Centre de recherche d'urbanisme, 1977), p. 11; A. Chazel and H. Poyet, *L'Economie mixte* (Paris: Presses Universitaires de France, 1963), p. 6.

9. Francois d'Arcy, *Structures administratives et urbanisation: La Société Centrale pour l'Equipement du Territoire* (Paris: Berger-Levrault, 1968), pp. 36-37.

10. P. Marchat, *L'Economie mixte* (Paris: Presses Universitaires de France, 1971), p. 13.

11. Chazel and Poyet, *L'Economie mixte*, p. 13.

time brought the private-sector housing industry to a literal standstill, and local governments were more interested now than they had been a decade before in exploring the SEM as a vehicle for a housing program. Several SEMs were formed in this period, mainly in Paris and Marseilles, and they were responsible for the construction of nearly 30,000 housing units in the years just prior to the war.

The emergence of the modern-housing SEMs on the local level dates from the 1950s. Parliamentary decrees of 1953 and 1954 allowed local governments for the first time to become majority partners in mixed corporations devoted to housing construction, renewal, and rehabilitation. This change, designed to allow greater governmental control over both initiation and implementation of housing programs, marked part of an emergent effort to fashion a comprehensive national housing policy.

The maximum public-sector financial share was put at 65 percent, and local elected officials now sat on the board of directors as a majority. The possibilities thus created for harnessing and directing private capital in the pursuit of publicly established urban goals stimulated a burst of organizational and then construction activity. Indeed, Castells speaks of the rapid development in this period "of a public and parapublic sector of social and subsidized housing" as a "spectacular transformation."[12]

In 1955 two umbrella organizations were created under the aegis of the quasi-public national banking institution, the *Caisse des dépôts et consignations*, to help establish

SEMs and to provide a variety of technical services. The *Société centrale immobilière de la Caisse des dépôts* (SCIC), the largest organization for the promotion of housing construction in France, and the *Société central d'équipement du territoire* (SCET), which serves mixed-economy corporations engaged in various urban and regional public works projects as well as many devoted to housing, oversee the operations of approximately 150 SEMs.[13] The services they provide range from engineering feasibility studies to comprehensive planning to computer programming. The *Caisse* itself, as we shall see next, provides a significant portion of SEM financing. Reflecting in part the historic special interest of the *Caisse* in financing low-income housing—which dates back to the HBM, or *habitation à bon marché*, movement of the late 1890s[14]—most modern housing SEMs initially devoted their energies to the construction of HLM *(habitation à loyer moderé)* dwellings aimed at the lower-middle and working classes.

The appearance on the French scene of mixed-economy corporations in such numbers may be explained in the first instance as a response to the precarious economic situation in France in the postwar period. In the years following the war the capital market was essentially moribund. Some short-term credit became available in the late 1940s, but such money scarcely suited a wholesale assault on the

12. M. Castells, *City, Class and Power* (London: Macmillan, 1978), p. 51.

13. Société centrale pour l'équipement du territoire (SCET), *1956-1976* (Paris: SCET, 1976), p.22; and E. Preteceille, *La Production des grands ensembles* (The Hague: Mouton, 1973), pp. 65-66.

14. Roger Priouret, *La Caisse des Dépôts* (Paris: Presses Universitaires de France, 1966), p. 418.

housing crisis.[15] All through the 1950s the state itself hovered on the edge of literal bankruptcy. Deprived initially of access to credit, the French state had to make all of its expenditures out of budgetary funds, effectively blocking plans for extensive capital projects. When loans gradually became available, the French government used its borrowing credit with the Banque de France to cover its payrolls. The government was in no position, then, either to raise or to spend the capital sums required for housing and rehousing a major part of the urban populace.

In the private sector, economic recovery was linked to postwar consumer demands and agricultural development. A historic reluctance on the part of the French to devote much of their income to housing kept private housing starts low after the war. In addition, rent controls established in 1914 and still in force in the early 1950s produced a pattern of such low rents that the average family had to spend only two or three percent of its income on housing.[16] In this context, the housing market offered little attraction to private investors.

The virtue of the mixed-economy corporation was that it provided the public sector with access to private capital—indeed, some measure of control over it—while at the same time guaranteeing in return a risk-free investment for the private partners to the arrangement, by charging local government with the sole responsibility for any financial loss.[17]

All SEMs operate under French laws designed to regulate private corporations, but they are formally more public than private in character. Each local *société* formed to construct or rehabilitate housing, usually with a specific area of a city and a specific project in mind, must submit its constitution and project plans to the city council for approval.[18] A board of directors is then established, with elected and administrative public officials holding 65 percent of the voting power. Among these is a representative from the national government who may exercise a veto single-handedly over any project deemed not to be in the public interest. This practice is consistent with the power of *tutelle*, the ability of the national government to veto or nullify, through the *préfecture*, any and all acts of local government on no more substantial basis than that it is deemed unwise. The remainder of the members of the board are representatives of private-sector capital and the monies invested by government-owned banks.

The private-sector partners in SEMs are largely institutional actors, many of which carry out quasi-public functions or possess quasi-public authority. For example, French Chambers of Commerce, to whom the right to condemn land for development purposes is occasionally delegated, are common sources of private capital in SEMs.[19] Private banks and savings and loan institutions also invest in such corporations. Typically, individual financial institutions and the Chamber of Commerce hold between 10 and 25 percent of the

15. W. Baum, *The French Economy and the State* (Princeton, NJ: Princeton University Press, 1958), pp. 26-27.

16. Ibid., pp. 278-79.

17. S. Magri, *Logement et reproduction de l'exploitation* (Paris: Centre de sociologie urbaine, 1977), p. 74.

18. Ville de Paris, Bulletin Municipal Officiel, *Débats du conseil*, 8 Aug. 1977.

19. J. Gozzi, Personal interview, 22 Mar. 1979.

shares of any given *société*. The remainder of the private sector share, between 15 and 30 percent, is held generally by the *Caisse des dépôts*. The *Caisse* is not a private institution. It is a government holding bank, but it operates independently of direct political control. It serves as a depository for postal savings accounts, pension funds of nationalized corporations, and the surplus deposits of savings and loan institutions, among others.[20] *Caisse* investments must be distinguished from state financing, for as d'Arcy notes, they are made with a banker's cautious concern for profitability.[21] The *Caisse* may be an actor of public origin, but the funds it invests have come from private owners.[22] Traditionally the *Caisse* invested these funds in government securities. Since 1955, however, the *Caisse* has used its deposits to underwrite what is regarded in law as the private-sector share of urban SEMs involved in housing.

If, on the one hand, the formation of urban SEMs was an economic response to the problem of capital aggregation in the postwar period, it was also designed as an administrative device to bypass antiquated and incompetent local governments. Although the situation has changed substantially in the last 20 years, local government in France in the 1950s was notorious for its lack of technically expert personnel.[23] Mayors and city councils committed to urban renewal and redevelopment found that they had no qualified civil engineers, computer technicians, architects, planners, or economists in municipal employ. Local governments were in no financial position to hire a corps of urban development experts. Indeed, even if cities had had the resources to expand their ranks, they could not have competed with private-industry salaries.

The mixed-economy corporations introduced a substantial degree of administrative flexibility in local affairs. Because the SEMs operate under the law of private corporations, they can establish salary levels competitive with the private sector. Furthermore, experts hired by SEMs are not civil servants and thus need not receive the sorts of job guarantees and fringe benefits that go with municipal employment. Although city officials initiate or contract for many SEM projects, they need not create a budget line for each new hire. Specialists are, in fact, often hired by SEMs only for the duration of a particular project. In short, city officials can engage a cadre of urban development technicians and direct them in the service of goals defined in terms of the public interest without going through the complex hiring procedures and making the long-term commitments required by civil service laws.[24]

Mixed-economy arrangements also enable local governments to move on projects much more quickly than if they were planned and administered entirely within the public sector. Since SEMs operate under the law of private corporations, they are able to avoid public scrutiny of their decision-making processes—despite the fact that elected officials sit on SEM

20. S. G. Wilson, *French Banking Structure and Credit Policy* (Cambridge: Harvard University Press, 1957), pp. 170-74.

21. d'Arcy, *Structures administratives*, p. 75.

22. Ibid., p. 41. See also Priouret, *La Caisse des Dépôts*, p. 426.

23. W. Saffran, *The French Polity* (New York: David McKay, 1977), p. 224. See also Priouret, p. 419.

24. M. Leroy, Personal interview, 29 May 1979.

boards—and their accounts. "Although one cannot admit this officially," the national director of Land Planning and Urban Affairs noted at a conference on the mixed economy in urban policymaking, "SEMs make effective action possible because they are not bound by the rules of public accountability."[25]

The emergence of the mixed-economy corporation also had a decided loosening effect in the rigidly centralized French political system.[26] Although the state holds a right to veto projects proposed by SEMs, it does not mandate action on the part of such corporations, as it does with municipalities. Program planning and implementation rest squarely with local SEMs. The role of the state, if it plays one at all, is reactive. The SEMs, acting under the laws of *sociétés anonymes* (private corporations), are not agents of national government, nor do they have to satisfy prefectural superiors in the *département*, as city officials must. Furthermore, unlike local governments, SEMs do not need prior approval of the state or *département* to undertake a project or establish a budget, although since 1976 the Minister of Equipment requires an annual budget report from SEMs explaining any deviations from budget projections. The mixed-economy corporation, then, is a comparatively free actor, standing outside a governmental system characterized by a tight hierarchy and often oppressive controls on subordinate jurisdictions. Since urban SEMs are dominated by local government officials, however, they

offer a means by which municipalities can escape to some degree their thoroughly dependent status. In the matters of housing as well as urban planning, the effective devolution of power has therefore occurred in France without making structural changes in the ancient pattern of intergovernmental relations.

Finally, it is important to note that the SEMs offered the French a way of bringing resources to bear on housing as a public problem without the complete socialization of the housing industry. Although some HLM housing is built by government housing agencies, a majority of low-cost units have been built by SEMs under contract to local housing authorities. SEMs are clearly very much tools of local government, but they retain certain important vestiges of capitalist enterprises. For a nation historically uncertain and divided about the possibilities and scope of a socialist state, the SEMs have represented what is widely deemed to be a very acceptable compromise.

THE MIXED-ECONOMY RECORD

Between 1965 and 1978 slightly under half a million new housing units for all income classes were built in France each year. Nearly 80 percent of these received some sort of governmental assistance.[27] Approximately one-quarter of the total were built by SEMs. Reliable detailed data pertaining to the SEM record in the decade prior to 1965 are apparently not published by any central organization.

Developments in the late 1970s show that despite continuing housing needs, mixed-economy arrange-

25. Colloques de Marly, *Les sociétés d'économie mixte*, p. 82.

26. SCET, *1956-1976*, p. 22; and J. E. Godchot, *Les sociétés d'économie mixte et l'aménagement du territoire* (Paris: Editions Berger-Levrault, 1958), p. 32.

27. M. Dresch, *Le financement du logement* (Paris: Editions Beger-Levrault, 1978), p. 230.

ments are playing a diminishing role in France, not only in the total supply of new dwellings, but also in the construction of low-income dwellings. Investments by urban SEMs in housing of all types fell from 79 percent in 1969 to 67 percent in 1975.[28] In part it would appear that the mixed economy simply began to defer to the relatively healthy private-sector housing industry, which rode to prosperity on the crest of an extravagant inflation in real estate. But SEM retrenchment in housing is also a response to a gradual withdrawal of state fiscal aid to municipalities for public works construction. Since 1962 such aid has declined slowly but steadily, and the vacuum has recently come to be filled by SEM activity. Mixed-economy resources at the local level have begun to be redirected from housing to the development of economic infrastructure: industrial parks, parking facilities, and, in places like Lyon and Grenoble, shopping centers.

Mixed-economy activity still devoted to housing is itself changing. The current concentration on small developments stands in contrast to the earlier production of *grands ensembles*, which took the form of veritible cities of new apartment blocks. Furthermore, beginning in the mid-1960s, SEMs began to build more and more moderate-income housing rather than focusing their efforts entirely on HLM projects for low-income groups.[29] Data for the 1965-71 period show that the average rental cost of SEM-built housing was twice that of HLM units built entirely by local housing authorities.[30] Finally, many mixed-

economy corporations involved in housing are engaged now in renovation rather than new construction. Indeed, more than half the major urban neighborhood renovation projects under way in France in 1979 were in the hands of SEMs. One estimate indicates that 50 of the approximately 150 housing-oriented SEMs are involved exclusively in the renovation of existing dwellings,[31] a response not so much to conservationist impulses as to the growing market for luxury addresses in the old central cities. Ironically, the old image of local mixed-economy corporations as builders of *logements sociaux* has given way in the face of SEM involvement, proclaimed on huge signs at the renovation sites, in the gentrification of popular or working-class districts.[32]

Despite the considerable growth of the private housing industry, SEMs will undoubtedly continue to play some role in French housing, in part for reasons of pure inertia: because they are there, they will be used.[33] In addition, there are few other major institutional actors in French society, outside of wholly public housing authorities, willing to put up housing for the poor besides the SEMs. Even in this increasingly small sphere, however, the role of the mixed economy is changing: since many SEMs are currently in financial difficulty, those that still engage in low-income housing projects lean more and more to the construction of mixed-income complexes, using middle-income rents to bolster revenues. It is evident that SEMs played a crucial role in the replacement and aug-

28. SCET, *1956-1976*, p. 69.

29. Leroy interview.

30. F. Godard, M. Castells, H. Delayre, C. Dessange, and C. O'Callaghan, *La rénovation urbaine à Paris* (Paris: Mouton, 1973), p. 109.

31. Colloques de Marly, *Les sociétés d'économie mixte*, p. 11.

32. Godard et al., *La rénovation urbaine a Paris*, p. 65.

33. Leroy interview.

mentation of France's housing stock in the 20 years after the mid-1950s, but it is equally clear that the SEM commitment to low-income housing is dwindling rapidly.

MIXED ECONOMY AND THE PUBLIC INTEREST

As permanent fixtures in the political economy of a nation, such mixed-economy arrangements appear to contain within them certain contradictions that, once they emerge, begin to undercut the best arguments for maintaining a commitment to the public-private mix.

There are at least four related problems inherent in the reliance on for-profit organizations in mixed-economy arrangements for the realization of public-interest goals that serve to compromise or weaken the public sector and those who depend on it. These are the profitability problem, the personnel problem, the coordination problem, and the unequal risk problem. While these have not all emerged to date with equal force in France, there is good reason to believe that the problems of mixed-economy arrangements are finally inescapable. The deterioration of public obligation, particularly, follows what is perhaps a universal logic.

Profitability

How mixed-economy corporations establish their agendas and the criteria they employ in doing so is a matter of vigorous debate in French local politics. Members of the French left, particularly the Socialists, suggest that profit criteria rather than social welfare values are the major determining factors in SEM decision-making. Critics on the left routinely cite as evidence

several controversial renewal projects in Paris, such as the transformation of the ancient Marais quarter into one of the highest rent districts of Paris by the *Société d'économie mixte de restauration du Marais* (SOREMA). There has been, as we have seen, an apparent shift of SEM activity in the 1970s away from new construction to renovation of old housing in response to the middle- and upper-class demand for central-city dwellings in historic neighborhoods. The involvement of SEMs in such activities simply seems to confirm for the French left the essentially capitalist character of such bodies, resulting in periodic calls by Socialist deputies and city council representatives for their dissolution.[34]

Spokespersons for the French center parties in local government view the SEMs in very different terms, arguing that they cannot be captives of private-seeking profit motives, for they "can only do what the city asks them to do."[35] To buttress the contention that the public interest is the guiding value in the choice of SEM projects, they point for proof to the fact that the majority of all housing units built by SEMs through the mid-1970s were for the working and lower-middle classes. It is the case, however, that while two-thirds of all housing projects built annually during the 1960s by SEMs were HLM, the yearly proportion of low-income housing has declined to less than half since 1969 and is still declining.[36]

34. Ville de Paris, Bulletin Municipal Officiel, *Débats du Conseil*, 27 Dec. 1976, p. 1254. Also, Colloques de Marly, *Les sociétés d'économie mixte*, p. 12.

35. Ville de Paris, 27 Dec. 1976, p. 1255.

36. SCET, *1956-1976*, p. 68; Leroy interview.

By their very nature, certain vital public services, such as the provision of low-income housing, do not return profits to the public treasury. In nonsocialist societies government assumes the responsibility for these services precisely because the private sector does not believe it can earn returns here. As Castells observes, "Public or semi-public housing... arises theoretically from a logic of service and not from profitability."[37] Pricing policy is a function of the fact that government does not have to pay dividends to shareholders. Even the collection of user charges is seldom sufficient to meet the break-even point, necessitating government subsidies from tax revenues. To finance such services with the help of private investment partners, however, is to change both the psychological and economic rules of the game. When there is a private investment partner, or a public partner using private money, as in the case of the *Caisse*, revenues must exceed the break-even line to keep the private money interested and/or available.[38] This must either drive up user charges or cause an increase in the tax subsidy. The French were not willing to increase significantly the tax subsidy, nor were they able politically to impose heavier user chargers—rents—on the poor. Rather than abandon subsidized housing activities altogether, however, local governments allowed SEMs to turn increasingly toward that sector of the housing market that could pay higher rents and thus provide returns to private capital, namely, middle-income consumers.

The mixed-economy partnership, it can be seen, enhances an option that government alone does not have in the face of so-called unprofitable services, namely, abandonment of the service. One possible private-sector response to an unprofitable line is to exit, that is, to shut down the line. Government is not in the same position, however. Government cannot easily determine, on the mere basis of cost, that because low-income tenants do not provide sufficient rents to cover the expenses of their public housing, it will get out of the low-income housing business. In nonsocialist societies the government is a supplier of services of last resort; it is therefore virtually locked in to the performance of certain functions, even if financially unprofitable, by a variety of moral and political considerations. But the private sector, while perhaps cognizant of such considerations, is freer to make choices on economic criteria alone. In a partnership with government, it may induce the latter to behave more like a private than a public actor, for the principal concern of the government then becomes the maintenance of the profitability of private investment. The SEM shift to mixed- and middle-income housing and luxury renovation in recent years can thus be regarded as good evidence of the end of a broad commitment to a social housing policy.[39]

The personnel problem

Freed from the constraints of a penurious civil service salary scale, the SEMs in the early years were able to lure skilled technical personnel—*urbanistes*—away from government service with relatively generous compensation. By virtu-

37. Castells, *City, Class and Power*, p. 22.
38. Godard et al., *La rénovation urbaine a Paris*, p. 77.

39. N. Evenson, *Paris: A Century of Change, 1878-1978* (New Haven, CT: Yale University Press, 1979), pp. 237-38.

ally capturing a whole generation of the best graduates of French technical institutes, the SEMs, presumably unwittingly, delayed the professionalization and growth of local government and administration.

Although the situation has changed somewhat and civil service salaries have begun to catch up to those in the private sector, local governments still rely heavily on SEM computer experts, economists, demographers, and planners. Compared, for example, with American or British local government, the presence of such technical personnel in municipal agencies is less common. The absence of a substantial pool of in-house technical employees denies local government a good deal of horizontal and vertical flexibility in its personnel administration. There are few skilled people who can be transferred from one project to another, from one department to another, or from technical to managerial positions within the same department.

Relationships between local government and a particular SEM and its technicians tend to be project-specific, that is, of a duration and character limited by the concerns and demands of a particular undertaking. Thus relationships between government administrators and technical personnel may be highly impermanent. No great fund of accumulated experience is created that carries over from project to project. The segregation of government from the technical staff it relies on means that a variety of start-up costs must be borne over and over again each time new projects are initiated.

Project decentralization

The creation of a different mixed-economy corporation to carry out each particular major urban redevelopment or housing project suggests that overall coordination, normally a strong suit of French administration, can be extremely difficult.[40]

Consider the Parisian case. Godard and his colleagues list 36 different renewal projects involving land clearance and housing construction in Paris during the 1966-69 period. Of these, 15 were being carried out by two public housing and renewal agencies. The other 21, however, were being conducted by 15 different SEMs.[41] It is true that the process leading to the approval of a particular project involves elaborate planning and consultation among the prefect, the city, and several national and local planning bodies, but once a project goes into the field the operations are no longer subject to effective centralized control. In Paris this has led, to give one example, to numerous violations by SEMs of the laws regarding relocating people displaced by land clearance. No central agency oversees the displacement process or follows up on those evicted from their dwellings.[42]

Unequal risk

Partners in mixed-economy corporations do not bear equally the burden of risk. Assigning all risk to local government in the SEM arrangement has ample justifications, of course. For one thing it was designed initially to attract private capital to public purposes in a period of tight credit. In addition, much of the private capital—particularly that portion held by the *Caisse des dépôts*—has not been

40. d'Arcy, *Structures administratives*, pp. 90-91.
41. Godard et al., *La renovation urbaine a Paris*, p. 128.
42. Ibid., p. 70.

invested directly by its owners. Thus, the reasoning goes, if the public sector is to use private capital without the direct consent of its owners, at least it should bear the risk of loss. But the government's obligation to bear all risk of loss, out of proportion to its investment, may induce excessive caution in the choice of projects. The patently unprofitable, even if it is socially justified, may be foregone in favor of more financially sound projects. Tying public money to private capital in a situation where only the former bears the risk of loss creates an inherent tension in the partnership that leads finally to the sort of mixed-income housing, gentrification, and economic development projects that increasingly command SEM resources.

CONCLUSION

As an adaptation to short-term problems in the credit market and as a reform device to develop and implement new public policies without undergoing the lengthy process of changing the capabilities of local government and its structural relationship to the state, the mixed-economy corporation in urban housing clearly performed well in France for nearly two decades. Not only did the SEM solve the capital aggregation problem and sidestep the issue of local government incapacities, but as a principal organ for the implementation of a social housing policy, it took a middle course between full socialization and the inefficiencies of capitalism.

The inherent tension in public-private partnerships, however, has caused a visible retreat from the initial social welfare goals that underlay the formation of the postwar SEMs. What is particularly

problematic about the increasingly entrepreneurial instincts of the housing SEMs is that the need for low-income housing still exists in French cities. Much of the burgeoning Algerian, central African, North African Jewish, and eastern Mediterranean European population is ill housed and unable to compete with the affluent French in the private housing sector.[43] Yet public-sector responsibility for such housing needs has all but deteriorated in the quest for more profitable ventures.

Naturally, we cannot conclude from this single case that private-sector, for-profit involvement in the provision of public services will inevitably transform the production of those services in ways inimical to the interests of the classes that cannot pay their share. But the case of the French mixed-economy corporations in urban housing is suggestive at least of the limits of such arrangements.

On the one hand the French experience with housing SEMs does nothing to cast doubt on the wisdom of vesting certain housekeeping functions in the hands of private contractors. A growing body of cross-national evidence suggests that private firms can manage garbage collection, tree-trimming, street repair, and so on more cheaply and more effectively than government.[44] What distinguishes these services from housing, of course, is that the former have virtually no social welfare component. They are not redistributive; they

43. M. Castells et al., *Crise du logement et mouvements sociaux urbains* (Paris: Mouton, 1978), pp. 80 ff.; and J. Minces, *Les Travailleurs étrangères en France* (Paris: Seuil, 1973), ch. 13.

44. Savas, "Municipal monopolies," pp. 486, 490.

have no special implications for the essential well-being of the have-not classes.

We may conclude by suggesting two conditions under which for-profit participation in the supply of public goods or services is problematic: (1) where the good or service is supplied on a selective or redistributive basis; and (2) where the potential recipients are nevertheless socioeconomically differentiated.

Housing supplied by the mixed economy in France is not available to everyone, but the potential clientele is still economically heterogeneous enough to allow certain groups to bid up its price. Private capital will generally respond to such competition, particularly in housing, where the basic costs of construction of low- and middle-income housing do not tend to differ as much as do the returns in rents. The government partner in such a situation, if it wishes to encourage the continued participation of private capital, must allow a shift to the more profitable market.

Government as the sole provider of a service, however, can resist this competition by accepting as a given the obligation to subsidize services to the lower classes. The French case, then, illustrates the extent of risk in entrusting private capital in quest of profits with social welfare responsibilities in situations in which the better off can outbid the poor for the service.

ANNALS, *AAPSS*, **459**, January 1982

Monetarists and the Politics of Monetary Policy

By JOHN T. WOOLLEY

ABSTRACT: Monetarist economists appear to have achieved a high level of success in having their policy ideas put into practice. The monetarists are analyzed here as a political group. They are characterized as a loosely organized group offering distinct policy prescriptions, closely aligned with neoliberal political forces. The supply of monetarists is discussed in terms of their relative numbers and shared socialization experiences. The demand for monetarist analysis stems from needs for policy prescriptions, from self-interest, and from need for ideological reassurance. This article concludes with the argument that monetarists' success depends on their ability to convince policymakers outside the Federal Reserve to adopt a monetarist line.

John T. Woolley, Ph.D., University of Wisconsin, Madison, has been assistant professor of political science, Washington University in St. Louis, since 1978. His publications include "Central Banks: Influence and Independence," *in* The Political Economy of Global Inflation and Recession, *Leon N. Lindberg and Charles Maier, editors (forthcoming). Current work, supported by a Social Science Research Council-Fulbright grant, includes collaborative research on the politics of monetary policy in Britain, France, Germany, and Italy.*

NOTE: Readers wishing more information on citations should contact the author.

PERIODS of crisis present opportunities to alter, to redirect, and to redefine the role the state plays in the economy and the way in which economic policy is made. To judge from many current commentaries, we are now in such a crisis: old understandings of how the economy and politics work no longer seem adequate; expectations are unmet; forecasts fail. The crisis is felt not only in the realm of economic thought but in political thought and in political life. The crisis is further revealed in the fact that serious consideration is given to the possibility of reversing the previously expanding role of government in the economy.

In recent years there has been intense discussion of the possibility of sharply altering the way in which monetary policy in the United States is conducted. On at least three occasions during the 1970s, the Federal Reserve has made—or has been obliged to make—moves in the direction of focusing policy on the monetary supply as an intermediate policy target. Such a change would represent a basic shift in the assumptions underlying U.S. monetary policy. The first year of the Reagan administration has been marked by a struggle between the administration and the Federal Reserve over the degree to which policy should follow a monetarist course.

Should the Federal Reserve firmly adopt a monetarist course, it will not represent merely a triumph of one theory of economic policy over another. Nor will it be simply another assertion of presidential power over the "independent" Federal Reserve. It will be a triumph of a broader kind of politics as well: a hard-won victory of a particular kind of ideological neoliberalism.

In this article, I discuss the politics of monetarist economists in the United States, examining their organization, their strategies of influence, and the conditions of their success. There is, implicitly, a broader theme here, too. The monetarists are not the only instance of economists who have organized and won political victories. Indeed, the predecessors of the monetarists could be examined in almost exactly the same terms. In a larger sense, then, this article is about the politics of economists—about how they organize and about how they help define the role of government in the economy.

This is not merely an examination of a change in government policy— that is, a change in monetary policy. Rather, this is a study of change in the conception underlying government policy. A condition highly conducive to such a change is that there be perceived failure of some sort—a crisis. However, crisis does not explain what kind of change will be made. Further, some changes, such as the rise to dominance of orthodox Keynesianism—the new economics —during the 1960s, appear not to have been preceded by crisis. Such changes reflect the emergence of a new dominant political coalition, a coalition that includes and is legitimated by a new set of economists.

The rise of the monetarists happens to have coincided with, and to have been facilitated by, apparent economic crisis. However, the monetarists' emergence was not entirely dependent on the crisis, nor has their success been due solely to the crisis. Rather, both have been the consequence of a conscious process of organization and persuasion. The process is indistinguishable from the kinds of processes undertaken by all manner of political groups. At the same time, however, the demand for the kind of analysis put forward by the monetarists has certainly been increased by the crisis in economic and political thought generally.

DIMENSIONS OF THE MONETARIST SUCCESS

The monetarists' success is revealed in several ways. They have become increasingly prominent in the popular media. They have become prominent—and permanently so—in academic discourse. They occupy important policy positions and have used those positions to increase the visibility of their views. Their recommendations are more and more evident in the policy choices of the Federal Reserve.

Monetarist economists hold ranking positions in the Reagan administration: Beryl Sprinkel is Undersecretary of the Treasury for Monetary Affairs; Jerry Jordan is a member of the Council of Economic Advisors (CEA). Monetarist thinking is fundamental in the administration's economic strategy. Monetarist economist Robert Weintraub, in his role of staff economist with the House Banking Committee, has for some years injected monetarist views into congressional action.

Recently a prominent monetarist journalist proclaimed that "hard-nosed monetarism" had become the dominant policy view at the Federal Reserve.[1] However, monetarists have announced the millennium before, only to experience a sense of betrayal later. I doubt that the Federal Reserve will consistently follow a course that would satisfy a monetarist true believer. Nonetheless, Federal Reserve policies are much

1. William Wolman, "Hard-Nosed Monetarism Takes Over at the Fed." *Business Week*, 15 June 1981, p. 32.

more nearly monetarist than ever before, and this has been evident in several actions taken during the 1970s.

In October 1979, the Federal Reserve announced that henceforth it was going to pay more attention to the behavior of the money supply and less attention to the movement of interest rates than it had previously. In 1975 Congress passed a concurrent resolution (HCR 133) requiring the Federal Reserve henceforth to announce monetary targets and to consult with Congress concerning progress in achieving those targets. The language of the resolution was ambiguous, but much more monetarist than anything that had come out of Congress before. In 1970 the Federal Reserve had changed its operating procedures to place more emphasis on a measure of bank reserves—a step clearly in keeping with the monetarist position. These actions were widely perceived as advances for the monetarists.

These events indicate that the rise of the monetarists is not simply a media phenomenon. However, the rise of the monetarists can be traced in the attention they have received in popular media. One indicator is plotted in Figure 1, which shows the ratio of an index of attention to monetarist economists to the same index for Keynesians for 1960-79.[2]

2. The index is the number of days per year on which one of the three monetarist (Keynesian) economists was cited in the *New York Times Index* divided by the number of pages of citations in the year—this last in order to control for varying completeness in indexing practices over the years. The monetarists were Milton Friedman, Karl Brunner, and Allan Meltzer. The Keynesians were Paul Samuelson, James Tobin, and Franco Modigliani. The Keynesians should do better on grounds of sheer prestige among economists; each has been president of the American Economic Association, whereas only one of the monetarists has been so honored.

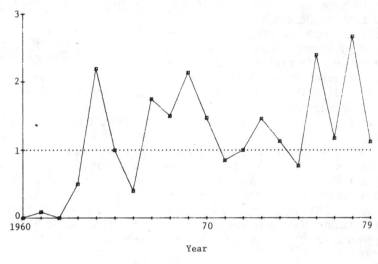

FIGURE 1
MEDIA ATTENTION TO MONETARISTS RELATIVE TO KEYNESIANS

Key: 0 = No citation of monetarists
        1 = Monetarist citations exactly equivalent to Keynesians
        2 = Twice as many monetarist citations
        3 = Three times as many monetarist citations

SOURCE: Source and index construction described in note 5.

The monetarists exceeded the Keynesians in media attention in seven of the most recent ten years, compared with only four of the preceding ten years.

THE MONETARIST PRODUCT: BASIC PRECEPTS

There are many varieties of monetarists, and there is disagreement among them on many specific points. Three distinct varieties of monetarism have been identified: that associated with Milton Friedman, that associated with Karl Brunner and Allan Meltzer, and the rational-expectations variant. Nonetheless, it is reasonably clear that there is a set of policy recommendations on which almost all monetarists agree and around which they unite. These include the following:

—the reserve base or similar measure should be the indicator of monetary policy;

—the money stock is the proper (intermediate) target of monetary policy;

—monetary policy should be guided by a monetary growth rule;

—the only appropriate targets of monetary policy are macroeconomic rather than, for example, preventing failure of specific institutions or avoiding other instabilities;

—inflation is a greater concern, relative to unemployment, than for most economists; and

—government intervention should be limited and reduced.

The defining characteristic of the monetarists is their insistence that monetary policy should be guided by a simple rule: achieve a steady, stable, low rate of growth in the money supply. Monetarists urge that policy not deviate from this monetary rule. They believe that there is no lasting tradeoff between unemployment and inflation, and they are particularly concerned with lowering inflation.

Monetarists are to be understood not simply as a group of economists participating in an obscure debate among economists about monetary theory. The monetarists are also a particular manifestation of a more general neoliberal—or, as the current analysts might have it, libertarian—political position. This broad ideological position is characterized particularly by mistrust of government; by the belief that exercise of government discretion— often as a consequence of misguided democracy—produces more harm than good; and by a desire to reduce government spending and to increase reliance on the free market. Monetarists should be understood as pressing specific elements in a neoliberal political program. The specific elements, of course, have to do with monetary policy.

These beliefs are held with a fervor that is almost religious. Observers have often called attention to the similarity between these disputes and theological arguments. The monetarists' own recognition of this fact is reflected in the metaphors they use to describe their efforts. Thus in October 1979 the president of the Federal Reserve Bank (FRB) of St. Louis, Lawrence Roos, likened his organization to "a preacher whose message is finally heeded."[3] Karl Brunner expressed

3. *Wall Street Journal*, 9 Oct. 1979, p. 7.

his religious attitude when he remarked, "All I can do is light some candles and keep up the pressure."[4]

THE SUPPLY SIDE OF MONETARISM

A recent survey of economists included questions about issues basic to the monetarist program. There are problems with interpretation of the published results,[5] but they constitute the only available indicator of the extent of agreement among economists with two monetarist principles. The relevant questions and the published responses are presented in Table 1. Divisions among various subsamples of economists are reported in Table 2.

Numbers

Figures in Table 1 indicate that economists substantially agree with one element in the monetarist program—stressing the money supply as a target. However, another element, the monetary rule, is overwhelmingly rejected. The lowest levels of agreement are found among the economists in leading graduate programs (Table 2). Other academic and business economists are more in agreement with the monetarist position. It seems accu-

4. *Wall Street Journal*, 12 Oct. 1979, p. 20.
5. The results are based on a rather modest 33 percent return in a stratified sample of economists. The research is reported in J. R. Kearl, Clayne L. Pope, Gordon C. Whiting, and Larry T. Wimmer, "A Confusion of Economists?" in *American Economic Association Papers and Proceedings, American Economic Review*, 69:28-37 (May 1979). The original sample included 100 economists in the top 7 graduate programs, 200 other academic economists, 150 economists in government positions, and 150 economists in private nonacademic employment. The aggregated results—for example, in Table 1—appear not to be weighted by the relative proportions of economists in each group.

TABLE 1

AGREEMENT AMONG ECONOMISTS WITH SOME PROPOSITIONS RELATED
TO THE MONETARIST POSITION (in percentages)

PROPOSITIONS	GENERALLY AGREE	AGREE WITH PROVISIONS	GENERALLY DISAGREE	SUM
1. The money supply is a more important target than interest rates for monetary policy	48	23	29	100
2. The Fed should be instructed to increase the money supply at a fixed rate	14	25	61	100

SOURCE: Adapted from J. R. Kearl, Clayne L. Pope, Gordon C. Whiting, and Larry T. Wimmer, "A Confusion of Economists?" *American Economic Association Papers and Proceedings, American Economic Review,* 69: 30 (May 1979), with permission of the publisher and the authors.

rate to regard general agreement with proposition 2 as characterizing true monetarists. Using this criterion, a generous estimate of the proportion of monetarists among all economists is less than 20 percent—even less among economists teaching in leading graduate programs.

Organization

Leading monetarists have been meeting semiannually since 1973, calling themselves the Shadow Open Market Committee (SOMC). They "shadow" the activities of the Federal Reserve's main policymaking body, the Federal Open Market Committee (FOMC). Although recent press reports about the SOMC have been rather brief, early reports indicated that the SOMC consisted mostly of academic economists. SOMC meetings are well organized and occupy an entire day. They involve 10 or more economists from all over the United States. Papers are presented, policy options are discussed, and a press release is issued, commenting on Federal Reserve policy and recommending an alternative course.

The SOMC is not the only organized manifestation of the monetarists. Monetarism is an article of faith at the Federal Reserve Bank of St. Louis. The St. Louis Fed is, in effect, a government-funded organizational center for monetarist economists. It publishes a monthly review that repeatedly has been at the center of the debate between monetarists and their opponents.

Particularly important in the organization of the monetarists are three policy entrepreneurs: Friedman, Brunner, and Meltzer. The obvious one is Milton Friedman. As far as the general public is concerned, Friedman alone has been monetarism's leading light. Friedman is known for his frequent columns in *Newsweek* and for winning the Nobel Award for economics. Perhaps more vigorous, if less well known, are Karl Brunner and Allan Meltzer. Brunner and Meltzer have organized an chaired both the SOMC and the Shadow European Economic Policy Committee (the latter "shadows" the Organisation for Economic Cooperation and Development, which it views as too Keynesian and activist). Brunner is closely associated with the activities of the Federal Reserve Bank of St. Louis through former students. In the United States, Brunner has founded two professional journals that greatly expanded

TABLE 2
BREAKDOWN OF RESPONSES TO QUESTIONS ABOUT MONETARIST
PROPOSITIONS BY SUBSAMPLE OF ECONOMISTS

SUBSAMPLE GROUP		PROPOSITION	
		1	2
Top academics*		1.6	1.3
	N	(.82)†	(.70)
		24	24
Other academics		2.3	1.7
	N	(.85)	(.76)
		73	77
Government		2.2	1.4
	N	(.82)	(.69)
		46	46
Business		2.4	1.5
	N	(.84)	(.69)
		56	55

SOURCE: Adapted from J. R. Kearl, Clayne L. Pope, Gordon C. Whiting, and Larry T. Wimmer, "A Confusion of Economists?" *American Economic Association Papers and Proceedings, American Economic Review,* 69: 31 (May 1979), with permission of the publisher and the authors.
NOTE: The main entry is the average score of respondents based on the following scores: disagree = 1; agree with provisions = 2; agree = 3.
*See note 5.
†Standard deviation.

the opportunities for airing monetarist arguments. Together, Brunner and Meltzer have edited the *Carnegie-Rochester Conference Series on Public Policy*—not an exclusively monetarist outlet, but one giving heavy play to monetarist arguments.

Production and socialization

There is, of course, some element of self-selection into the monetarist camp. I have pointed out that monetarism is an element of contemporary neoliberal thought. One would expect persons already in agreement with such ideas to associate with others of like mind. Unfortunately, with available data it is not possible to say much about this process.

However, one can observe that prominent monetarists have often shared certain socialization experiences. Prominent monetarists have tended to have Ph.D.s from the University of Chicago, to have been associated with Brunner/Meltzer—

via UCLA, Ohio State, Carnegie-Mellon, or Rochester—or to have links to the Federal Reserve Bank of St. Louis, or some combination of the three. Of 21 prominent monetarists —including all members of the SOMC for whom data could be discovered—10 have Ph.D.s from Chicago. In addition are Friedman, Brunner, and Meltzer. Six of the remaining eight have a close and direct link to Brunner, Meltzer, Friedman, or the Federal Reserve Bank of St. Louis. (See Table 3 for the raw data.)

Of course, many economists besides Brunner, Meltzer, and Friedman have contributed to the development of monetarism, so it is not surprising that there should be experiences of monetarism other than through these three major routes. Nevertheless, with a very high probability, monetarists are produced by other monetarists. What cannot be argued is that monetarists always produce other monetarists. Similarly, some mone-

TABLE 3
ACADEMIC BACKGROUNDS AND CAREER EXPERIENCES OF
NOTABLE MONETARISTS

NAME	Ph.D.	CHICAGO FACULTY	OTHER CAREER EXPERIENCES
Andersen, Leonall	Minnesota (1962)	—	FRB St. L., 1962-74
Brunner, Karl	L.S.E. (1943)	—	Cowles Foundation Fellow (U. of Chi.), 1949-50; UCLA, 1951-66; Ohio S. U., 1966-71; Rochester, 1971-; SOMC
Cagan, Philip	Chicago (1950)	1955-58	NBER, 1953-55; Brown, 1958-65; Columbia, 1965-
Christ, Carl	Chicago (1952)	1955-61	Johns Hopkins, 1961-
Dewald, William	Minnesota (1963)	—	Ohio S.U., 1963-; Editor, *JMCB*
Friedman, Milton	Columbia (1946)	1948-	Hoover Inst., 1977-; NBER, 1937-45, 1948-
Jones, Homer	Chicago (1949)	—	FRB St. L., 1958-71; SOMC
Jordan, Jerry	UCLA (1969)	—	FRB St. L., 1967-75, Pittsburgh National Bank, 1975-80; University of New Mexico, 1980-81; CEA, 1981-
Laidler, David	Chicago (1964)	—	Manchester, 1969-75; W. Ontario, 1973-
Lucas, Robert E.	Chicago (1964)	1975-	Carnegie-Mellon, 1964-75.
Mayer, Thomas	Columbia (1953)	—	Mich. State, 1956-61; U. Cal. Davis, 1961-; SOMC
Meigs, A. James	Chicago (1960)	—	Argus Research; Claremont Men's College, 1975-; SOMC
Meiselman, David	Chicago (1961)	1958-62	NBER, 1955-58; Government, 1962-66; Macalester College, 1966-71; VPI, 1971-; AEI Adjunct Schlr., 1976-
Meltzer, Allan	UCLA (1958)	1964-65	Carnegie-Mellon 1957-; SOMC
Poole, William	Chicago (1966)	—	Hopkins, 1963-69; staff BGFRS, 1969-73; Brown, 1974-; Brookings Panel, 1970-77; FRB Boston. Consultant
Rasche, Robert	Michigan (1966)	—	U. Penn. 1966-72; Michigan State. 1975-; FRB St. L., 1976-77; SOMC
Sargent, Thomas	Harvard (1968)	—	Research Assoc., Carnegie-Mellon, 1967-68; Minnesota, 1971-
Schmidt, Wilson	Virginia (1952)	—	George Washington U., 1950-66; Treasury, 1970-72; VPI, 1966-; SOMC
Schwartz, Anna J.	Columbia (1964)	—	NBER, 1950-; SOMC
Sprinkel, Beryl	Chicago (1952)	—	Harris Trust and Savings Bank, 1952-81; Treasury, 1981-; SOMC

TABLE 3 Continued

NAME	Ph.D.	CHICAGO FACULTY	OTHER CAREER EXPERIENCES
Weintraub, Robert	Chicago (1954)	—	CUNY. 1956-65; U. Cal. Santa Barbara, 1965-76; Cong. Staff, 1964, 1975-.

SOURCE: *American Men and Women of Science: Social and Behavioral Sciences,* ed. The Jacques Cattell Press (New York: Browker, 1978); "Biological Listing of Members," *American Economic Review,* 68 (Dec. 1978): monetarist work. Lucas and Sargent represent the rational-expectations variant of monetarism.

NOTE: FRB = Federal Reserve Bank; UCLA = University of California, Los Angeles; SOMC = Shadow Open Market Committee; NBER = National Bureau of Economic Research; *JMCB* = **Journal of Money, Credit, and Banking;** CEA = Council of Economic Advisors; VPI = Virginia Polytechnic Institute; AEI = American Enterprise Institute; BGFRS = Board of Governors, Federal Reserve System; and CUNY = City University of New York.

tarists have been produced by educational programs famous for producing Keynesians, for example, MIT, Yale, and Harvard. Nonetheless, the tendency is clearly to the contrary.

THE DEMAND FOR MONETARISM

Monetarism has not succeeded simply because it exists, but because it responded to real needs. Here my analysis must be primarily suggestive. There are three basic kinds of needs to which the monetarists respond. First, at the instrumental level there is a need for a solution to a policy problem—a solution the monetarists claim to provide. Second, the monetarist arguments serve the self-interest of some influential groups. Third, in a period of ideological disarray, monetarism responds to a need for ideological order and certainty.

As a policy program, monetarism is more clearly addressed to the problem of inflation than the mainstream Keynesian analysis that preceded it. In this respect, the monetarists make a policy claim that may appeal to many on purely instrumental grounds.

The focus of monetarists on controlling inflation may make mone-

tarism attractive to groups whose interests are particularly affected by inflation. In the abstract, it is conventionally argued that net monetary creditors are especially harmed by inflation. Within this category fall most important financial institutions. It is of some interest to note that while early SOMC meetings were supported at least in part by grants, there have been in-kind contributions from Argus Economic Research, *Business Week,* and the brokerage firm, Morgan Stanley & Co. Thus available evidence indicates that monetarists have been supported by organizations that, one would expect, have their own financial interests clearly in view.

Finally, as I have mentioned previously, monetarism is itself a component of a larger ideological structure. Monetarism performs both for mass publics and for elites the kinds of functions that ideologies are supposed to perform: it explains current events, it justifies a course of policy, and it provides a simple, clear-cut evaluation of government behavior. Monetarism can perform this function for both mass publics and for elites.

The recent rise of monetarism relative to the established Keynesianism is, I believe, significantly due to the ideological aspects of monetarist doctrine and to its linkage with a larger conservative political movement. It is important that in a period of widespread feeling of crisis and disarray, this movement presents a conceptually simple analysis. This analysis specifies culprits who are regarded as personally responsible for our problems—the Federal Reserve Board—and presents an apparently uncomplicated solution: control the money supply.

THE MONETARIST POLITICAL STRATEGY

Like most economists, monetarists account for the behavior of policymakers by reference to a model of rational decision makers seeking to optimize the attainment of various goals. Following the logic of this model, monetarists would assume that the Federal Reserve is composed of rational actors, but monetarists would also observe that the Fed fails to adopt the appropriate—monetarist—policymaking procedures. Why would rational actors behave in such a fashion? The monetarists appear to infer that the Federal Reserve is politically constrained from following a correct policy path. That is, the monetarists appear to adopt an assumption that the organization engages in an optimizing process that includes yielding to external political threats—an assumption that many analysts of Federal Reserve behavior have also found productive.

If one did follow such an analysis, a particular political strategy would be implied, a strategy of trying to alter the nature of the political constraints operating on the Federal Reserve. In fact, this appears to be the kind of strategy the monetarists have adopted. In order to influence

their ultimate target, the Federal Reserve, the monetarists concentrate on three intermediate targets: the president and Treasury, the Congress, and the press. This strategy is clearly a complex one, although, as I have shown previously, the monetarists have been quite successful in getting substantial press coverage, much of which has been intended to place the Federal Reserve on the defensive.

Through the efforts of House Banking Committee (HBC) staffer Robert Weintraub, monetarists have had modest success in creating the presumption of congressional support for monetarist policy. For example, one can observe (Table 4) that appearances by economists increased dramatically after Weintraub began to serve—1975 and after. In contrast to appearances before the Joint Economic Committee (JEC), it is clear that Weintraub also increased substantially the probability that monetarists would be called to testify before the Banking Committee.[6]

An examination of the process leading to the passage of HCR 133 in 1975 provides further evidence of monetarist influence on congressional behavior. HCR 133 directed the Federal Reserve to consult with Congress on monetary policy, and it used a very monetarist formulation. Weintraub's important role in this legislation was one of furthering its monetarist direction. The monetar-

6. Counted as monetarists appearing before the HBC are Brunner, Meltzer, Christ, Dewald, Jordan, Laidler, Meigs, Meiselman, Poole, and Sprinkel, all in Table 3, and William Fellner, Darryl Francis, and John Lindauer. Counted as monetarists when appearing before the JEC are Brunner, Weintraub, Christ, Alan Greenspan and, perhaps implausibly, Herbert Stein. Also see notes to Table 4.

TABLE 4
APPEARANCES FOR TESTIMONY BEFORE THE HOUSE BANKING COMMITTEE (HBC)
AND THE JOINT ECONOMIC COMMITTEE (JEC) BY MONETARISTS AND
NONMONETARISTS, 1970-79

	HOUSE BANKING COMMITTEE		JOINT ECONOMIC COMMITTEE	
YEAR	MONETARIST	NONMONETARIST	MONETARIST	NONMONETARIST
1970	0*	0	1	3
1971	0	2	2	6
1972	0	0	0	14
1973	1	6	0	9
1974	1	0	0	10
1975	3	5	0	15
1976	3	3	0	10
1977	7	4	0	6
1978	3	4	0	11
1979	2	3	3	6
Total	20	27	6	90

SOURCE: Lists of appearances and information on substance of testimony are drawn from Congressional Information Service, CIS Annual Abstracts, vols. 1970-79 (Washington, DC: CIS, 1970-79). JEC counts are based only on testimony at hearings on the Economic Report of the President. HBC counts refer to all hearings dealing with macroeconomic policy and the performance of the Federal Reserve (exact list of hearings available on request).

*Tallies are limited primarily to academic economists and economists with independent research organizations, such as Brookings and the American Enterprise Institute. Economists employed primarily by business and testifying primarily as to the effect of policies on particular industries are excluded, as are trade association economists. Exceptions are Beryl Sprinkel and Jerry Jordan. Also excluded are economists testifying as government officials. See also note 6.

ist approach of the House committee has, if anything, strengthened since 1975 and is plainly evident in committee reports commenting on monetary policy.

The effort to focus presidential pressure on the Federal Reserve has culminated in the appointment of two monetarists, and SOMC members, to high positions in the Reagan administration: Beryl Sprinkel at the Treasury and Jerry Jordan at the CEA. It should be noted as well that another CEA member, William Niskanen, is also a Chicago Ph.D., and a student of Milton Friedman.

CONCLUSION: MONETARISTS, POLITICAL GROUPS, AND FEDERAL RESERVE BEHAVIOR

Monetarists cannot be excluded from the category of political groups on the grounds that their arguments are supported by theory and data. Indeed, many successful—and unsuccessful—political movements can claim some kind of theory and evidence supporting their positions. However, scientific debate regarding fundamental issues is rarely conclusive in resolving policy debates. Finally, contests are decided on the basis of votes, power, persuasion, or authority, not scientific proof.

It is unusual to describe economists as an interest group. This approach may be irritating to economists, whether monetarists or not, who view their role as advocates in policymaking as logically connected to their research. Still, it is not possible to distinguish monetarists from at least one category of political group—the public interest group (PIG)—which has been closely studied.[7] At the descriptive level, the monetarists' degree of organization, or disorganization, is the equivalent of that of other PIGs, as is their level and sources of finance, their organizational structure and history, and their strategies. It may be objected that monetarists are not a monolithic group, that they do not carry cards, subscribe to given creeds, uniformly support the proclamations of their leaders, or even make tax-deductible contributions. However, all of these are true of public interest groups as well.

The monetarists are distinguished from most PIGs in the extent to which they have been politically successful. In understanding this success—and its limits—one must understand two routes available for attempting to influence the Federal Reserve. The first route is the direct route: the route of attempting explicitly and directly to confront the Federal Reserve about its course of policy. The second route is one of attempting to influence the Federal Reserve indirectly, by pressure from either Congress or the president. The first route is one highly restricted to elites who possess special expertise: economists and top financial officials. The second route is the one ordinarily taken by organized interests, such as labor and the construction industry, who wish to alter Federal Reserve policy.

Most interests have had more success using indirect rather than direct routes to influence the Federal Reserve. Indeed, this appears to be true of the monetarists, despite the fact that they are well represented within the Federal Reserve,

through the Federal Reserve Bank of St. Louis. The success of the indirect route is a function of the structural and substantive characteristics of Federal Reserve decisions: decisions are paradigmatically incremental; that is, critical decisions are hard to identify, impacts occur only with a substantial lag, and the relationship between policy impacts and policy decisions is consequently obscure.[8] External responsiveness stems in part from the Federal Reserve's apparently undemocratic structure and its consequent vulnerability to criticism, precisely on grounds of its lack of responsiveness. Externally, the Federal Reserve defends its independence and future policy autonomy through a combined strategy of dazzling opponents with technical virtuosity and partially yielding on politically sensitive issues that appear to enjoy considerable support. The Federal Reserve relies in large part for political protection on its claim to special technical expertise. It is precisely when that expertise came most into question during the 1970s that the Federal Reserve came under the sharpest political attack from Congress and elsewhere.

Monetarists share with all economists the characteristic that their relationship to the Federal Reserve is not merely that of an interest group—even a public interest group—to target officials. As economists, monetarists do not simply argue for their own view of desirable public policy; rather they also

7. Jeffrey M. Berry, *Lobbying for the People: The Political Behavior of Public Interest Groups* (Princeton: Princeton University Press, 1977).

8. For further discussion of these characteristics and the overall nature of Federal Reserve relationships with external actors, see John T. Woolley, *The Federal Reserve and the Political Economy of Monetary Policy* (Ph.D. diss., University of Wisconsin, Madison, 1980).

offer an evaluation of the technical quality of the Federal Reserve's performance. This provides the monetarists with access via direct pressure. However, as interpreters of the Federal Reserve's practices for other political actors, the monetarists gain access to indirect routes of pressure. The most important factor facilitating monetarist indirect pressure on the Federal Reserve is their alliance with their conservative compatriots.

Conditions for success

Monetarist successes appear to have been greatest when they have indirectly pressured the Federal Reserve, especially when they are in concert with a strong neoliberal ideological coalition. This reveals much about the conditions for politically constraining the Federal Reserve.

The monetarists succeed insofar as they oblige the Federal Reserve to focus exclusively on only one, intermediate policy target—the money supply—and to be concerned with only one major problem, or ultimate target—inflation. Always in the past, apparent monetarist successes have proven to be short-lived because of the impossibility of achieving this single-mindedness. Monetarists could believe that they had succeeded in altering Federal Reserve behavior only because they incorrectly understood the logic of the system's behavior. The Federal Reserve has not been optimizing across a few goals simultaneously; rather, it has tried to reach a satisfactory level (not an optimum) in one goal at a time. The nature of those goals and the importance attached to various ones of them have been determined substantially by prior political conflicts. Thus for short periods of time the Federal Reserve could appear to follow a monetarist strategy—until a new or different problem came to dominate policymaking.

In trying to alter Federal Reserve behavior the monetarists have pursued a reasonable political strategy. However, in the long run their success depends not merely on having monetarists in key policymaking positions, but on doing away with the problems that have in the past generated the political forces to which the Federal Reserve has been sensitive. This is not very likely. Alternatively, the monetarists must generate political forces that neutralize any groups striving to distract the Federal Reserve from a steady money-supply-oriented, anti-inflation policy. This is also a substantial task that will require the deep commitment both of White House political officials and of congressional leaders to the monetarist approach. This is not impossible to achieve, but it requires a level of willingness to ignore constituency concerns that is highly unusual in representative government.

Book Department

INTERNATIONAL RELATIONS AND POLITICS

RICHARD S. KATZ. *A Theory of Parties and Electoral Systems.* Pp. xii, 151. Baltimore: Johns Hopkins University Press, 1980. $12.95.

This short, well-written, comparative treatise deals with causal relations between electoral structures on one hand and party and campaign behavior on the other. In particular, Katz examines how select electoral structures affect the choice and formulation of electoral issues, the ideological posture of parties, and the degree of cohesiveness and divisiveness of party organization. A rationalistic paradigm is employed: legislators are rational actors seeking reelection by one way or another. From such simplistic assumptions, the behavioral characteristics of British, Irish, and Italian parties are deduced against the context of their respective electoral structures. These deductions are offered as predictions and are tested using data from the International Comparative Political Parties project and questionnaires distributed for this study.

The empirically tested findings contain few surprises. They include observations such as the following: PR systems tend to promote ideological articulation and differentiation among parties in marked contrast to single-member plurality systems; matters of considerable import to parties give rise to noticeable internal party debate; split and transfer voting lead candidates to emphasize personality and locality instead of issues; intraparty preferential voting encourages diffused party leadership; large districts in a PR system foster more parties than moderate-sized districts in a single-member plurality system; and PR ordinal—as opposed to categoric—choice lists spark intraparty rather than interparty campaign competition.

All in all, in view of the pedestrian nature of the tested predictions, the only significant question for political science that follows is why so much methodological concern and energy needs to be expended to prove what knowledgeable political observers have long taken for granted? This work though is not entirely without merit. As a case study in vintage behavioral political science, it constitutes a tightly worked exercise. But the claims made are far too extravagant, if not presumptuous. Electoral structures, it is stated, are critically important because they can be equated with the core of the definition of Western democracy. Accordingly, the present methodological approach, Katz argues, can provide a scientific understanding of democratic institutions. If applied to an extended study of electoral systems, this methodology would promise a clarification of democratic theory, explanation of elite political behavior, and with sufficient data even an understanding of mass political behavior.

The credibility of these macro claims, however, is undermined by a failure to explore and explain fully the limited micro topics addressed here. Electoral structures defined as independent variables are treated as if they had developed and operate in political vacuums. No thought is given to the roots that electoral structures have in the political, social, and economic matrices of nations. If macro political questions are to be tackled scientifically, an auspicious beginning will require wide-ranging scholarship, and not merely a declaration of faith that electoral structures are independent variables that go to the quick of democratic political life. Common sense suggests that political science should not ignore electoral structures. But it suggests also that there is more to the essence of democratic theory, and that the key to a scientific understanding of democratic politics is not simply and so easily found. It might be asked, for example, How much would a prodigious study of American electoral structure tell us about the actual distribution of power in the United States? Probably, little. What would such a study tell us about the behavior of elites like David or Nelson Rockefeller? Again, very little. In concluding, Katz almost concedes as much. "The important factor," he writes, "is not the substance of the empirical findings, but rather the method by which the hypotheses tested were derived." This is a book, then, of method; little else seems to matter.

PAUL L. ROSEN

Carleton University
Ottawa
Canada

RICHARD W. MANSBACH and JOHN A. VASQUEZ. *In Search of Theory: A New Paradigm for Global Politics.* Pp. xxv, 559. New York: Columbia University Press, 1981. $25.00.

Students of international relations have long lamented the unsatisfactory theoretical underpinnings of their field. If theory in the social sciences should allow one to describe, explain, and predict events, then indeed the development of theory in international relations is underdeveloped.

Professors Mansbach and Vasquez acknowledge this weakness and place the blame squarely on the dominance of the realist paradigm in the thinking and writing of international relations since World War II. They find, as have others, that this state-centric model is inadequate to deal, for example, with multinationals, the Common Market, and the phenomenon of interdependence. They question also the assertion of a clear boundary between domestic and global politics and the assumption of an overarching struggle for power.

The two authors thus begin by describing The Decay of an Old Paradigm and embark on the construction of a more satisfactory paradigm centering on issues and actors (Chapters 2 through 8). Many of the elements of their paradigm are derived from findings in American politics as well as from related social sciences. It is impossible to describe the richness and complexity of the paradigm in a short review. It must suffice to mention just a few of the ideas presented.

The model begins with issues, their formation, their placement on a global agenda, and their salience. A case study is presented of issue transformation in Indochina since World War II. The other major focus is an actor dimension. Variables such as similarity, relative status, and prior patterns of interaction help determine the issue positions of actors. Actors allocate values according to interaction rules formed mostly by trial and error. Thus, the Korean War showed that unlimited war is currently illegitimate, just as it was during the classical balance-of-power era and that limited wars are possible in a nuclear age. As a case study of actor contention, the authors devote part of one chapter to an analysis of the causes of war and argue that change in the status hierarchy of actors is the key variable because this disrupts prior patterns of interaction.

The third part of the book, Practice, consists of three chapters in which the authors look at history with the aid of their model, beginning with the Peace of Westphalia and continuing to the present. In a separate chapter on the cold war, the authors argue that the cold war began to be transformed into detente after the Cuban Missile Crisis proved to both major actors that the cold war could not be "won," leading to the dormancy of the transcendent stakes of communism versus capitalism and the rise of new, more concrete stakes.

Mansbach and Vasquez have performed a valuable service in synthesizing in a coherent way many of the findings of the past decade. Since much of their paradigm builds on recent behavioral research, readers unfamiliar with quantitative techniques should be warned that some of the text will be difficult to follow. At times, in their effort to prove the value of their model, they become a bit too deterministic:

In light of their prior pattern of disagreement, dissimilarity and rapid rise to the first and second ranks in the status hierarchy, it may have been inevitable that the United States and the Soviet Union would drift apart after the defeat of Hitler [p. 421].

The authors see their work as a beginning—a path leading to better theory in international relations. This attempt to bring structure and coherence to the field will be welcomed.

WAYNE PATTERSON
Saint Norbert College
De Pere
Wisconsin

GORDON TULLOCK. *Trials on Trial: The Pure Theory of Legal Procedure.* Pp. xiii, 255. New York: Columbia University Press, 1980. $20.00.

At the outset, Tullock assures his readers that this book is an exercise in the pure theory of legal procedure, by which he seems to mean a theory without "the necessary statistical and other empirical bases for a less theoretical work." His impatience with Anglo-Saxon law, especially its American version, soon propels him into demands for fundamental reform. His proposals are offered as issues for empirical research, which he regards as sadly neglected in every domain of jurisprudence. Most of his readers will agree with him as to that; but, to say the least, the research he calls for would be extraordinarily difficult to carry out. Yet Tullock is a positive man; regardless of the feasibility of the studies he recommends, he leaves no doubt about the findings he expects them to produce.

To put the matter bluntly, Tullock is a revolutionary. It is his opinion that "the bulk of procedural rules used in Anglo-Saxon courts are useless or positively perverse." If American jurisprudence is made over to his liking, it will be nearly unrecognizable. The ancient common law will be jettisoned in favor of a code, probably based on Justinian. Trial procedures will be revised to assure that the information considered by the court will be as complete as possible. Appellate review will be narrowly limited, if it survives Tullock's empirical tests at all. Judges may be paid a lot more than they get now, thereby "obtaining really superb quality personnel." On the other hand, many law schools will close, and many practicing lawyers will have to give up their profession and turn to such occupations as the selling of vacuum cleaners. It is not at all certain that the U.S. Supreme Court will retain its lawmaking prerogatives, but Tullock calls attention to its peculiar singularity: alone among all the supreme courts in the world, it maintains this power of unmaking and making laws.

These reforms are the culmination of the pure theory to which Tullock addresses himself in the first ten chapters of the book. It is presented as a basis for the "truly scientific approach," to law that is so lacking now. That approach is not necessarily limited to the discipline of economics, but it is plain that Tullock regards the methods of the economist as the most appropriate for research.

We are first led through an economic analysis of the relationship of the costs of litigation to the accuracy of judicial decisions. A succession of diagrams demonstrates that where the quality of the evidence before the court is high, the probability of a correct decision is also high. We then learn that as resources are invested, the quality of the evidence improves accordingly, although the diagrams do not clearly allow for the effect of diminishing returns.

From this laborious exposition, lawyers could calculate the cost of resources needed to make a successful case for their clients and compare the investment required with the probable gain or loss from a winning lawsuit. Neither an economist nor a lawyer, I cannot judge how helpful these diagrams will be to those who must make decisions about pursuing litigation. It seemed to me that so far as they went they charted what every honest lawyer ought to know intuitively and then scrupulously tell his client.

Economists inhabit a world in which everything has its price. Anything that cannot be assigned a monetary value must be left out of the equations. It is not surprising that Tullock candidly allows that he is not very interested in "fairness," if that is defined as "in accord with certain ancient customs"—not the definition that would have occurred to me—and, whatever the definition, not readily translated into a dollars-and-cents value. Instead, Tullock believes that legal procedure should aim at accuracy and low cost, values that are readily quantified and put into condition for cost-benefit analysis. I think that most observers of our system of justice are also interested in the attainment of these objectives, and that they share Tullock's discontent with the capriciousness and costs of the present system. Many of his suggestions for change would increase accuracy and reduce costs, and if that were all there were to reform of the courts, we would be well advised to follow Tullock's lead into a new and more efficient system for the dispensation of justice.

But after the courts have established the fact by whatever system and within whatever constraints of due process, their most difficult tasks remain to be done. The facts have to be related to the aggravation or mitigation of penalties, to the assessment of punitive damages, and to other exercises of discretion. Human nature being what it is, and human transgressions being what they are, there is no way to eliminate discretion from jurisprudence or to guide it by a diagram or an algebraic equation. It is there, and best guided by a principle of consistency that necessitates the use of precedent. Without the exercise of discretion, fairness would disappear, and the law would indeed be guided by cost-benefit analyses. It may well be that the Roman law and its derivatives can guide discretion as well as the common law, but Tullock does not consider this case, nor is it clear that he thinks it important.

Who can contemplate the American system of justice—its delays, its continuances, its manipulations of the rules of due process, its invitations to indolence, and its opportunities for the complete obstruction of justice—without agreeing with Tullock that radical changes must be made? Close out the common law, he urges; terminate the appellate processes and design procedures that will move litigation rapidly, efficiently, and economically, leaving neither lawyers nor their clients any incentive for needless lawsuits or for dragging them through the years once they are initiated. Tullock does not insist that these improvements should be undertaken forthwith. There should be research; his laments about research that has not been done are frequent, and his demands that research should be done are urgent, if not always obviously practical. He would like to make a comparative study of the accuracy of the European and Anglo-Saxon models, but does not suggest a methodology for this useful investigation. He would like to have empirical research to "establish whether appellate courts are desirable or undesirable," and so would I—if I could think of a way of doing it.

Readers of this idiosyncratic adventure in pure theory will be left with many questions that Tullock thinks ought to be answered in the interests of the improvement of theory. In the absence of any way of proving any of Tullock's points, or of disproving them either, this book serves a valuable purpose in calling attention to how the law ought to be. The role that Tullock has chosen for himself has been too infrequently played; he works in the direct tradition of Jeremy Bentham, that indefatigable but always optimistic censor of the law. Unfortunately, this censor has chosen revolutionary change rather than meliorism. Things will have to get even worse before they get better. But this book is an indispensable step toward documenting how bad things really are.

JOHN P. CONRAD

American Justice Institute
Sacramento
California

MITCHEL B. WALLERSTEIN. *Food for War—Food for Peace: United States Food Aid in a Global Context.* Pp. xxii, 312. Cambridge: MIT Press, 1980. $30.00.

Mitchel B. Wallerstein, a lecturer in the departments of political science and nutrition at MIT, has written an interesting survey and analysis of American food policy from 1954 to 1980. His thesis essentially revolves around the shifting locus of food policy. The USDA desired to reduce commodity surpluses and expand commercial markets while the State Department wished to use food as an adjunct to foreign policy.

Under the auspices of the Eisenhower administration, the Agricultural Trade Development and Assistance Act of 1954 (P.L. 480) was legislated. It included both the promotion of agricultural markets and the giving of humanitarian aid. At that point in time, the farm bloc prevailed and the emphasis was on the fostering of new markets. Secretary of State John Foster Dulles thus lost out to Ezra Taft Benson, the secretary of agriculture.

Agricultural Secretary Orville Freeman, in the Kennedy administration, shifted the policy objectives of P.L. 480 to foreign aid. In 1966 he got the Food for Peace Act and thereby committed the Johnson administration even further in that direction.

The advent of the Nixon administration in 1969 signaled a major shift back to free-market agriculture. Earl Butz, the new secretary of agriculture, responded to the unprecedented commercial demand for U.S. agricultural exports and promoted the adoption of the Agriculture and Consumer Protection Act of 1973. This reduced domestic price supports and encouraged farmers to sell abroad, which included wheat sales to the Soviets for the first time.

In the Ford administration, Secretary Butz continued this market-oriented approach in the face of Democratic opposition. Senator Hubert Humphrey (to whom the author dedicated his book) persuaded Congress to pass the Food Development and Assistance Act of 1975 to meet the world's hunger needs. Secretary Kissinger, at the Rome Food Conference, wished to use food as a diplomatic tool but was unable to do so, due to budgetary restraints.

The Carter administration operated under the Food and Agriculture Act of 1977. This responded to the petrodollar drain by seeking markets and suggested the international sharing of food resources. Many recipients of American aid now demanded food as if it were an American obligation.

Although the American food program has been a mixture of self-interest and altruism, it has never exploited the world with "food power" analagous to OPEC's manipulation of oil prices.

This study will be of value to agricultural historians and political scientists interested in world politics.

FREDERICK H. SCHAPSMEIER
University of Wisconsin
Oshkosh

AFRICA, ASIA, AND LATIN AMERICA

PETER S. CLEAVES and MARTIN J. SCURRAH. *Agriculture, Bureaucracy, and Military Government in Peru.* Pp. 329. Ithaca, NY: Cornell University Press, 1980. $22.50.

A lucid chapter in Latin American history, this informative volume will be of particular interest not only to Americanists but also to political scientists, economists, and social planners.

At once a case study in directed change, including land reform—a lively topic these days, especially in Central and South America—it is also a case study in political, and particularly bureaucratic, processes, as well as one in military government. Documented are the attempts at agrarian reform in Peru, the third largest country of South America, on the part of the military government that assumed power there in October 1968. In the authors' opinion, these efforts "surpassed all other such efforts in Latin America, except the Mexican under Cardenas and perhaps the Cuban."

The sources are quite varied. Consulted were government documents, legal codes, official statistics, published speeches, memoirs, and news accounts of the time; and there were interviews with "major and minor figures," both inside and outside government.

As early as 1965 some of the more influential officers of the Peruvian Army had come to believe that the prevailing land tenure system was at odds with their responsibilities for maintaining national security. After taking control of the government, these men, in an attempt to carry out their primary goals of "economic nationalism, industrialization, national security, income distribution, and social mobility" under the leadership of General Juan Velasco Alvaredo and his immediate successors, came consciously or unconsciously to experiment, in sequence, with three different "state models" that "for the purposes of this study, can be labeled centralism, corporatism, and liberalism." None of the three models, however, in the opinion of Cleaves and Scurrah, fitted well into "the natural contours" of the Peruvian social system.

Against a background of land concepts and land practices under the Incas, and also of what Cleaves and Scurrah consider to be "the three major themes" of post-Conquest Peruvian history—a large indigenous population, the important role of the state, and civil-military relations—there are documented here various actions of agrarian character of this government, their successes and their failures. Included are the formulation and reformulation of agrarian legislation over a period of six years; the accompanying attempts to set up and administer agrarian cooperatives and an agrarian court system, as well as to "create official interest groups" among the middle and lower classes; the Chira-Piura irrigation project, to illustrate the ways in which the early "centralist approach" affected relations between the state and regional elites, "poor peasants," and international institutions; the erosion of certain of the original policies because of "increased differentiation within the State," in addition to serious financial difficulties; and conflicts between different ministries over policies of land use, all of which reflected disagreements not only over what constitutes ideal economic and social arrangements but also, basically, over human nature.

No attempt is made to advance a theory of agrarian reform. After pointing out briefly the "shortcomings" of similar attempts in Bolivia, Guatemala, Mexico,

Cuba, and Chile, however—at least as far as agricultural production, on one hand, and the incorporation of rural workers into full political participation, on the other, are concerned—the authors note that certain generalizations do emerge from this study that might serve "as reference points toward an understanding of similar efforts in Latin America, Asia, Europe and Africa."

The 23-page bibliography will delight specialists. Titles, with the exception of a few in German, French, and Portuguese, are almost equally in Spanish and in English. Appended are notes on the 134 interviews obtained, including a five-page table identifying the occupation or affiliation of each informant, and the date and length of the interview.

DONALD PIERSON

Leesburg
Florida

MELVIN GURTOV and BYONG-MOO HWANG. *China Under Threat: The Politics of Strategy and Diplomacy.* Pp. xi, 336. Baltimore: Johns Hopkins University Press, 1981. $22.95.

China Under Threat is a timely and serious effort by Gurtov and Hwang to examine the substantive nature of Chinese foreign policy. Gurtov and Hwang are particularly concerned with the interplay between Chinese foreign policy initiative and such factors as domestic stability, desires for economic and/or political development, and local perceptions of the nature of external threat.

For over 30 years now, Western scholars have sought to clarify the motivating impulses for and nature of the international behavior of the People's Republic of China. All too frequently the close proximity to the events and manifestations of Chinese behavior as well as the sometimes unwitting tendency to view China as an unthinking, or only "Mao think" socialist monolith—or in a few cases the last savior of oppressed humankind—have led us to perceptions of China that fail to take into account the inevitable dynamics of a large nation and the equally inevitable political decisions based on national interest and sophisticated assessments of domestic or national need.

This study by Gurtov and Hwang will certainly not be the final word on elucidating Chinese foreign policy, but it is an important contribution to the growing number of sophisticated and insightful analyses of Chinese domestic and foreign policy. The recognition that China is indeed a changing—and changeable—nation has caused scholars to search more carefully for the social, historical, and economic elements that permit and/or cause that change.

Gurtov and Hwang reiterate the now generally accepted notion that Chinese foreign policy initiative stems from three distinct impulses or outlooks, namely, the Asian, the socialist, and the revolutionary. They recognize that these impulses are interactive in nature and intimate that there may be a new impulse emerging—the modernizing impulse, an impulse that is distinctive in that preoccupations with revolutionary behavior, anti-imperialism (Asian impulse), and socialist development may in certain instances be given a back seat or at least second priority as industrialization and economic development become the foremost concerns.

In developing their conceptual model the authors use five case studies wherein China is involved directly in conflicts with external forces. The events include the Korean War, the Taiwan Strait crisis, the Sino-Indian border war, Vietnam, and the Sino-Soviet border clashes of 1969. It is demonstrated that in each case there is dynamic interplay between the foreign policy initiative and the domestic political circumstances and conditions.

Gurtov and Hwang present several propositions that they believe characterize the nature of Chinese foreign policy. These are:

—The chief purpose of foreign policy in China is to protect and promote the radical socialist revolution at home.

—A quiescent (non-threatening) international environment is the optimum condition for radical socialist development.

—Economic performance is considered by Chinese leaders to be the key to national security and international legitimacy.

—Chinese sensitivity to external threat is highest at times of domestic political weakness or conflict.

—Domestic weakness magnifies external threats and may lead to misperceptions or miscalculations of the opponent.

—The most dangerous aspect of external threat is its subversive influence on revisionist elements within the country.

—Foreign policy becomes a domestic political issue by addressing economic or political choices that are under debate.

—Domestic stability promotes conditions that are favorable to foreign policy initiatives.

—Domestic instability discourages foreign policy initiatives.

The study is well written and does present some thought-provoking alternatives for serious China watchers. Likewise, the search for understanding China must continue.

ARVIN PALMER
Northland Pioneer College
Holbrook
Arizona

YOUNG C. KIM. *Japanese Journalists and Their World.* Pp. 226. Charlottesville, VA: University Press of Virginia, 1981. $15.00.

Young C. Kim's purpose is to elucidate the world of those Japanese journalists who report for Japan's four major dailies, *Asahi, Yomiuri, Mainichi,* and *Sankei,* which account for around half of the country's total newspaper circulation.

His research during a six-month period of 1975-76 consisted of examining the available literature on the subject and of conducting in-depth interviews, in Japanese, with 40 reporters, 17 officials of the Foreign Ministry and the Ministry of International Trade and Industry, and 9 parliamentarians representing five political parties, including the Communist. English translations of Professor Kim's Interview Schedule for Reporters, and other works, are reproduced in an appendix.

Among Professor Kim's more significant findings and conclusions are these: each of the four papers thoroughly tests 1000 to 3000 college graduates each year and hires 10 to 20 of them; few women are employed; because reporters are elevated to managerial posts within about two years, columnists of stature do not emerge; increased government handouts make it difficult for a reporter to obtain a scoop; political reporters are careful not to undermine parliamentary government and the electoral system; the absence of byline articles stultifies individual initiative; the social standing of reporters has risen appreciably since 1945; parliamentarians think more highly of reporters than do government officials; top bureaucrats oppose the marriage of their daughters to reporters; reporters can legally be compelled to disclose their news sources; Japanese courts hold that freedom of reporting is indispensable to democratic government; before normalization of Japanese-Chinese relations in 1972, Japanese reporters consistently glorified developments in China, offering little criticism; Japanese reporters vehemently and persistently condemned America's involvement in the Vietnam War: *Asahi* is most pro-Chinese and anti-American of the national dailies; the United States fares better than the USSR in the Japanese press; most Japanese officials do not feel that the public has a right to know about government affairs; some Japanese believe that the Communist party infiltrated the Federation of Newspaper Workers Unions in order to influence the editorial policy of the press; newspapers are afraid to investigate rumors of corruption in high government circles; newspapers are susceptible to manipulation by the government; to prevent a drop in their nationwide circulation, newspapers stand for neutrality in foreign policy; reporters seem more impressed with the government's ability to use the press than with their own ability to influence government policy; officials feel that the press is overly critical of the government; the press exerts little influence on foreign policy; taboo requires that the emperor be described with "polite expression."

The author succeeds well in explaining why the "substantive content" of newspapers is what it is. He might have further enriched the study by placing Japanese journalism, a Western import, in historical perspective, by spelling out the impact of the Allied occupation on the press, and by briefly characterizing the world of the reporters for *Akahata*, the Communist party organ.

The book has too many misprints. The index is inadequate. There is no bibliography.

JUSTIN WILLIAMS, Sr.
Washington, D.C.

NANCY PEABODY NEWELL and RICHARD S. NEWELL. *The Struggle for Afghanistan.* Pp. 236. Ithaca, NY: Cornell University Press, 1981. $14.95.

The authors of this first book-length treatment of Russian intervention in Afghanistan are enthusiastic supporters of the anti-Marxist insurgency. For them the issue in Afghanistan is simple: "A large nation has attempted to take away the independence of a smaller nation by force." Their obvious purpose is to provide an understanding of this conflict and invoke the aid of the free world for the Afghan people: "Outside assistance is . . . vital not only to the Afghans, but to anyone opposed to Soviet expansionism."

The Newells show how successive Afghan governments set the stage for Soviet invasion by depending on Moscow for military and economic aid. By the mid-1950s the Soviet Union supplied virtually all the equipment and training for the Afghan army and air force. Muhammad Daoud attempted to stop his country's drift toward the Soviet orbit in the 1970s by attracting Iranian and Pakistani investment and economic assistance. Eventually Daoud found he had to divert much of his energy toward expelling the Parcham wing of the Marxist People's Democratic Party of Afghanistan, whom he had placed in key positions of the government.

The excellent analysis of the ensuing struggle between the Communist Khalq and Parcham factions enlarges our understanding of Afghan Marxism and of the radical reforms that are so alien to Afghan traditions. Khalq is shown to have rural and lower-middle-class roots and better organization, while Parchamists have ties with the urban upper-middle class and are less doctrinaire. The authors attribute conflict between the two Marxist groups to ideological differences, class origins, and to the blood spilled at one another's hands since the 1978 coup.

The authors' account of the economic and social dislocations of the war is reinforced daily by news reports of food shortages in Kabul and by the presence of two million refugees in Pakistan. The Newells argue that the agricultural cycle has been wrecked by "the flight of labor and breakdown of transportation and marketing." It seems more likely that agricultural activity remains undisturbed except where military operations occur, and that transportation is interrupted only in areas held by the Soviets.

Unlike the Newells, we should not be surprised that extensive Soviet academic research on Afghanistan failed to make the Soviet leadership weigh the wisdom of invasion in December 1979. Moscow arguably anticipated bitter resistance, but doubtless calculated that the potential gains appeared to offset the inherent costs. By ensuring the life of a Marxist regime in Kabul—no matter how unpopular with the Afghan people—the Soviets hoped to avoid the spread of Islamic fundamentalism contiguous with the borders of its own central Asian republics. Furthermore, the combat experience—the Soviet army's first since 1945—in addition to geopolitical factors, may justify the continued occupation of Afghanistan.

J. DANIEL MOORE
Washington, D.C.

JOHN J. SEILER, ed. *Southern Africa Since the Portuguese Coup.* Pp. xix, 252. Boulder, CO: Westview Press, 1980. $24.50.

An Associated Press account in national newspapers in mid-April 1981 indicated marked apathy and ignorance about the world outside the United States by American university students, as determined by the results on a 101-item multiple-choice examination administered to 3000 students in 185 universities. This particular news item supplements, rather than supplants, the findings about foreign language skills noted by Illinois Congressman Paul Simon in his 1980 study, *The Tongue-Tied American: Confronting the Foreign Language Crisis* (New York: Continuum, 1980).

These two indicators suggest that what has often been termed the attentive public is becoming smaller or less attentive and that the college-bound student and college graduate need to become more concerned with and knowledgeable about the world overseas. These indicators might also suggest to Southern Africa watchers that they reasses carefully both the breadth and the depth of American interest in the southern third of the African continent. This region seems to have attracted zealots of the Right and of the Left with the seeming paradox that the thoughtful, nondogmatic, doubting center is underrepresented in Southern African studies. Although the current secretary of state may have a special rhetorical fondness for the term "crisis," that particular noun is perhaps the most hackneyed term in the lexicon of Southern African research and publication. The region has become an intellectual playground for those who embrace the class-oriented mode of analysis as well as for those who

seize upon the variable of race as the one that far outstrips competing variables in explanatory power.

Consequently, Dr. Seiler's contribution is all the more welcome at this juncture. He is an unusually gifted scholar whose knowledge of the sources on Southern Africa and whose ability to stay abreast of current developments are matched by his skill in writing lucid and crisp English prose. His monthly newsletter on Southern Africa, *The Seiler Report,* as well as his previous publications in learned journals, are ample evidence of his gift for analysis and expository prose that is mercifully free of jargon and ceaseless moral hectoring. His edited volume consists of a brief introduction, thirteen component chapters, and a short concluding chapter. He wrote one of the thirteen chapters and co-authored a second chapter. Of the remaining eleven chapters, all but one are written by single authors. As expected, there are separate chapters on Angola (by Douglas Wheeler), Mozambique (by Keith Middlemas), Zaire (by Crawford Young), Transkei (by Roger Southall), and Zimbabwe (by Professor Utete); four chapters devoted to South Africa; one concerned with Namibia; another devoted to the Cuban factor (by Maurice Halperin); one considering the Soviet factor (by Christopher Stevens); and one that embraces the region and its relationship with the rest of the continent.

One can, of course, quibble about whether this or that chapter should have been included or not, or about whether this nation or that was given too little or too much attention. These problems plague any writer who attempts to assume the role of editor. Such a role is all too often a thankless task and is one most readily appreciated by those who have attempted the task themselves, as the reviewer can attest from personal experience. The quality of editing is exceptionally high and the standard of prose and documentation is uniformly exemplary. The very solid index, the decent maps, and the editorial consistency of the authors' endnotes all help to make this book eminently worthwhile as a reference source for public and university libraries. But that is not all. The contributors are recognized authorities in their fields, and Dr. Seiler has selected academicians from different disciplines and from a wide geographic range of universities in North America, the United Kingdom, and Southern Africa. These scholars present the reader with an admirable blend of ideological and methodological preferences and skills. To harness such a talented group was a real challenge, and the editor has met the challenge with marked success.

Dr. Seiler's volume addresses itself to both the domestic and the foreign dimensions of the policies of the nations included in this regional study, and the analysis has an especially solid regional focus. The book will appeal not only to undergraduate and graduate students but also to the literate general public, and it should be issued in a paperback edition that should be revised to include a selected bibliography of English language sources. Those concerned about the policy preferences that the new administration in Washington, and particularly that portion of the Department of State headed by Assistant Secretary of State for African Affairs Chester A. Crocker, has made will find Dr. Seiler's volume all the more significant, although it certainly does not reflect or necessarily endorse those views about Southern Africa that Dr. Crocker and his aides have embraced.

RICHARD DALE

Southern Illinois University
Carbondale

RAYMOND F. WYLIE. *The Emergence of Maoism: Mao Tse-Tung, Ch'en Po-ta, and the Search for the Chinese Theory, 1935-1945.* Pp. viii, 351. Stanford, CA: Stanford University Press, 1980. $25.00.

Raymond F. Wylie's book *The Emergence of Maoism* is mainly concerned with the ideological and political process that led to the dominance of Mao Tse-tung's thought in the Chinese Communist Party (CCP). It focuses on the Yenan Period from 1935 to 1945 with special reference to Ch'en Po-ta's influence on Mao's thought. The author gives a detailed account of the development of Mao's theoretical leadership in the CCP from the Tsunyi Conference in 1935, when Mao began to assume party leadership, to the Seventh Congress of the CCP in 1945, when "Mao Tse-tung's thought" was officially incorporated in the party constitution as a guiding principle.

Wylie is very perceptive in saying that the ascendancy of Mao as a theoretical leader in 1943 was caused by internal and external political development, not only because of the efforts of Mao and Ch'en or the genuine acceptance of Mao's ideological supremacy by most of the CCP leaders. The book is well-researched and Wylie has consulted numerous sources on the subject. This is one of the most exhaustive studies of the intellectual relationship between Mao Tse-tung and Ch'en Po-ta.

In his attempt to prove that Mao was influenced by Ch'en in his theoretical formations, Wylie carefully compares the similarities between the two men's intellectual orientations, especially their common interest in the Sinification of Marxism. The difficulty is that influence cannot be quantified precisely. Furthermore, Wylie often concludes that Ch'en has influenced Mao on certain questions without providing concrete evidence.

Mao was a complex person and his thought was influenced by many factors, both theoretical and practical. Although Ch'en has played a major role in promoting Maoism, his influence on Mao's thinking should not be exaggerated. Mao's thought has many components. It is doubtful that Ch'en has significant input in all of them, such as military affairs. Ch'en's major contribution to Mao's thought is that he has helped refine and articulate Mao's ideas because of his better training in philosophy and Marxism.

The book would have been more useful to political scientists had Wylie placed greater emphasis on relating Mao's Sinification of Marxism to the general problem of adaptation of alien ideology by the developing nations. The epilogue brings the data of the book up to the post-Cultural Revolution period. It would help the reader's understanding of the emergence of Maoism if the book also included a brief chapter on Mao's intellectual development before 1927. This is the least researched period in the study of Mao's thought. These are the formative years of Mao's intellectual growth. An investigation of this period may enhance our knowledge of the intellectual roots of Maoism.

Incidentally, Mao's formal education did not include college. The Hunan Provincial No. 1 Normal School, which Mao attended from 1913 to 1918, was a high-school-level institution, not a normal college, as erroneously reported in many Western publications, including Wylie's book. This error is serious when Mao's theoretical leadership is examined, because it puts Mao in a different category in terms of formal academic training.

With Mao dead, Ch'en imprisoned, and the new leadership of China in the process of reassessing the role of Mao in the Chinese communist revolution, this book is an important and welcome addition to the literature on Mao Tse-tung's thought.

GEORGE P. JAN
University of Toledo
Ohio

EUROPE

MICHAEL BALFOUR. *The Adversaries: America, Russia and the Open World, 1941-62.* Pp. xv, 259. Boston: Routledge & Kegan Paul, 1981. $25.00.

The Adversaries is written as though the author visualized himself seated in front of a fire in an otherwise cold and damp London flat as he regaled a somewhat reluctant auditor with his "interpretive framework" for a study of East-West relations, 1941-62. Somehow, though, we continue to feel the cold and the dampness. A teacher of politics, later information officer in the British zone of occupied Germany, then teacher again, Professor Balfour divides his chapters into chronological blocks of ice with the lively titles "1941-5," "1945-7," "1947-9," and so on to chapter 7, "1961-2," ending with "Concluding Reflections," and a sigh of relief, at least from the reader.

On first encountering the book, an interested reader immediately notices some significant omissions from the index—a book's menu, playbill, or scorecard. Although the volume purports to analyze over 20 years of America, Russia and the Open World, the author finds no reason to include discussion of Vladimir Ilyich Lenin; Marxism-Leninism; Leonid Brezhnev, who was a force in Soviet politics long before 1962, the end date of the book (Balfour completed it, however, in 1979); or Mikhail Suslov, kingmaker, chief ideologist—its Archbishop Laud, in other words. The omissions keep adding up. In place of the ones I have mentioned, Professor Balfour does find room for unbalanced discussions of Henry A. Wallace; Georgy Malenkov, the pudgy Kremlin also-ran purgee after Stalin's death; U.S. "suspicions" of Russia—mostly groundless, in the author's opinion, but worth over a dozen pages; house-building, East and West; and something called, with initial caps, Winds of Change. The latter is characterized by the author, quaintly, as the "staircase of history" resounding with the "clatter of clogs and the tinkle of tiaras coming down. . . . The Winds of Change are always blowing." Profound, what?

A major event of one of Balfour's time frames, 1957-60, was the Soviet launching of Sputnik I. It is amusing, if sad, to read the author's questionable assessment that the Soviet rocket and MRBM buildup to the contrary, the "U.S. remained less accessible to a Russian attack than Russia was to an American one, though the American public as a whole did not realize this." Professor Balfour has confused the meaningless bomber gap of the pre-Sputnik era with the meaningful missile gap of later years, which continued to widen into a yawning case of gaposis between U.S. and Soviet missile-building, to the latter's advantage. Calling Sputnik a traveler—in context, it means satellite in Russian—Balfour pooh-poohs the concern over it in America as an instance of "putting an outsize cat among the pigeons—and even more among the hawks." Ignoring the revelations of 1961 in *The Penkovsky Papers*—which, as far as purloined papers are concerned, are far more significant for an understanding of East-West problems than, say, the more widely-read drivel contained in the Pentagon Papers—Balfour assesses Khrushchev's attitude toward modernizing the Soviet armed forces—by stepping up Soviet ICBM development—as if the late Soviet leader had been a paragon of a peacemaker. On the other hand, Colonel Oleg Penkovsky, high-ranking officer of Soviet military intelligence, had an entirely different insight into his boss, Khrushchev, whose colleagues often quoted his boasting about "showering our missiles" upon the imperialists. At very least, Khrushchev says in his memoirs, they should be used as elements in Soviet Machtpolitik in the Nuclear Age. An instance of this, of course, was the 1962 Cuban Missile Crisis. A mere storm in a teacup, our author assures us, as he offers to pour more of the same: "Kennedy had nothing to lose leaving the missiles in Cuba. . . . [But] inaction by Kennedy might well have led to his impeachment."

Stirring the fire once more to relieve the unsettling claminess, we settle into Concluding Reflections. Reflections they are, but of what? Cure-alls, of course. The Western half of the adversarial relationship could be much improved, Balfour thinks, by following small-is-beautiful: cut consumption, he advises; "reduce their standards," cut demand. Draconic compulsion may be necessary, "undertaken by the state or by a state-authorized body." Meanwhile, the East, he believes, will accelerate the revolutionism of their creed "by judicious action." They will attempt to achieve their goals "short of large-scale war." But, we ask, are such local wars as those of Korea in the fifties, Vietnam in the sixties, Ogaden in the seventies, and Afghanistan et al., in the eighties "judicious" exertions by Soviet-backed proxies that fall "short" of being open combat? Moreover, Balfour is confident that the "Communist world is sure of what a nuclear war would be like." Undoubtedly. But the Soviets claim in their military writings that a nuclear war—for them—is both "winnable" and "survivable." They also claim that "national-liberation wars"—ignored by Balfour—are justifiable acts of violence by a minority of Communist-trained guerrillas seeking to impose Soviet-style "socialism" on the masses of peasants in Third World countries. "Many people, if given the choice," Balfour pontificates, "would prefer prosperity to freedom." Like the workers and farmers of economically bereft Poland? What choice are they making? Ditto the millions of refugees and boat people preferring freedom to Communist prosperity, or promises of the same.

ALBERT L. WEEKS

New York
New York

RANDOLPH L. BRAHAM. *The Politics of Genocide: The Holocaust in Hungary*, Vols. 1 & 2. Pp. xxxv. 594 (Vol. 1), x, 1269 (Vol. 2). New York: Columbia University Press, 1981. $60.00.

To the recent outpouring of studies on the Holocaust, the present volumes recounting the terrible destruction of Hungarian Jewry add a definitive chapter. Written by the acknowledged authority on the subject, Professor Randolph L. Braham of the City College of New York, it would perhaps be inappropriate, given its subject matter, to describe the work as a labor of love. Nevertheless, the author has clearly been impelled in his prodigious efforts by something more than the usual scholarly motivations, including assumably, the loss of his own parents in the Hungarian maelstrom.

In his preface, Braham defines his purpose as the provision of a clear perspective on the complex of "historical, political, communal and socioeconomic factors" that led to the decimation of Hungarian Jewry. In addition to this essentially descriptive task, the author has also undertaken the critical analysis of the Holocaust in Hungary in the context both of that nation and of the world at large. In both these endeavors, the descriptive and the analytical, Braham as admirably fulfilled his goals.

Organized into 32 chapters, the study proceeds in roughly historical sequence, punctuated, however, by occasional chapters that abandon strict chronology in favor of the development of some tangential, but related, theme. In addition to his text, the author has provided a number of valuable appendices, including a chronological summary of relevant events, several essential reference lists, a glossary, and three useful indexes. Each chapter is replete with copious documentation, but, regrettably, there is no bibliography, an omission particularly unfortunate in a work that will be used, by many, primarily as a reference.

As Braham emphasizes, the modern history of Hungarian Jewry is full of paradox. Thus, following the famous Compromise *(Ausgleich)*, which created the Dual Monarchy of Austria-Hungary in 1867, Hungarian Jews received legal emancipation and entered a golden era of prosperity that lasted through World War I. During this time, despite occasional outbreaks of anti-Semitism, Hungarian Jews worked out a highly profitable *Interessengemeinschaft* (community of interest) with the ruling aristocratic elite and enjoyed an unparalleled degree of social and economic prosperity culminating in the legal recognition of Judaism in 1895. Ironically, however, it was precisely this condition of relative luxury that caused the Jews to develop a myopic social and national outlook that ignored the sufferings of the oppressed masses and national minorities of Hungary. It was this alienation that sowed the seeds of Jewry's persecution after 1918.

Following World War I, defeated Hungary was severely truncated by the victorious Allies and then subjected to sharp social and economic dislocation by the abortive Communist regime of Bela Kun. In response to this double buffeting, a counterrevolutionary reaction brought to power Admiral Miklós Horthy under whose leadership rightwing authoritarianism held sway in Hungary for the next twenty-five years. During this period the Jews of Hungary were subjected to the earliest anti-Semitic legislation of the interwar period in Europe, and a general atmosphere of anti-Jewish discrimination pervaded the country under the influence of a variety of ultra right-wing political parties. On the baffling array of these protofascist movements Braham is especially elucidating, particularly as regards the programs and personalities of the two key figures in Hungarian fascism, the opportunistic Gyula Gömbös and the mystical nationalist Ferenc Szálasi.

With the onset of World War II still another paradox enveloped Hungarian Jewry. Thus while the other Jews of Europe were subjected to systematic persecution, Hungarian Jews, despite some harsh legal and economic discrimination, were for several years left largely alone. Again, however, this relative luxury had the effect of lulling Hungarian Jewry into a false sense of security, which rendered them all but totally unprepared to contend with the anti-Semitic onslaught that began with the German occupation of March 19, 1944. Thereafter, notwithstanding the frantic resistance of the local Jewish leadership, the Nazi Final Solution was applied to Hungary's Jews with unprecedented speed and ferocity. It is to an incredibly detailed analysis of this program of progressive isolation, expropriation, ghettoization, deportation, and, finally, liquidation that the bulk of the author's attention is devoted.

In his preface, Braham expresses regret that his study contains "a number of gaps." From the context of this remark it is apparent that he is referring to the continued inaccessibility of certain source materials, particularly those reposing in Hungarian archives. However that may be, it seems unlikely that the melancholy story of the Holocaust in Hungary, which Winston Churchill once called "probably the greatest and most horrible crime . . . in the history of the world," will ever be more judiciously or meticulously recorded.

JOHN W. LONG

Rider College
Lawrenceville
New Jersey

DIMITRIE DJORDJEVIC and STEPHEN FISCHER-GALATI. *The Balkan Revolutionary Tradition.* Pp. xv, 271. New York: Columbia University Press, 1981. $20.00.

Although there has lately been a steady increase in studies of the Balkans, a region usually known as The Powder Keg of Europe, most of them have been focused on politics, while the treatment of the sociocultural background has tended to be rather minimal.

Since the present work gives us a valuable interpretation of the Balkan history within the framework of the historical geopolitical trends in the Balkans, Djordjevic and Fischer-Galati's contribution is definitely welcome. They bring order and meaning to the chaos and confusion of centuries of rebellion, accepting the popular interpretation that the turbulence was largely a function of the geopolitical location of the Peninsula and of the relentless struggle for control of Constantinople, the Eastern Mediterranean, and the Near, or Middle, East that has been waged by contenders for political and economic power. But they also assert that, in the last analysis, the history of the Balkans and of its revolutionary traditions was conditioned by the historical retardation of the area as much as it was by its unfortunate location. They demonstrate that the tradition of revolutions was rooted in the desire for emancipation from foreign domination and agricultural servitude, highlighted by continual, explosive political and social confrontations between the forces of Western European modernism and those committed to retaining Balkan traditions. Djordjevic and Fischer-Galati show how in the modern era this tradition developed into peasant masses attaining their goal of land and nationalist leaders attaining power in independent states.

The revolutionary implications for the Balkans today are serious indeed. In fact,

despite the seriousness of the prevailing political social problems, the Balkan Communist parties [have been] unable to make headway in a political order characterized by nationalism and factionalism among "bourgeois" political organizations. The Balkan revolutionary tradition made its reappearance only as war, invasion, and destruction of the state establishment in Yugoslavia, Greece, and Albania rendered other forms of resistance impossible. It should be noted, however, that in Romania and Bulgaria, where the armies were in control, and where nationalist aspirations were satisfied, revolutionary actions still reflected political and social polarizations of prewar and wartime years, exacerbated, however, by the cruelty displayed by foreign forces of occupation and/or by Communist propaganda and indoctrination. Nevertheless, the revolutionary manifestations represented the first chapter of the Cold War which followed the victory of the anti-Fascist coalition [p. 236].

Even the civil war in the Balkans, which took place under foreign occupation, "did not alter Balkan revolutionary traditions to any significant extent."

The thesis of the collaborators is supported by numerous studies in foreign languages. In short, any bona fide specialist in the Balkans should consider this work a must.

JOSEPH S. ROUCEK
City University of New York

ROBERT L. HOFFMAN. *More Than a Trial: The Struggle Over Captain Dreyfus.* Pp. vii, 247. New York: Free Press, 1980. $14.95.

In *More Than a Trial: The Struggle Over Captain Dreyfus*, Robert Hoffman attempts to fill in the background of the Dreyfus Affair by reconstructing the states of mind of the partisans on both sides of that struggle. In so doing he performs an exercise in what Max Weber called *verstehen*.

The book starts out strongly, but the sense and purpose of the chapters starts unraveling about halfway through. The first two chapters quickly review the principal events of the case. The third chapter is a sketchy background portrait of Dreyfus as a man. There is not enough to justify a separate chapter on this subject, because as a person Dreyfus was almost irrelevant to the case. Hoffman is interested in social roots and ramifications, and by his own intentions should have left Dreyfus the man a few paragraphs in the first two chapters. Chapter 4 describes the underlying conflicts in French society that were exacerbated by the Affair—the antagonism of Catholics, Monarchists, revanchist patriots mortified by the defeat in the Franco-Prussian War, and anti-Republicans of all sorts, toward republican, anticlerical, liberal, and socialist forces. The next chapter takes up the subject of the fantasy world of the anti-Dreyfusards, one inhabited by forces of evil embodied in a syndicate supported not only by Jews but by freemasons and Protestants conspiring against the Church, the army, and the nation. Hoffman's illustrations of these paranoiac imaginings are colorful and fascinating. Chapter 6 continues with the exploration of the state of mind of the anti-Dreyfusards, providing a clear explanation of why, although often highly educated and literate, they were so willing to believe any outlandish story that tended to support Dreyfus's guilt and so unwilling to believe the overwhelming evidence that argued against it. But the next five chapters string anecdotes together in a way that palls, in spite of the interest the reader may have for the stories.

One of Hoffman's most interesting observations comes in his conclusion, where he questions the role of the Dreyfus Affair in the conventionally viewed history of anti-Semitism. "Alfred Dreyfus," he says, "was not persecuted because he was Jewish: the decisive factors in actions by officials against him would have been little if any altered had he been a Gentile." More important than religious bias was the need of the French General Staff to cover up its mistakes and maintain its reputation and morale.

In reconstructing the states of mind of both sides of the struggle, the book's long series of anecdotes entertain the reader, at least up to a point. They are fascinating and make good reading, but they do not take the place of more concrete and original historical material. One is left with the feeling of having eaten several desserts without being served the main course. For such fare the reader must look elsewhere. For these reasons, I must conclude that since it does not provide new interpretations of the known data or new data that make us reinterpret the Affair, the book should be considered a supplement to the existing literature, albeit an interesting one.

WILLIAM R. BEER

Brooklyn College
New York

PAUL MARER and JOHN M. MONTIAS, eds. *East European Integration and East-West Trade.* Pp. xvi, 432. Bloomington: Indiana University Press, 1980. $32.50.

Since the implantation of the Soviet-type system in Eastern Europe at the end of World War II, the question of the economic integration of the socialist countries has surfaced time and again in both scholarly literature and the popular media. Integration, often rather loosely defined and usually coupled with such adjectives as "further," "broader," or "tighter," sounds particularly newsworthy. Actually, however, the movement toward integration, that is, toward coordination of foreign trade, output specialization, or supranational investment allocation and economic planning, has made little headway among the socialist countries during the past thirty years.

The main reason for this is easy to understand. The Soviet-type system of centralized planning is predicated on the notion of *autonomous development* of each country. Furthermore, this development specifies as its priority, growth for industry in general and for producers' goods—capital goods and materials—in particular as well as the subordination of foreign trade to the needs of the domestic plan. When the Soviet-type system was imposed in Eastern Europe, *all* of these countries began following an identical pattern of industrialization. With the exception of Yugoslavia, expelled from the socialist camp in 1948, only Hungary has been able to reorient some of its priorities, and even then in a limited way since the 1960s. For all of the other countries, economic cooperation is circumscribed by and subordinated to the same imperatives of the domestic plan and its basic options.

In the late 1940s, faced with an effective Western strategic embargo, these countries formed a Council of Mutual Economic Assistance (CMEA). Characteristically, CMEA was not meant to create a multilateral common market, to lead to an extensive coordination and specialization in manufacturing, or to turn into a supranational investment allocator. CMEA's movements toward foreign trade coordination, manufacturing specialization, or investment cooperation has always been sporadic and encumbered by innumerable rules and constraints intended to preserve the autonomy of each country's centralized economic plan. Due to development along similar lines and the absence of proper price signals, cooperation in foreign trade cannot but take the form of bilateral bartering. Given the constraints of the domestic output plans and given the absence of proper price signals, specialization in manufacturing cannot go beyond some technical apportionments of some limited production tasks—for example, production of trucks of given weights in this or that CMEA country. Finally, in the absence of competitive goods from world markets, the interchanges between the socialist countries cannot but involve products increasingly lagging in technology.

When opening toward the West became possible in the late 1960s, all the Soviet-type economies, starting with the USSR itself, turned their attention toward the expansion of their ties with the developed countries. Throughout the 1970s Soviet and East European trade with the West increased about nine times at current prices, while their international indebtedness increased *pari passu.* As the burden of their international debt has reached impressive proportions, it is easy to understand that the 1980s could hardly lead to a further expansion of the ties with the West—except perhaps for the USSR, which still has, or might have, some tradable commodities such as oil, gas, and gold.

This book consists of a number of papers originally presented at a Conference on East-West Trade, held in Bloomington in 1976, and of some additional papers commissioned subsequently. It comprises four parts. The first surveys classical and neoclassical aspects of international trade theory. The second contains, notably, a study on differences in foreign trade behavior between centrally planned and market economies. The third is focused on CMEA's financial system and on industrial policies. The fourth and last deals with "individual countries' perspectives," particularly Bulgaria's, Romania's, and Poland's relations in CMEA. Of particular note are the essays of Hewett, Wolf, and Vanous. The first of these compares foreign trade predictions and outcomes on the basis of "systemic" characteristics uncorrelated with central planning or the policies associated with it. The second establishes a framework for analyzing adjustments of the centrally planned economies to external disturbances in their East-West trade. The third, in many respects problematic yet quite stimulating, presents an econometric model of intra-CMEA trade. Most of the essays with a specific country focus are generally well documented but add little to the clarification of the analytical issues at hand.

NICOLAS SPULBER

Indiana University
Bloomington

JOSEPH L. NOGEE and ROBERT H. DONALDSON. *Soviet Foreign Policy Since World War II.* Pp. vii, 319. Elmsford, NY: Pergamon, 1981. $35.00 Paperbound, $10.00.

ALVIN Z. RUBINSTEIN. *Soviet Foreign Policy Since World War II: Imperial and Global.* Pp. viii, 295. Cambridge, MA: Winthrop, 1981. Bibliography and index. $15.00. Paperbound, $9.95.

In 1981, two books on Soviet foreign policy were published. They had nearly identical titles, approximately the same number of pages, and generally the same area of coverage. In addition, they were authored by scholars with strong and established reputations whose writings command the attention of anyone interested in the topic. But the similarities quickly become irrelevant as the reader examines the content and discovers that each makes a different contribution to the reader and the field.

The Nogee-Donaldson study is a deeper and more analytical study than the work by Rubinstein. The former is more concerned with ideology as it relates to policies and practices than is the latter. Nogee and Donaldson organize their study in such a way to allow the reader to become acquainted both with the ideas and the polemical styles of Soviet leaders, while at the same time learning how fact informs ideology and forces the Soviet thinkers either to torture logic and make the facts fit their

"Procrustean bed" or to "jerry-build" new theoretical formulations to account for a chaotic world they neither control nor accurately predict. While both volumes use a loose chronological stucture, Nogee and Donaldson hold more closely to it and make more interesting comparisons within a particular era than does Rubinstein, who overdivides his material into several compartments, leaving it to the reader to remember what was written in a previous section in order to appreciate the full impact of a particular event or statement upon the world at large.

As a teaching tool, the Nogee-Donaldson volume is a more challenging and slightly more difficult book than its competitor. It offers its reader a plausible explanation for Russian outrage over the U-2 flights in the early 1960s and the missile gap issue—both of which played important roles in the 1960 U.S. presidential election and contributed to the arms race of the next decade. The reader also will find a well-rounded and highly interesting account of unity in the socialist camp in Nogee and Donaldson's discussions of the Hungarian uprising in 1956, the Czechoslovakia invasion of 1968, and the implications of both for the current problems in Poland. Most useful of all is their explanation of the emergence of polycentrisim and the career of detente—both subjects of continuing interest to scholars and laypersons alike.

While similar discussions and more are to be found in the Rubenstein book as well, the treatment is less detailed, less well documented, and, as noted above, sometimes broken up and treated in several chapters, thus reducing its impact on the reader.

Of particular value in both books are the bibliographies. While both volumes divide their bibliographies by chapter, the Nogee-Donaldson study offers brief annotations that can be exceedingly helpful to the reader unfamiliar with the range and diversity of scholarship available in this field.

For the instructor looking for a single volume with which to introduce the subject to a general reader, just interested in becoming acquainted with the broad topic, both of these books are equal to the task. While some will be put off by the scholarly and serious presentation of the Nogee-Donaldson book, others might find Rubinstein's attempts at humor to be out of place. However, on balance both might join this reviewer and choose the Nogee-Donaldson study as the more challenging introduction to this exciting field of study.

JOSEF SILVERSTEIN

Rutgers University
New Brunswick
New Jersey

URS SCHWARZ. *The Eye of the Hurricane: Switzerland in World War Two.* Pp. xviii, 169. Boulder, CO: Westview Press. $18.00.

Throughout World War II Switzerland strove with political economic and military power to maintain neutrality on its own terms. Initially, the Swiss opposed any attack on their territorial integrity and rejected any foreign intervention unless Switzerland expressly requested it; even then, the Swiss refused to support either side militarily and pledged strict equal treatment without further obligations. Internal and external pressures to support one side or the other ebbed and flowed. The Swiss struggle to retain its neutrality, told here by a Swiss army veteran who also served as a wartime journalist in Berlin and in Switzerland, is filled with some proud and a few sad moments.

At the war's outbreak, Switzerland altered its cantonal federalism when Parliament gave the Federal Council sweeping authority and then elected the first commander-in-chief of the armed forces since World War I. The Federal Council received a mandate not only for maintaining the security, independence, and neutrality of Switzerland, but also, as Schwarz correctly emphasizes, for defending Swiss economic interests and ensuring economic survival. Contradictions abounded. A large army obviously helped to maintain neutrality but also

disrupted the precarious wartime economy. The military leaders planned for resistance to the last soldier, but the best defensive positions abandoned half of the land and three-quarters of the population.

Switzerland had not existed in economic isolation. Swiss rationing and a restructuring of domestic food production enabled the Swiss to survive agriculturally, but Swiss industry could never be independent. In return for coal, oil, iron, and export privileges, the Swiss, through numerous deals, provided Germany with precision tools, ball bearings, arms, ammunition, and dairy products, plus enormous financial credits. Swiss contribution to the Allied war effort, while substantially smaller, nonetheless included ball bearings, machine tools, stopwatches, and jewel bearings.

The Eye of the Hurricane is a fascinating blend of memoir and history told from a Swiss viewpoint. The reader will find exotic spy stories and tragic tales of refugees. Schwarz proudly chronicles Swiss humanitarian activities, especially those of the Red Cross, but thoughtfully questions Swiss actions concerning displaced persons. The controversial Swiss medical mission to the Russian front receives careful analysis, particularly with regard to later Russian antagonism. Unfortunately, Schwarz's topical organization often leads to a repetition of events. The strength of the work, however, lies in its account of the economic and moral strains the war placed on the Swiss nation.

CHARLES JOSEPH HERBER

George Washington University
Washington, D.C.

BRUCE G. TRIGGER. *Gordon Childe: Revolutions in Archaeology.* Pp. 207. 37 illus., index. New York: Columbia University Press. $22.50.

Bruce Trigger has written an admirably researched and carefully written book covering the professional life of

Gordon Childe, one of the twentieth century's most influential archaeologists. Childe, an Australian and a Marxist, was trained at Oxford by Sir Arthur Evans and Sir John Myers. In 1957, at the age of 65, he died of injuries resulting from a fall under still puzzling circumstances. Most feel that suicide was the motive, but as Trigger points out, the case is far from clear if all the evidence is examined.

In his life Childe brought order to virtually the entire corpus of Old World prehistory through his books and scores of scholarly articles. His first book, *The Dawn of European Society*, published in 1925, was the model of its day for the presentation of a regional archaeological synthesis. It is a work that covers the prehistory of Europe through the Middle Bronze Age and is the result of Childe's tireless digging in libraries and a monumental correspondence with field-workers of the day and those in charge of Museums and other collections of prehistoric artifacts. The fact that *The Dawn* is in print today, in its sixth edition, is sufficient testimony to its author's genius. It was this book, and its far less successful companion volume, *The Aryans*, that led Childe in 1927 to the newly established Abercromby Chair of Archaeology at the University of Edinburgh and to a position as one of the few professional archaeologists of the day. Childe's other major synthetic works—*New Light on the Most Ancient East, Man Makes Himself, What Happened in History*, and *The Prehistory of European Society*—have assured him a place of prominence in the intellectual history of the Western world.

The success Childe enjoyed as a scholar seems to have been largely due to his even-handed treatment of most basic interpretive issues and his gift of clarity as an author. But Bruce Trigger makes it clear that this man was neither fully understood nor appreciated by his contemporaries. Childe's wildly shifting turns of emphasis and his unsuccessful search for a larger meaning to the syntheses he was so gifted at creating lend a sense of confusion to the more abstract aspects of the man's thought. All this Trigger rather nicely brings out in the book. What remains obscure is a full understanding of what the confusion, or apparent confusion, results from. Why the shifts of emphasis, why the unevenness in so great a mind? There was, after all, the Childe who was a sometimes silent, sometimes vocal Marxist who in his home would make his guests aware of his distaste for, and fear of, totalitarianism and would then gleefully cite Stalin as an authority in his professional papers. There are highly respected and knowledgeable prehistorians today who feel that Childe abandoned Marxism in the last decade or so of his life. But his complexity leads other, equally reputable scholars to the opposite view. Trigger admits that a resolution of the problems that lie at the root of this aspect of Childe's life is beyond his capabilities and the scope of so short a book. But let us not forget them, since they are possibly the most significant aspect of Gordon Childe, a curiously gifted scholar.

GREGORY L. POSSEHL

University of Pennsylvania
Philadelphia

UNITED STATES

DESMOND BALL. *Politics and Force Levels: The Strategic Missile Program of the Kennedy Administration.* Pp. xxvi, 352. Berkeley: University of California Press, 1981. $27.50.

Desmond Ball very ably presents an analysis of a subject that has not been studied nearly enough, the Kennedy administration's decision between 1961 and 1963 to push to a total of 1710 American strategic missile launchers. Given that the current breakdown of SALT negotiations hinges to a great extent on the Soviet missile procurements that followed these American nuclear forces and on the American procurements that must follow such Soviet procurements, it might be high time to have a discussion (à la Vietnam) concerning how we got into this quagmire.

Ball has collected a great deal of material on the decisions as they were made, examining the documents and interviewing many of the principals. He offers explanations that relate to American electoral politics as well as to bureaucratic politics, and to the inherent difficulty of formulating U.S. national intelligence estimates concerning the original Soviet missile program of the later 1950s. The book is definitive, but it is also very well written and would work well for courses in U.S. defense policy. Moreover, it is must reading for any researcher in the field.

The American missile buildup escaped such careful scrutiny until recently perhaps because, unlike Vietnam, it was long considered an American success story, a very wise and proper step. As the 1980s now torment us again with Soviet missile threats and American counterthreats, it is appropriate that bureaucratic politics theories, and other theories of pathology, also be tested against this case.

Ball does not endorse any simple bureaucratic politics model by which the U.S. Air Force and Navy turn out to be the only villains. Secretary of Defense Robert McNamara and his team of "rational activists" also come in for a fair amount of criticism, as does President Kennedy. If there is anything unsatisfying about the Ball book, it is that he gives us a very mixed verdict in the end on whether the American missile expansion was predetermined. Was this the inevitable working out of the career self-interests of the "semi-sovereign" portions of the Navy and Air Force? Or was it more a series of miscalculations and mistakes by Kennedy and McNamara, in their estimates of what was needed to neutralize any Soviet threat?

Desmond Ball has clearly become one of the more serious and readable authors on strategic matters. This book supplies the other side of the coin for what was analyzed by Arnold Horelick and Myron Rush in 1966 in *Strategic Power and Soviet Foreign Policy* (University of Chi-

cago Press): the 1950s Soviet move into missiles that provoked the American response of the 1960s. Perhaps what we are missing most now—but how can we get it?—is an equally detailed and informed account of the Soviet decision since then to acquire a multitude of large new missiles through the 1970s.

GEORGE H. QUESTER

Cornell University
Ithaca
New York

J. RICHARD BUEL. *Dear Liberty: Connecticut's Mobilization for the Revolutionary War.* Pp. xix, 425. Middletown, CT: Wesleyan University Press, 1980. No price.

If the record of other states during the revolutionary war for mobilization is comparable to that of Connecticut, we may be able to answer the question, How did the Revolutionary fathers win the war for American independence? They did not. The British lost the war, simply because their field commanders pressed for rather than avoided a decisive engagement on the field of battle. Had the conflict continued, Buel implies, the ability of the Whig governments to sustain and finance armed forces would have collapsed totally. Indeed it had done so in Connecticut well before the surrender of Cornwallis at Yorktown, although the state did not experience major British naval and military incursions during the last years of the war.

Buel bases this highly factual—almost excessively so—account on the voluminous Revolutionary archives of the state and the correspondence of Governor Jonathan Trumbull and Commissary-General Jeremiah Wadsworth. The result is not flattering to the ancestors of the DAR. The picture that emerges is one of a highly contentious but essentially parochially minded people enthusiastically entering into what they expected to be a short but decisive struggle to win republican rights. In outlook and financial and economic resources they were not prepared for the long, drawn-out war that followed. This tale is one of petty bickering and patriotic and rhetorical posturing but concern primarily for local interests. Attempts to raise men and money for the Continental war effort generally gave way to concerns for the immediate security and financial interests of the particular town or immediate neighborhood. Connecticut's economy, dependent on the export of agricultural surpluses, could not adequately fulfill the demands of the army and the militia and fell victim to British pressures. Without transforming the society, the effort to mobilize resources inflicted wounds that did not heal during the lifetimes of those who experienced the war. As a consequence of the harsh trial of the Revolution and the hardships of the years following, most of the state's Federalist leaders developed a passion for order and a horror of republican ventures in foreign policy during the closing years of the century, when war meant conflict with the British and the closing of the state's essential export trade. Not until there was a shift to industry for an internal domestic market was the foundation laid for new attitudes.

J. M. SOSIN

University of Nebraska
Lincoln

WILLIAM A. BULLOUGH. *The Blind Boss and His City: Christopher Augustine Buckley and Nineteenth-Century San Francisco.* Pp. xvi, 347. Illus., notes, bibliography, index. Berkeley: University of California Press, 1979. $19.95.

Few institutions in American urban history deserve more attention than the boss and his political machine. "If the boss has been a characteristic of the city," historian John M. Allswang writes, "it can equally be said that the city has been a characteristic of the boss." Both traits are quite evident in William A. Bullough's political biography of Christopher Augustine Buckley. Drawing heavily on newspapers,

government reports, and the reminiscences of Buckley and other local bosses, Bullough skillfully places Buckley's public career within the context of San Francisco's late-nineteenth-century growth. The result is a thorough explanation of the city's fragmented politics and an enlightening account of its transition from a rambunctious boomtown to a mature metropolis.

San Francisco in the 1870s and 1880s needed a leader who could organize physical expansion, coordinate economic and political power, and reconcile immigrants to their new environment. Bullough clearly shows that Buckley, despite his blindness, provided dynamic leadership. He built a Democratic machine that considerably influenced local and state politics, selected capable persons for important elective offices, mediated between the city government and competing business enterprises, and furnished essential services to immigrant workers and their families. These things were done at serious costs, however. Bullough observes that Buckley and his counterparts in other cities "took from the rich and poor alike and retained much of what they obtained." More damaging was Buckley's failure to recognize crucial demographic and social changes in San Francisco and meet effectively the dissatisfactions of influential residents with public facilities. Bullough points out major community problems such as inadequate water supplies, badly paved streets, and corrupt fire and police departments.

These deficiencies in municipal services aroused the wrath of reform-minded politicians, businessmen, and professional people. Determined to impose their vision of efficiency and centralized authority on the city government, they seized control of the local Democratic organization and ended the Blind Boss's dominance over San Francisco. Bullough concludes that reform programs meant the eventual reduction of popular participation in city politics and government. Reform movements, while undermining traditional expressions of mass democracy, also promised citizen groups direct access to public decision-making without the meddling of the boss and with the assurance that their demands would be more readily answered. This significant development goes well beyond Bullough's investigation. He has brilliantly illuminated the complex interrelationship of industrialization, urban growth, and political change in late-nineteenth-century America.

MARTIN J. SCHIESL

California State University
Los Angeles

JEROME M. CLUBB, WILLIAM H. FLANIGAN, and NANCY H. ZINGALE. *Partisan Realignment: Voters, Parties, and Government in American History.* Pp. 311. Beverly Hills, CA: Sage Publications, 1980. $20.00, Paperbound, $9.95.

Was 1980 a year of partisan realignment in this country, or, at least, will it be so recognized some years from now? This is the question that analysts of American elections have posed for us every four years. But if we accept the historical analysis of Clubb, Flanigan, and Zingale, we must now ask a different kind of question: In the years to come, will President Reagan and other Republican leaders take advantage of the opportunity for realignment created by the 1980 election? The voters have taken the first step in rejecting Democratic leadership. Will the Republicans govern effectively and curry and sustain the voters' favor?

This new view of realignment shifts the emphasis from voters' attitudes to leaders' behavior, from "critical" elections to the interaction of leaders and led over longer stretches of time. It at once gives the electorate less and more credit than conventional explanations: less by not reading much more than a simple repudiation of incumbents into the vote in turnover years, and more by assuming that successful new leaders will be rewarded at the polls and, equally, that opportunities for realignment will be missed when leadership fails. The rewards, according to this book, are more likely to take the shape of an across-the-board increase in the successful party's support than in differential changes among demographic groups, as commonly supposed.

The realignment cycle goes through periods of stability, mid-sequence adjustment, and decay. For some 14 years after the elections of 1860, 1896, and 1932, the presidency and both houses of Congress were controlled by a single party, with a greater than usual margin of control in Congress. The parties took clear opposing positions on salient national issues. Voting in Congress was relatively polarized. These were periods of successful, or at least plausible, national leadership. After a time each realignment decayed. The government became divided, policymaking turned incremental, third-party movements appeared, partisanship declined, and the incumbent party ultimately was removed.

Clubb, Flanigan, and Zingale also offer an assessment of the decline and, as some would have it, demise of political parties in the United States. They attribute lower levels of partisanship today to specific cultural and institutional changes—urbanization and the primary, for example—and reject the notion that a point of no return has been passed—a speculation of Walter Dean Burnham, originally a fourth member of the research team. This section is the weakest, I think, if only because of a total absence of comparative testing.

The book is recommended in company with the works of Burnham, James L. Sundquist, and Everett C. Ladd, Jr.

ROBERT J. SICKELS

University of New Mexico
Albuquerque

WARREN I. COHEN. *Dean Rusk* [*The American Secretaries and Their Diplomacy*, Vol. 19]. Pp. xii, 375. Totowa, NJ: Cooper Square, 1980. $22.50.

Born in 1909 to genteel poverty on a small Georgia farm, Dean Rusk made his way by sheer ability and industry up an educational ladder that was topped by a Rhodes Scholarship at Oxford. During World War II he rose to the rank of colonel in the army, and both in the field, where he was on General Stillwell's staff, and later in the Pentagon, where he was highly regarded by top-ranking civilian and military personnel, he established an enviable record. Transferring to the Department of State, he held positions in which he shared in important foreign policy decisions of the Truman administration. In 1952 he left the government to become president of the Rockefeller Foundation and from that post returned to Washington in 1961 to become President Kennedy's secretary of state. Under Kennedy and his successor, Lyndon B. Johnson, Rusk held this position for eight years. No one else, except Cordell Hull, has ever been secretary of state so long.

Dean Rusk was a "good soldier." He presented his views forcibly, but if overruled, faithfully observed administration policy. Both Kennedy and Johnson liked a secretary of state who would tell them things they wished to hear. When Johnson said later that "Rusk had the best understanding of the way I wished to move," he revealed much about himself and his secretary.

Philosophically, Rusk was a Wilsonian internationalist, an anticolonialist, and a devout believer in the UN Charter. In the Far East he was convinced that Chinese communism must be contained and thus approved American efforts, already begun by the Eisenhower administration, to prevent communization of South Vietnam by local communists aided by North Vietnam and China. Even so, these efforts were only to prepare South Vietnam to defend itself. Step by step, however, the secretary's

hopes were disappointed: the war was not Vietnamized, but Americanized, and soon the United States was so deeply committed that there seemed no way out short of policy reversal and withdrawal. This was recommended by Assistant Secretary of State George Ball and other Atlanticists, but their advice was rejected, and when Johnson and Rusk relinquished power in January 1969, no end to the war was in sight.

Cohen concludes his well researched book with the subjective judgment that Rusk, among his other failings during the Vietnam War, "betrayed . . . the interests of his country" and that for these alleged offenses "much may be said in mitigation, but never enough."

JENNINGS B. SANDERS
Kensington
Maryland

JOHN E. FERLING. *A Wilderness of Miseries: War and Warriors in Early America.* Pp. xv, 227. Westport, CT: Greenwood Press, 1980. $25.00.

A Wilderness of Miseries is a timely and important book. Drawing on the insights of the new military history, with its emphasis on the interactions of war with the broader web of social activities, John Ferling has shed considerable new light on the military experience of colonial America. He has also offered some of the most interesting and provocative observations by any current historian on the impact of conflict both on those who bore arms in early America and on the societies for which they fought. The entire work reflects a careful reading of the sources on Ferling's part—sources on contemporary attitudes toward martial affairs, military leadership, and specific wars—and painstaking thought about their meanings.

Professor Ferling's arguments are refreshing; in an area long dominated by traditional battles-and-leaders histories, they represent some genuinely new thinking. He holds that the nature of colonial warfare led Americans to accept a severe, even brutal, brand of conflict as their normal mode of fighting. It also inclined them toward a willingness to fight largely unknown in contemporary European populations. In fact, while European wars were becoming the business of professional armies, with rules that discouraged civilian participation, Americans moved toward a concept of total war. Colonists routinely saw militia duty, fought Indians, and grimly accepted the fact that their civilian populations were fair game for enemy raids. Savagery, not restraint, characterized such combat as Americans struggled to survive in the New World. Ultimately, Ferling concludes, these patterns had a dramatic impact on the War for Independence, helping to explain the aggressive colonial response to the British in 1775 and the ferocity that marked the civil phase of the conflict. By then, colonials were simply used to resorting to arms in times of crises and fighting savagely when they did so. It was the American way.

Ferling builds his case with real skill, and while some of his conclusions will very likely provoke debate, *A Wilderness of Miseries* is on the whole compelling stuff. In fact, it deserves a wide and careful reading, and my guess is that it will spark a number of similar, perhaps regional, studies to test further its central ideas. I hope it does. In any case, Ferling's is a first-class book, and it should hold the interest of military historians for some time to come.

MARK EDWARD LENDER

Rutgers University
New Brunswick
New Jersey

CLAIRE KNOCHE FULENWIDER. *Feminism in American Politics: A Study of Ideological Influence.* Pp. xiv, 167. New York: Praeger, 1980. No price.

Not only is *Feminism in American Politics* an impressive scholarly work; it is also well written and beautifully organized. Fulenwider's initial objective is to evaluate feminism as a social movement and to examine feminist political views to determine whether they can be classified as an ideology. After carefully analyzing the origins, structure, process, and ideology of feminism, the author concludes that feminism does, in fact, qualify as a social movement. Feminist political ideology includes a perception of social reality that is oppressive to women and that results from an ideology of institutionalized sexism. As a political ideology, the goal of feminism is ending sexist practices and attitudes and achieving full equality for women in all areas of life. Historically, female oppression is seen as tied to the norms of patriarchy, the nuclear family, heterosexuality, and the female reproductive system. Women come to believe that their relationships with men are part of a personal condition that has little to do with their political condition. The question asked by Fulenwider is, Does feminism make a difference in the relationship of the electorate to the political system? To answer the question the author used primary data from the 1972 and 1976 CPS American National Election Studies, conducted by the Center for Political Studies of the University of Michigan. The data included a large representative cross-sectional sample for each year and a three-wave panel study (1972, 1974, 1976). A section of the questionnaire included 11 items dealing with sex roles, women's issues, life values, and the women's liberation movement. Fulenwider found increasing support for feminism among the U.S. electorate between 1972 and 1976 and a strong relationship between feminism for people with high cognitive ability and conventionally liberal ideology. Differences in the way feminism is understood and translated by women and men implies that feminist ideology has both cognitive and psychological components. Study results indicate that feminists are less likely than other women to believe that conventional political participation will be effective, yet they are more likely to have high political interest and a high sense of citizen duty. For minority women, approval of protest was much greater than for white women and had increased dramatically between 1972 and 1976. Concurrently, disenchantment with traditional efforts toward systemic change were evident as feminism among minority women clearly predicted dissatisfaction with the political system. Strong support was found for the contention that political ideology is formed as a product of socialization and life situation variables and that this influences political attitudes, which in turn influence political behavior. The strongest effects of feminism on political participation are seen among minority women, a group with little political clout and the greatest feeling of absolute deprivation.

Fulenwider speculates that the impact of feminism will increase in the future as awareness of sex-based inequities increases and as men give feminist demands more validity. Changes in sex roles will result in increases in political efficacy and activity for women, although minority women may be less active due to their sense of political alienation.

In her concluding chapter, Fulenwider notes, "Political and social change can come either at the rate of the caterpillar's crawl or the speed of its metamorphosis into a butterfly." The influence of the Reagan administration and the Moral Majority may have postponed the flight of the butterfly.

LES LEANNE HOGT
Wichita State University
Kansas

JAMES L. GARNETT. *Reorganizing State Government: The Executive Branch.* Pp. xviii, 243. Boulder, CO: Westview Press, 1981. $25.00.

In this volume the author attempts to answer three basic questions about state reorganization efforts: Why do state reorganization efforts occur? How are the organization efforts conducted? What forms do executive branches that have been reorganized take? In order to answer these fundamental questions Professor Garnett systematically examines all of the reorganization efforts that have occurred between 1900 and 1975. This effort results in a data base of 151 state executive branch reorganizations.

In order to determine why reorganization attempts are made, the author first reviews the various theoretical perspectives, such as the socioeconomic determinants approach, the reorganization as diffused innovation perspective, and reorganization as adaption to modernization. Professor Garnett provides us with a synthesis of the various theoretical perspectives in order to "take advantage of the collective strengths and compensate for the shortcomings of individual approaches." The third chapter is an excellent overview of the various forms that reorganization efforts have taken as well as an attempt to determine what criterion should be used in evaluating reorganization efforts. These related tasks lead the author to develop a new "modified typology," which is used to determine the degree of reorganization reform. In Chapter 4 the author discusses the various strategy alternatives available to bring about the adoption and implementation of reorganization decisions. Professor Garnett presents the reader with an excellent comparative overview of the different methodologies used to study executive reorganization as well as his own systematic quantitative approach. The author's work meets all the standards for vigorous value-free research and leads him to conclude that state reorganization adoption has been more successful in New England, the Southeast, and the Far West. Further reorganization efforts occur more frequently at an early point in a governor's administration, and most attempts are made by statute rather than by constitutional amendment or executive order. The last chapter presents the author's conclusions and guidelines for practitioners for translating the research findings into policy actions, and a thoughtful section devoted to possible directions for further research.

This volume is well written, concise, and yet meaty with pertinent findings. Professor Garnett has done a commendable job in bringing conceptual order and empirical systematic research methodologies to the study of reorganizing the executive branch of state government. This work should result in an increased awareness of a field of inquiry that has been long neglected. I believe it would be a valuable addition to the library of anyone interested in public administration or state and local government.

JOHN S. ROBEY

East Texas State University
Commerce

DORIS A. GRABER. *Crime News and the Public.* Pp. xviii, 239. New York: Praeger, 1980. $17.95.

Are the media somehow obsessed with the reporting of crime, especially vicious or bizarre crime? Most of us in the criminal justice field probably think so. Doris Graber examines this popular belief along with a number of others in a carefully and well-designed study. As such, this book fills an important gap in criminal justice knowledge.

Although Graber notes that she has worked as a news reporter, this experience is not allowed to bias her in any way. Yet it is apparent that her reporting experience has trained her in what to look for and the areas of reporting upon which to focus. She leaves very little of the process of reporting crime untouched and does a well-balanced job of presenting her results.

The findings are of great interest for two important reasons. They support some of the more popular assumptions many of us have had about the media coverage of crime. On the other hand, the study produces some surprising findings, especially in the area of what seems to be a disjunction between people's perceptions of crime and the way the media report it. This goes against the widely held suspicion that the news media somehow "brainwash" people by their biased or selective reporting. Graber shows that this assumption is by and large not true. Examples of some of her interesting findings follow.

The similarity in the amount and type of crime news reporting from one newspape to another, or across local TV stations, or across national TV stations is strikingly the same. At each level of reporting the amount and type of coverage are almost identical. This she attributes to the set pattern of the "news beat," which essentially relies on the police blotter as a relatively easy means of developing news stories.

Yet the coverage of violent crime and street crime is far and away overreported by the media compared to what is recorded in the police crime reports. There is, very definitely, a selective reporting process.

Even though over the period studied—more than a year—the newspapers reported that 21 percent of the criminals were black as opposed to 70 percent white, the panel of respondents who were interviewed had their own ideas: in their view, 61.4 percent were black and only 7.4 percent were white. In this case, the newspaper percentage conforms closely to that reported by the FBI Uniform Crime Reports.

Similarly, the panel of respondents perceived that the victims were 41.3 percent black and 54.3 percent white, whereas the newspaper reported only 23.6 percent black and 67 percent white. The difference here between the panel and the media is remarkable and offers considerable food for thought to those who presume that there is some kind of conspiracy between the media and the "powerful" to misinform the public that most crime is committed by blacks and the poor. Graber takes the opportunity with such results to show that the "radical criminologists" may not be wholly accurate in their claims. She notes that the people have made up their own minds.

The views of the panelists seemed to be that crime is not "an interclass phenomenon where the poor prey on the rich.

Rather, it is a self-destructive battle where the poor prey on the poor." Yet a fascinating question arises: If the public has acquired these perceptions of the nature and causes of crime—respondents were also found to adhere to a personality/situation type of causal theory of crime—one may well ask where they got these views, especially given the fact that these so-called theories are very much in line with the accepted explanations of crime that are currently taught in most of our criminal justice classrooms.

What are we to conclude from this? That criminal justice research has filtered down to the public by some wonderful process that produces popular views closely following those of the leading researchers? Or is it that our current explanations of crime are simply reflections of common knowledge?

I dare not pursue this line of questioning further. This fascinating study has raised many more questions than it answers. It is to be hoped that it will spawn a vast array of research into the question of this strange social reality of crime.

GRAEME NEWMAN
State University of New York
Albany

ALBERT K. KARNIG and SUSAN WELCH. *Black Representation and Urban Policy.* Pp. xiii, 179. Chicago: University of Chicago Press, 1980. $20.00.

Drawing in part on their own original research and in part on other recent studies, and using data from more than 250 cities, Karnig and Welch have attempted a twofold study: of conditions that contribute to or inhibit the nomination and election of black mayors and city council members, and of the impact of the election of black officials on urban policy. Their conclusions are for the most part rather tentative and not particularly surprising.

During the seventies there was a dramatic increase in black representation at the municipal level, but blacks still constitute less than one percent of elected officeholders in the nation. There are sharp regional differences. The proportion of black mayors is much lower in the South and Northeast than in the West and Midwest. The small number in the South is attributed in part to lack of educational and economic opportunities.

Not surprisingly, the size of the black population is the best predictor of the election of black officials, but socioeconomic variables such as level of education and economic status are also important. There is fairly conclusive evidence that district rather than at-large elections favor black candidacies. When blacks are in a minority they have little chance of electing a mayor, but once blacks are in a majority there is a rapid and enormous tipping in favor of the election of blacks. In 1978 in cities with black majorities less than 20 percent had white mayors.

The effects of the election of black officials on policymaking are more difficult to measure and raise more complex questions. There are many obstacles to translating black representation into policy. For example, the values and objectives of black officials, who are usually successful members of the middle class, do not always lead to policies desired by the mass of black voters. Moreover, the winning of a few council seats or even a mayorship does not necessarily mean power in decision-making. The continuing power of white bureaucrats and the financial power of the private sector as well as a declining tax base can thwart black mayors. The cities with the largest percentages of blacks and the largest black political representation are likely to be the most financially distressed. The limited powers of local governments and restrictions imposed by state laws and state legislatures also inhibit efforts of black municipal officials.

Karnig and Welch have chosen to make a study of aggregate data analyses of a large number of cities rather than an in-depth study of a smaller number. As such this little volume is useful, but it leaves unexplored many more complex questions.

EMMA LOU THORNBROUGH
Butler University
Indianapolis
Indiana

JÜRGEN KOCKA. *White Collar Workers in America, 1890-1940: A Social-Political History in International Perspective.* Pp. v, 403. Beverly Hills, CA: Sage Publications, 1979. $25.00. Paperbound, $12.50.

Jürgen Kocka rejects the received thesis that white-collar workers have formed the natural clientele of fascist movements. However much it fits the German case, it fails in the American. Kocka also cites British and French trends to strengthen his argument that it is historical experience and not some status-specific reflex that best accounts for the sociopolitical outlook of white-collar workers.

Kocka draws on both statistical and literary materials. He reveals a shrewd grasp of American historiography and displays a refreshing independence of mind. But sparse sources dictate a skewed picture of the American white-collar labor force. Retail clerks and draftsmen loom large, while general office workers and female secretarial and bookkeeping employees receive little attention. Public employees are excluded altogether. Kocka is good on the relationships between education and employment, weaker on the important subject of changing work structures.

The events of the 1930s provide the crucial test of Kocka's thesis. Using public opinion polls, Kocka contrasts the strong support for the New Deal and the opposition to race- and labor-baiting among American white-collar workers with the right-wing orientation of their German counterparts. Collective protest in America, he notes, flowed largely through the two labor federations and was not subsumed in fascist or authoritarian movements.

Kocka dismisses the notion of a distinctive American national character as a fiction. Yet he does point to the contrasting historical experiences of Germans and Americans as the key to sociopolitical behavior. Germany's powerful corporative, statist, and even feudal traditions, he believes, most satisfactorily explain the proclivities of her white-collar workers for right-wing politics. Without the burden of this past, however, American workers identified with the dynamic capitalist order, willingly embracing its risk-taking features while limiting collective protest to bread-and-butter concerns. Louis Hartz and David Potter, neither of whom is prominently cited, would find Kocka's story familiar.

Notwithstanding its occasional omissions and minor factual errors—for instance, Kocka misunderstands the code-making process of the National Recovery Administration—*White Collar Workers* is a significant contribution. It is packed with information about a much-neglected subject. Its comparative historical approach is provocative and compelling. And Kocka's explicit effort to put historical sources to work in seeking answers to basic questions of political and social behavior while at the same time eschewing sectarian homiletics is both refreshing and convincing.

ROBERT H. ZIEGER
Wayne State University
Detroit
Michigan

DANIEL C. MAGUIRE. *A New American Justice: Ending the White Male Monopolies.* Pp. xiii, 218. Garden City, NY: Doubleday, 1980. $9.95.

In this book an established writer on ethics and theology attempts, with some success, an advocacy of affirmative action. The author's approach is a provocative one, which asserts at the outset that we have been operating for two hundred years in America under "a rigid quota system" that has "institutionalized and legalized" a 90 to 100 percent white male monopoly of the principal power centers in business, government, and the professions. He states his conclusions in the first chapter and then sets out to defend them. In the process he (1) offers a stinging critique of the neoconservative views of Nathan Glazer and Robert Nozick, (2) distinguishes between remedial and preferential affirmative action, and advocates both, (3) develops criteria to identify those who should qualify for preferential relief, and (4) argues a theory of "distributive" justice that does "justice to justice" by including a component of "mercy" and the principle that "justice for all means preference for some."

In Glazer's neoconservative preferences, Maguire sees the stereotypically American tendency to applaud justice but settle for order and stability. In Nozick's theory of justice, Maguire sees a thinker hamstrung by traditional American individualism. The result of such order-oriented, individualistic approaches, even at their best, is an argument for faith in our folkways, concentration on individual rights and equal opportunity, and enforcement of nondiscrimination on a case-by-case basis. Maguire argues, instead, for a fundamental change in the patterns of distribution.

The author's criteria for identifying those groups that should qualify for social and distributive justice are sufficiently stringent that only blacks, American Indians, Puerto Ricans, Mexican-Americans, and women fall within the criteria—with blacks favored as the "prime and paradigmatic" recipients. These groups should receive both remedial affirmative action—special tutoring or job training, for example— and preferential affirmative action, with race or sex counted as a plus factor in hiring or admissions. The phrase "to each according to his need" is argued to be "a principle of justice," and, regarding the groups identified above, Maguire argues that social and distributive justice require "sufficient sharing to meet what is minimally due to [them] ... their essential needs."

The book is generally well written. It is clearly passionate. Disturbingly, though, its language is often too cute, even hip: "So that what I am about might be clear, I shall state. ..." The abstract thinking is clear and convincing. Many of the descriptive assertions, apparently intended to be empirical generalizations, are at best questionable; for example, is it really true that minorities today are "demanding a complete overhaul in the power structure" of society? And I think students of the American judiciary might quarrel with the author's advocacy of a philosophical function, in moral discourse, for the Supreme Court analogous to that "performed by the universities in medieval Europe." All in all, however, I find myself persuaded by the principal argument of the book and I find the book a useful critique of the neoconservative position on affirmative action.

WILLIAM C. LOUTHAN
Ohio Wesleyan University
Delaware

DAVID L. PORTER. *Congress and the Waning of the New Deal.* Pp. xiv, 169. Port Washington, NY: Kennikat Press, 1980. $13.50.

Some, though not all, historians have viewed the New Deal as passing through two fairly distinct phases, the first extending from 1933 to 1934 and the second from 1935 to 1938. In *Congress and the Waning of the New Deal,* David L. Porter discovers a third stage, one spanning the years 1939-40. Porter examines the legislative history of six so-called reform measures during this period: the extension of the presidential power to devalue the dollar and purchase foreign silver, the broadening of transportation regulation to include waterways, the continuation of the reciprocal trade agreements program, the renewed funding of the Works Progress Administration, the reorganization of executive agencies, and the restriction of political campaign activities on the part of federal officeholders.

"This book," Porter explains, "concentrates on the battle within Congress between the New Dealers and the bipartisan conservative coalition." But the book also attempts to show that the battle did not always pit President Roosevelt and the New Dealers against Republicans and conservative Democrats. Porter takes into account the sectional as well as the partisan interests of senators and representatives and also the influence of pressure groups, both those of private enterprisers and those of federal bureaucrats. In analyzing congressional votes he makes use of roll-call data supplied by the Inter-University Consortium for Political Research at the University of Michigan.

Porter succeeds in establishing his point. Clearly, on the basis of his evidence and argument, the reform spirit persisted after 1938, arising from diverse sources and taking a variety of shapes. The makeup of the opposition as well as the sponsorship depended on the nature of the particular proposals. As Congress turned from one issue to another, there was a kaleidoscopic realignment of forces. Thus, for example, Southern Democrats parted from Northern Republicans to continue supporting the New Deal monetary and trade policies, divided among themselves on the regulation of water transport, and rejoined the Republicans to oppose work relief and executive reorganization and to favor the Hatch Acts, which originated as anti-Roosevelt reforms. To understand the full complexity of the struggles, however, one must carefully read the entire book, and rather difficult reading it is.

RICHARD N. CURRENT
University of North Carolina
Greensboro

JEFFREY A. SMITH, *American Presidential Elections: Trust and the Rational Voter.* Pp. xiii, 207. New York: Praeger, 1980. $20.95.

One is almost tempted to say that the presidency is "too much with us." Few would disagree that the growth of the executive institution in this country has had a profound impact on the nature of the American political process, while the last several decades of presidential scandal, presidential abuse of power, presidential electioneering and ambitions, and a frightening series of presidential assassination attempts would seem to make us all weary of the subject.

Anything but. Not only do we realize that we understand the institution and how it functions only dimly, but as social scientists we realize that we recognize only partially the implications that the modern presidency has for a multitude of related variables, or what we might learn from the institution and related political behavior. Smith's book is in this vein, and offers some novel and intriguing insights into a well-researched aspect of the political system.

Specifically, Smith is offering an alternative hypothesis explaining American electoral behavior. He eschews, on a number of grounds, two major categories of electoral behavior models: the voter-as-spectator category, containing the "naive model of the democratic citizen" (Schumpeter and Berelson) and the social-psychological model (Lazarsfeld, Campbell, Miller, Stokes, Converse et al.); and similarly, the voter-as-consumer models, that of the rational voter (Downs, Key) and that of the new issue voter (Miller and Leviton, Nie-Verba-Petrocik, Pomper). In contrast, Smith offers a perspective that views the American voter as investor. Using secondary data originally collected by the SRC/CPS, and focusing closely on the 1976 election, Smith develops an argument that posits trust as a critical variable in voters' decisions to participate in elections—the personal context—and their preference among candidates—the institutional context.

Whereas recent models have argued the basic irrationality of the American voter, Smith's assumes the opposite, and his hypothesis contends that change in electoral behavior in recent years is better explained by the dissonance the rational voter perceives between the democratic ideal and "normal" American politics. Trust figures here, he argues, and the data show as much. In effect, voters act toward elections much as investors act toward their financial decisions; political participation "is viewed as an investment in the political system and the candidates as the agents whose performance will determine the value of that investment." Smith's interpretation of the data suggests that this value, like others, has diminished over the years, the response of the rational voter being to invest less in the process.

An intriguing argument and interpretation of the data, this. Smith has brought into sharp focus some of the deficiencies in the assumptions of the extant models and has raised some valid questions concerning how the data are employed therein. While not entirely convincing—theory-confirming case studies on his hypothesis are now in order—Smith's work provides new vistas for students of electoral behavior. The 1980 presidential election seems tailor-made for such a study.

KENT MORRISON

University of Utah
Salt Lake City

WILLIAM N. STILL, Jr. *American Sea Power in the Old World: The United States Navy in European and Near Eastern Waters, 1865-1917.* Pp. xi, 291. Westport, CT: Greenwood Press, 1980. $29.95.

Professor Still's exhaustively researched book spells out in detail for the first time the role, or nonrole, of the U.S. Navy in European-Mediterranean affairs during the half century that this nation matured as an industrial power, between the end of the Civil War and the American entry into the great European world war. Without a raison d'être for maintaining a naval presence in the North Atlantic during the long Pax Britannica (1815-1914), the Navy instead found its ships increasingly involved in disputes resulting from the tedious dem-

ise of the Ottoman Empire. The Navy designated these ships, which operated singly and independently between the Baltic Sea and the coasts of Africa as the European Squadron until 1905, when regular tactical Atlantic Fleet units began to make specific visits for diplomatic purposes as the Navy took its place among the world's leading navies.

The last third of the nineteenth century was notorious for imagined diplomatic threats and resulting crises suggesting the potential use of the Navy's antiquated warships. Many of the incidents of these and the immediately subsequent years now appear uproariously funny, especially as Still tastefully relates them. Like the time the cruiser *Pittsburgh's* bandmaster, unable to find the national anthem of Palestine—not knowing it was not a nation—to render honors played "Lena, She's the Queen of Palestina!" Or the 15-gun salute fired by the steam sloop *Lancaster* at Kronstadt, almost bringing on a counterattack by an uncomprehending Russian general. Incidents involving the Moslem world continued unabated since the original less-than-happy encounter of the Barbary wars of 1801-06.

The actual impact of the presence of warships is exceedingly difficult to measure, and the precise scholar might squirm at Still's frequent equivocations: "probably," "for some reason," "more than likely," "undoubtedly." But sea power is a most subtle force, a mysterious elixir to U.S. citizens abroad and undefinable quantity and quality to diplomatic historians. Still is perhaps most successful in his narrative when he has energetic admirals as his focus, notably Louis M. Goldsborough, David G. Farragut, Henry Erban and his flagship captain Alfred Thayer Mahan, and the notorious William A. "Red Bill" Kirkland. Lacking overseas bases, these men kept their handful of fewer than half a dozen ships operating from comfortable anchorages like Villefranche (French Riviera) and Lisbon on purely mundane matters until the Egyptian crisis of 1882 and the unsuccessful attempts of U.S. warships to pressure the Ottoman government to submit to several demands, usually related to overseas missionaries, during the 1890s.

The American victory over Spain in 1898 changed the role of the United States in European affairs, and President Teddy Roosevelt used his new battleships to play an unprecedentedly active role in the Mediterranean during 1901-09. This part of the story has been told many times before but never from the perspective of the operating U.S. naval forces afloat, making Still's contribution to the literature a unique and important one. Especially new is his treatment of U.S. naval activities in Turkish waters from the 1890s to 1917, a prelude to the important postwar work there of Admiral Mark L. Bristol.

The only annoying error is obviously the fault of proofreaders and editors who could not accept the spelling of the steam sloop-of-war *Juniata*, named for a river in Pennsylvania and persistently gave two other renderings in this otherwise fine book.

CLARK G. REYNOLDS

Charleston
South Carolina

WILLIAM STINCHCOMBE. *The XYZ Affair.* Pp. 167. Westport, CT: Greenwood Press, 1980. $23.95.

Partisan politics in the infant American Republic, while profoundly affecting the crisis with revolutionary France in the later 1790s, were not responsible for the famous XYZ affair. The causes lay in fundamentally different views held by French and American officials, the former believing that the United States had abrogated the alliance concluded with France in 1778, while the latter blamed the French for violating American rights in prosecuting war with Britain. Strained relations between the two countries helped to clear away any emotional attachments to republicanism and revolution, and while the differences between the two

governments were fundamental, they were manageable.

This is not a study on how the two revolutionary republics resolved their differences by diplomatic means, but on why for two years they did not. Neither side wanted war. President John Adams was committed both to the treaty signed by John Jay with Britain and to American neutrality in the conflict between Britain and France. The French regarded the Jay Treaty as an alliance between Britain and her former colonies. Within the American administration and the Congress domestic politics counted more than the policy to be pursued with France. In Paris, too, internal politics colored foreign policy. But the issue of policy became moot when the Directory refused officially to receive the American envoys and the foreign minister, Tallyrand, demanded a loan to France and a bribe for himself, not an uncommon practice for the French government of the time. Tallyrand and his associates had turned the ministry of foreign affairs into a commercial venture, an instrument to raise funds for investment in North America, a region safe from the vicissitudes of European wars and French political instability. Neither the envoys of the United States nor Tallyrand wanted war, but while John Marshall, Charles C. Pinckney, and Elbridge Gerry sought a prompt agreement, Tallyrand wanted to prolong negotiations.

By delaying, he and his associates did not intend to risk the peace, but to reward themselves. In this goal they had the aid of a corps of Americans living in France, merchants, students, and speculators, who feared an open break between the two countries. These expatriates would not acknowledge what Marshall and Pinckney perceived: naked power underlay French action. The turning point came following the return of Marshall and Pinckney to the United States and the publication of their dispatches recounting the demand for the loan and bribe. The American Congress then unilaterally cancelled the alliance with France, undertook to expand the army, and dispatched ships against the French West Indies. Given the consequences of these actions, Stinchcombe's discussion—a paragraph —is surprisingly brief. Concluding that the United States was preparing for war, the French government reversed itself, eliminating commissions to privateers preying on American commerce, relaxing embargoes against American ships in French ports, and releasing American seamen imprisoned in French jails.

The obvious lesson, one Stinchcombe does not discuss, is that diplomacy without force is impotent. The way was now clear for another diplomatic mission to settle outstanding differences. From the XYZ affair many Americans gained the conviction that France could not be used against Britain and that their country ought to have little to do with any European power. Perhaps another conclusion was more appropriate: a weak nation could not afford the luxury of standing alone when confronted by a power willing and able to exert force in the Western Hemisphere. Common ideology and form of government were not sufficient to unite national interests. The American republic did need alliances, but not permanent ones.

J. M. SOSIN

University of Nebraska
Lincoln

CHARLES WARD, PHILIP SHASHKO, and DONALD PIENKOS, eds. *Studies in Ethnicity: The East European Experience in America.* Pp. viii, 254. Boulder, CO: East European Monographs. Distributed by Columbia University Press, New York. $17.50.

As American scholars continue to be fascinated by the immigrant experience, *Studies in Ethnicity* is welcome for its focus on less familiar elements of a generally familiar story. This book pulls together essays on language, literature, and institutions among oft-neglected groups such as Serbs, Croats, and Czechs, as well as Poles and Jews, exemplifying both the similarities and the dissimilarities among these peoples. As a collection of individual conference papers on different aspects of life among immigrants from a variety of backgrounds, it lacks evenness and cohesiveness. (It also lacks physical quality: there are an appalling number of typographical errors.) But its broad scope is actually its chief asset. Editors Charles Ward, Philip Shashko, and Donald Pienkos recognize that there are many useful approaches to the immigrant experience, some of which have not been adequately explored.

In this regard, the opening section on language maintenance is particularly interesting, with articles on the way in which Croatian- and Polish-Americans speak their mother tongues, on the linguistic impact of adjacent ethnic groups, and on problems in teaching the Czech language in America. Unfortunately, all but the last of these essays promise more than they deliver. Narrow, unsystematic research techniques, an apparent unwillingness to probe deeply, and the authors' use of technical terms comprehensible only to trained linguists leave the reader more frustrated than enlightened.

The section on immigrant organizations is more solid, if more traditional. There are good articles on the lack of cohesiveness among Czech Americans, on the factors differentiating the Jewish experience from that of other East Europeans, and on the problems of the Orthodox Church in America. Essays on Polish and Serbian immigrant organizations are useful, though rather pedestrian, while another on the role of the parish in assimilation contrasts Polish traditions of tolerance with American traditions of intolerance, a bizarre conclusion. But the author of that essay deserves credit for trying to come to grips with the precise way in which Old World differed from New World culture.

The final four papers on ethnic writers in America, are like the rest of this volume, promising but uneven. There are stimulating personal comments by an exiled Czech novelist and less stimulating comments by a Polish American theater director. An essay on four novelists dealing with immigrant life is interesting but haphazardly presented; another, ostensibly on Serbian writers in America, actually discusses only two: scientist Michael Pupin, whose autobiography was published in 1922, and Dragoslav Dragutinovic, a post-World War II refugee poet. The analysis is good, but a comparison between men with such totally different backgrounds employing such different literary forms does not lend itself to generalizations on Serbian writers. Nevertheless, *Studies in Ethnicity* aids us in understanding the special experience of Americans of East European heritage.

LAURA L. BECKER
Clemson University
South Carolina

SOCIOLOGY

DONALD APPLEYARD. *Livable Streets.*
Pp. xvii, 382. Berkeley: University of California Press, 1981. $27.50.

Donald Appleyard has written what should be a significant contribution to the area of urban design and planning. Although that in itself would be a major achievement, if it were the only fruit of Professor Appleyard's labor his text would be simply excellent. It is, however, much more than that: it is outstanding. This latter accolade is due to the fact that *Livable Streets* not only will be useful to professional planners and policymakers, but also will provide a source book for laypersons interested in reclaiming their streets and neighborhoods.

Appleyard's claim is that livable streets, places where human life can creatively prosper rather than merely exist, are quickly vanishing from our cities. The principle culprit behind the usurpation of city life is automobile traffic. Appleyard painstakingly describes how traffic, with its attendant fumes,

noise, dirt, vibration, and danger, is steadily decreasing the quality of life for urban residents. He reports that the problems that traffic creates are of greater concern for street residents than is crime.

The problems created by traffic, though widespread, are not insurmountable. The excitement generated by this book is brought about by Appleyard's claim, and documentation from case studies, that the reduction and slowing down of traffic can allow for the construction of safe and enjoyable urban communities. He describes the success of the Dutch Woonerf, a residential area within which the street is shared by vehicles and pedestrians. This is accomplished by eliminating through traffic, considerably slowing down motorists—to 9-12 miles per hour—planting trees and shrubs, constructing outdoor furniture, and making other changes designed to convey the impression that the street is being used by the residents as well as the motorists. Although Woonerf-like residential yards are rare in U.S. cities, Appleyard details smaller-scale attempts, in St. Louis, San Francisco, and other American cities, to create protected neighborhoods.

The formula for the successful rebirth of street living is not exclusively to be found in the efforts of professional planners and traffic managers, however. If one lesson is to be learned from these prior attempts at creating improved urban residential areas, it is that the way to create livable streets is through grass-roots organizing. Nor will the creation of safe and pleasant residential areas require drastic and expensive modifications. In several chapters at the end of the book, Professor Appleyard proposes some modest changes that could, nonetheless, produce substantial improvements in street livability, such as speed limits, turn prohibitions, undulations, and diverters. Appleyard persuasively argues that whatever the temporary inconvenience for motorists—and these are not to be underestimated, he warns—the costs must be borne. The alternative is less acceptable: the demise of livable streets.

In sum, Appleyard has written a timely and important book. It is well documented and exceptionally well written, although a reader not acquainted with social science material might find the reporting of survey data somewhat dry. My hope is that the book does not simply sit on the well-stocked library shelves of professionals but that it gets into the hands of neighborhood organizers so that the reclamation may begin. Therein lies the excitement that Appleyard has generated.

RAYMOND PATERNOSTER

University of South Carolina
Columbia

ROBERT K. FULLINWIDER. *The Reverse Discrimination Controversy: A Moral and Legal Analysis.* Pp. xi, 300. Totowa, NJ: Rowman and Littlefield, 1980. $22.50. Paperbound, $9.95.

This book is a critical evaluation of the major moral and legal arguments swirling around the controversial public policy mandating the preferential hiring of blacks. Overall, the philosophical and legal reasoning behind this issue is found wanting. Lawmakers, by and large, are taken to task for decisions in this area that are ambiguous, arbitrary, contradictory, and without a sound moral foundation. The ideas of moral theorists who advocate employment favoritism for blacks either as a means of compensation or as a form of distributive justice are dismissed both for their practical inability to redress the grievances of victimized blacks and for their unwarranted denial of the basic rights of all citizens, especially the right to be employed solely upon the basis of job-related qualifications.

Only the philosophy of social utility provides a strong substructure for policy designed to hire blacks on a preferential basis. In essence, Fullinwider contends that societies are justified in deciding that reverse discrimination is beneficial. This position is supported by solid reasoning, which, among other

things, convinces that neither the U.S. Constitution nor basic moral tenets guarantee a person that right to be selected for a job only on the basis of qualifications pertaining to that job.

While long on the moral and legal discourse that surrounds the issue of preferential hiring, this book is short on evidence that summarizes the empirical impact of reverse discrimination decisions. Readers who desire to know how many blacks have benefited through these programs, and at what expense to whites, should look elsewhere. The support accorded social utility as a rationale for employment favoritism is not introduced until well into the book and probably will catch some by surprise. There is no early warning that the author intends to take a stand on the reverse discrimination controversy. If anything, most of the material is presented in a value-neutral, albeit lively, style. To the opponent of preferential hiring the Hitchcock-twist near the end will probably be disquieting. To the advocate of this policy, the surprise ending, assuming one survives the devastating critique of reverse discrimination, will likely be a relief—maybe even a moral charge for greater change.

JAMES LAMARE

University of Texas
El Paso

JAMES B. LEMERT. *Does Mass Communication Change Public Opinion After All? A New Approach to Effects Analysis.* Pp. x, 253. Chicago: Nelson-Hall, 1981. $17.95. Paperbound, $8.95.

This book presents a new research model for the media's impact on public opinion. It seeks to furnish a more firmly grounded basis for media impact study, claiming that the results of former and more traditional media research are inadequate. The fault is perceived in the hitherto widespread assumption that public opinion is simply the sum total of everybody's attitudes.

Lemert, who is director of communications research at the University of Oregon School of Journalism, brings to view and criticizes the "simple reductionist" approach of mass communications researchers that he sees as having been dominant since the work of Lazarsfeld in the 1940s. He shows a strong grasp of research done in this field, which he summarizes. His thesis is that the media tend to affect public opinion not so much by altering the minds of folk but rather by engendering changes in such variables as participation and power. Citing Ernest Nagel, he seeks the need for "correspondence rules" that link individual and collective concepts.

The work furnishes many examples from the political events of the last ten years, some as recent as the Iran hostage situation. Several examples are given of ways in which the media provide situation definitions whose impact can be appreciable, though nobody is aware of them. Another neglected area is that of whether and when the mass media produce lowered political participation.

Lemert discusses the phenomenon of mobilizing information, information that helps people to act on attitudes they already possess. Other topics include power discrepancies among participants, public opinion polls, and the link between public opinion and decision makers. Lemert points the way to a new type of research, claiming that it is not merely those interested in the mass media who need this research but scholars in other social sciences as well. He provides many testable program statements and hypotheses that should prove thought-provoking and stimulating to all those engaged in public opinion research. For example, research into attitudes has usually stressed two kinds of changes, attitude change and attitude reinforcement, neglecting attitude formation and attitude object change. Similarly, research has traditionally concentrated on issue-centered attitudes, but equally significant are attitudes on political participation. In addition to participation and power, research models should take account of the "influence framework" and mobilizing information.

This is a book that public opinion researchers cannot afford to ignore.

JOHN E. OWEN
Arizona State University
Tempe

ARTHUR MARWICK. *Class: Image and Reality in Britain, France and the USA Since 1930.* Pp. viii, 416. New York: Oxford University Press, 1980. $19.95.

Teachers of introductory sociology courses frequently meet with resistance from undergraduates to the idea that modern societies are class societies. Professor Marwick's study of class in three modern societies should persuade disbelievers that class does not simply exist in the minds of social scientists, but also in the minds of ordinary men and women. Although he defines class as inequalities of power, wealth, income, working conditions, lifestyles, and culture, Marwick is not concerned with social scientific definitions or theories; indeed he takes an explicitly atheoretical approach and means by class "what people in everyday life mean by it." If he were not so explicitly atheoretical, Professor Marwick might be suspected of a phenomenological approach to the subject, but his concern to explore the reality of social class by starting from the evidence is that of the historian, not the social scientist.

Although the basis for selection is unclear, the evidence amassed for and about the existence of class in Britain, France, and America is rich and varied, for both the thirties and the period since World War II. Official images of class range from those to be found in census data to those contained in the speeches of politicians. Unofficial images include the views of a French socialist peasant and the American factory girl in the thirties who was, in her own words, "bursting with red-hot revolt." The mass media, in the shape of the BBC, Hollywood films, and the French cinema, are also used as sources of popular ideas and portrayals of class and class structure.

It is certainly not a static image of class that emerges from this study, and the author shows that World War II acted to some extent as a catalyst in the movement toward modernization and the postindustrial society of advanced technology and multinational capitalism. All three countries under discussion have experienced a relative expansion of white-collar occupations, increased social mobility, and some affluence, but other developments—the decline of the French peasantry and increasing class consciousness on the part of the American working class—reflect the different historical context of each country. However, Marwick rightly takes issue with those theorists of the sixties who interpreted such changes as heralding pluralism and the end of ideological and class conflict. He concludes that class inequality remains real and similar to that which existed in the thirties—particularly the power and wealth of the upper classes. Despite these conclusions and his lavish use of varied and interesting evidence, Professor Marwick fails to explain how class creates and recreates inequality. This reviewer would suggest that we can only understand class by the application of theoretical tools to raw evidence.

ROSAMUND BILLINGTON

Hull College of Higher Education
North Humberside
England

GEORGE PETER MURDOCK. *Theories of Illness: A World Survey.* Pp. xv, 127. Appendix. Pittsburgh: University of Pittsburgh Press, 1980. $9.95.

In this brief book George Peter Murdock looks at patterns of theories of illness that have developed in a regionally stratified sample of 139 societies excluding modern urban-industrial societies. Thirteen theories of illness are divided into two major divisions: theories of natural causation—with the following five subtypes: (1) infection, (2) stress, (3) organic deterioration, (4) accident, and (5) overt human aggression—and theories of supernatural causation—with eight subtypes that fall into three distinguishable groups: theories of mystical causation: (6) fate, (7) ominous sensations, (8) contagion, and (9) mystical retribution from breach of taboo; theories of animistic causation: (10) soul loss and (11) spirit aggression; and theories of magical causation: (12) sorcery and (13) witchcraft. While the definitions of these thirteen theories are brief but adequate, their illustration is sometimes overly condensed. Murdock recognizes that some contemporary forms of treatment, like acupuncture and chiropractic and faith healing, fall into a twilight zone between natural and supernatural theories of causation; he then excludes them from further analysis.

After noting that supernatural theories predominate in primitive societies and after discussing the methods and limitations in comparative ethnography, Murdock examines twenty-five correlations—most of them between theories of illness within certain geographical and linguistic areas. He scores the theories of illness on a four-point scale that ranges from the theory being the predominant cause recognized by the society to its being of auxiliary importance, unimportant, or absent. Spirit aggression theories and witchcraft theories, for example, are found predominantly in the circum-Mediterranean region; sorcery theories and techniques are found in sub-Saharan Africa, the insular Pacific, and both North and South America. Other illustrative correlations are a relationship between witchcraft theories and patrilineal or double descent, as well as the use of substantial bride-price customs. Sorcery and witchcraft theories tend to be antithetical; witchcraft theories are likely to be found in stratified societies while sorcery theories are found in preliterate societies. Spirit aggression theories predominate in nonpastoral societies. Murdock usually explores the bases for the correlations he finds.

This cross-cultural study of diverse theories of illness and their relations to the ideational and structural components of culture is provocative, although occasionally sketchy. It provides many useful hypotheses and ideas for more detailed research by medical anthropologists and sociologists.

DUANE F. STROMAN

Juniata College
Huntingdon
Pennsylvania

CHARLES R. TITTLE. *Sanctions and Social Deviance: The Question of Deterrence.* Pp. xx, 346. New York: Praeger, 1980. $26.95.

This study of the relation between so-called sanction fear and future deviant acts raises again the question, How is society possible? By way of answer, Tittle offers several more specific questions that sociologists and criminologists ought to find useful in their own research.

It will come as no surprise that Tittle finds informal sanctions to be far more important than formal ones in deterring deviance. Policymakers may be somewhat surprised by Tittle's finding that the poorest of all sanctions is the perceived severity of a jail sentence.

While the study demonstrates that sanction fear is a significant independent predictor of estimates of future deviance, its value lies in Tittle's refinement and critique of theories of deviance prediction and deterrence generally. He is concerned to discover whether and how sanction fear is related to other theoretical and status variables. Among theoretical variables, only moral commitment and differential association can claim, with sanction fear, independent predictive power. As for status variables, sex, age, and degree of religious involvement are significant, but not class, race, and marital or labor force status. Taken together and in an absolute sense, none of these variables is an important factor in conformity.

Tittle suggests a number of refinements in explanatory logic as well as a few important caveats and provocative questions. Lest we dismiss too quickly the role of formal sanctions in social order, we ought first to explore the possibility that formal sanctions contribute to the character of the informal, moral climate of everyday life. In any case, Tittle warns, the sooner sociologists give up one-variable theories, the better. A good theory of deterrence will be interactive and systemic.

As for future work in the field, this study makes two important points. First, since in all cases variation within categories is greater than variation among them, we should look more closely at individualistic variables. Second, the predictive power of sanction fear seems to depend on the sensitivity of perception, or the subjective evaluation of sanction threats. To the extent that this aspect of perception can be equalized, differences on all other dimensions fade away. Thus, for example, differences between males and females in estimates of future deviance seem to depend entirely on differential sensitivity of perception of sanction threats. Why should this be so? The implication is that the answers to the question of sanctions and deterrence are to be found in understanding how we construct reality.

JOEL S. MEISTER

Amherst College
Massachusetts

ALLEN M. WEST. *The National Education Association: The Power Base for Education.* Pp. ix, 303. New York: Free Press, 1980. $15.95.

WENDY PETER ABT and JAY MAGIDSON. *Reforming Schools: Problems in Program Implementation and Evaluation.* Pp. 230. Beverly Hills, CA: Sage Publications, 1980. $20.00. Paperbound, $9.95.

These two volumes share an interest in education and a concern for the analysis of change. But they differ dramatically in scope, perspective, methodology, and style of reportage. One is a historical survey of the National Education Association (NEA) from its centennial anniversary in 1957 to 1980, with an emphasis on tracing changes in the NEA and its political involvements. The other documents a project under federal grant to evaluate the Pupil Change Study in rural education, emphasizing analysis of the process of evaluation and utilizing sophisticated contemporary statistical procedures. These are divergent books, and are discussed separately in what follows, but they have a further common element that deserves comment prior to separate treatment. Each is written in a personalized manner by people in positions to know a great deal about the topic and also to have an interest in the outcome. Allen West was a member of the highest levels of NEA staff during over 30 years with NEA. Wendy Abt, of Abt Associates, joined the described evaluation project two years after it was initiated and was an active participant in the debates over evaluation design and intentions chronicled in the book. This personal involvement and interest of authors in both books is a consideration in any critique.

The National Education Association is a personal history of the NEA during a time of great growth in the association and a number of crises. West begins with a very brief overview of the first 100 years of NEA and suggests some themes that West contends are long-standing NEA positions—for example, civil rights and equality, establishment of education at the cabinet level, states' rights over educational matters, and adaptation to changing social conditions. The rest of the book treats the years between 1957 and 1980, when West rose in NEA staff positions to head of the membership division, then to deputy and acting executive secretary of the NEA. The themes in this part of the book are change, bargaining, equality, legislative action, and unity. Each chapter attempts to document the movement of the NEA toward increasing political power and political action.

There are many good things about the book. Certainly, an insider's views of what transpired during a period of turmoil in education and society is a valuable addition to the literature on education. And NEA has obviously risen in political power and influence because of more teacher militancy and a late decision to enter political activities by endorsing candidates. The long-standing NEA goal of a Department of Education was achieved under President Carter, who received NEA support. That same department is now under serious threat and the NEA's activities will be interesting to observe.

Unfortunately, West is not a critical historian of the organization. He provides a broadly positive view of NEA achievements, downplays its errors and internal strifes, portrays AFT in negative stereotypes without equal criticism of NEA, and leaves the generally knowledgeable reader wondering if the insider ever understood the outsider's interpretations of NEA activities. For example, the NEA, according to West, was a strong advocate of civil rights and equality for women and minorities. While that is partly true, West does not raise a question about why it took until 1964 for the NEA to abolish dual representation of separate black and white teacher associations in the southern states. Even then it took until 1970 for all but two states to merge black and white teacher associations under the NEA. Similar critical questions are avoided with regard to women in the association. Another area West almost ignores is the protection of academic freedom for teachers, to which the NEA has given some attention, but very little, and certainly not in times of major censorship like the 1950s and again now. There are also some side trips into trivia that are distracting because the relationships are not shown. Grover Cleveland's election and the cornerstone of the Statue of Liberty are interesting artifacts, but add nothing to the book. In all, the book seems to be one of false modesty and NEA adulation.

Reforming Schools is also a personal account that moves from relating the political environment and interactions surrounding debate over proper evaluation approaches in a federally funded project, to elaborate graphic displays of the data. The first part of the book is very interesting to anyone concerned with research and evaluation. It points out the disparities between pure and real evaluation, between differing views of the right approach, between differing interpretations of changing federal grant guidelines, and between time periods. The first part is enlightening and seldom found in evaluation books. It is really a political treatise on the nexus between public grants for evaluating intervention to improve schools, and private concerns that contract to evaluate those projects.

The second part of the book provides data showing that the project appeared to fail in changing academic achievement of students in several schools in rural areas. Yet the research was flawed, as admitted openly in the book, and the intentions and approaches changed over time. The book illustrates major problems in conducting evaluation studies in schools without good controls and design. The self-justification in the book may be ignored to get at the broader issues of importance to those interested in improving program evaluation.

JACK L. NELSON

Rutgers University
New Brunswick
New Jersey

ECONOMICS

DIANE E. GOLD. *Housing Market Discrimination: Causes and Effects of Slum Formation.* Pp. x, 304. New York: Praeger, 1980. $26.95.

A man in the Crown Heights neighborhood of New York City had this problem: every morning he would see the same vicious dog asleep under his car parked at the curb, creating the problem of how to get in the car and close the door without getting his ankle torn. Dogs control the streets of Crown Heights. But that is only one kind of trouble. *Housing Market Discrimination* by Diane E. Gold is a litany of complaints about conditions of life in low-income neighborhoods of New York. Dr. Gold is an accounting professor at CUNY; the book appears to be the outgrowth of graduate student research.

Most of the book presents responses to a lengthy questionnaire that the author administered to a set of community spokespersons. These questions were not quantitative but rather along the line of, How has this neighborhood changed? The style is reportorial, and the prose is often colorful; a heap of junk and garbage is called "a sour effluvium of neglect and despair."

The list of complaints is long but never trivial. Drug addicts use apartment corridors as toilets. Colonies of rats thrive in filthy, abandoned houses. Medicaid mills rip off the taxpayer by issuing prescriptions in small quantities, forcing patients to return. Schoolchildren are not allowed to take books home to study. Recreation facilities have disappeared. Arson is commonplace. Building inspectors promise landlords that for fifteen dollars they won't come back. Police sit in their cars drinking beer. Absentee landlords and merchants systematically gouge the poor. Gentrification, particularly by militant Hasidics, crowds poor blacks out of the little territory they held.

There are complex syndromes. Former homeowners are now absentee landlords who neglect their properties to the extent that, for example, the fire department shuts off the tenant's heat because of a dangerous fixture. The frustrated tenant dumps garbage around the building. The landlord, claiming he intends to move back, evicts the tenant and in due course relets the building at a much higher rent. Because of the high rent, tenant families double up; they use too many electric appliances, overloading the circuits and causing a fire that destroys the building. Demand for remaining buildings is intensified, encouraging other landlords to skip maintenance.

Another sequence starts with pilfering in food stores by impoverished, idle youth. Nonresident storeowners react by raising prices and offering only damaged and unwholesome food. Resentment leads to more pilfering. Still another chain involved the construction of many high-density project buildings for welfare tenants in what had been a showcase middle-income black neighborhood, concomitantly with placement there of many foster children from other parts of the city. The area is effectively cut off from potential employment opportunity because it is remote and the bus fare is very high. Unemployed youth soon brought serious crime and drug problems. The high-density projects were not accompanied by increased garbage collections, so huge quantities of garbage sit in bags on the curbs until the bags are ripped open by uncontrolled dogs; then rats breed in the refuse.

Perhaps the most serious problem was caused by the Section 235 federal housing subsidy program, which held out the promise of homeownership to families of very limited income. A speculator could buy a dilapidated house for $3000, bribe an FHA appraiser to value it at $12,000 and get a mortgage for that amount on behalf of a hopeful but ill-informed welfare family; the bank would not check the family's credit because when default occurred—as it did in vast numbers of cases—the FHA would make up the loss and acquire the nearly worthless building, which would then sit empty, attracting vandals and filth, filling the neighborhood with rats, until one species or another of arsonist came along.

Gold reacts to this wealth of unpleasant information by suggesting that the facts about housing in U.S. cities substantiate a specific theory put forth some time ago by Karl Marx. The argument is not at all clear, but the upshot is that Gold decided to test the hypothesis that in slum neighborhoods, under capitalism, house rent and housing quality are negatively correlated, while in nonslum neighborhoods rent and quality are positively related. She developed elaborate census and public agency data for a set of test and control neighborhoods and extracted a set of factors by principal components analysis. Apparently these factors were then regressed against rents; the reader will have difficulty sharing Gold's view that the results are significant, or that they prove the Marxian thesis.

It may not matter much. Indeed, if she is right and conditions in these New York neighborhoods reflect a capitalist plot, that would mean the people responsible for this melange of evils know what they are doing. Unfortunately, New York City probably isn't a capitalist plot.

WALLACE F. SMITH
University of California
Berkeley

PENELOPE HARTLAND-THUNBERG. *Trading Blocs, U.S. Exports, and World Trade*. Pp. xiv, 197. Boulder, CO: Westview Press, 1980.

Trading blocs have proliferated worldwide during the postwar years. They have had significant impact on the volume and direction of international trade. This book analyzes these blocs in terms of their growth and impact on the U.S. international trade.

It begins with a succinct summary of the theory and practice of trading bloc formation. Basically, trading blocs emerge as a form of regional self-help organizations, in order to achieve economic goals. However, their effectiveness depends very much on political factors. Hartland-Thunberg illustrates this theme with a careful analysis of the emergence of the European Economic Community (EEC). Even though the United States was skeptical in the beginning, the idea was actively promoted on political grounds in the interest of stability. The EEC is well in the process of achieving its economic goals, although the political ones have proved somewhat more inscrutable. As for the United States, its overall trade with the rest of the world declined during the 1960s. Hartland-Thunberg argues that this decline is not to be attributed to the emergence of the EEC, but rather to the overall policy framework followed by the American administration. She points out that the overvalued U.S. dollar, a booming war-related domestic economy, and the presence of excess capacity in Europe and Japan are the factors that would go to explain the decline in exports by the United States during the 1960s.

Export performance continued to lag during the 1970s as well, but due to a different set of circumstances. She points to the wide divergence in the business cycle phases of the U.S. vis-à-vis the European economies, expansion in the EEC membership and the rising oil prices and related problems.

Even though U.S. exports to the EEC region declined, private investment in manufacturing capacity soared. This was partly due to the financial incentive that was inherent in locating facilities in the region and partly due to exchange rate considerations. The overall political climate is favorable for foreign investment, although codes of conduct and terms are not uniform. The EEC, however, has a goal of developing such an arrangement. In view of persistent overcapacity in the wake of the post-1974 energy regime, foreign investment in the EEC regions is likely to level off.

What are the immediate prospects for growth in U.S. international economic activities? Hartland-Thunberg is skeptical about any further spectacular growth. She argues that the higher energy prices have made the current structures obsolete. If nation-states take highly protectionist measures instead of adjusting to the reality of higher energy prices, she sees a slowdown in trade. She argues also that the prospects seem to point to a strategy of

import curtailment rather than export promotion as a means of bringing about a balance in international payments. She sees some evidence in support of such a development in the probable slowdown of conservative Middle Eastern countries in the wake of the fundamentalist Islamic revolution in Iran, a judgment that is highly speculative at this time.

Of all the trading blocs that are discussed in the book (a total of 13), only the EEC seems to have been successful. Why is this so? Hartland-Thunberg makes the argument that this outcome is due to the vision of its leaders. The trading blocs formed among the less developed countries have failed, basically because these countries have not been able to establish and articulate common points of interest. Further, the EEC countries are at similar levels of economic and political development, whereas, the LDCs that have attempted to form trading blocs are at different stages of development. An exception has been the surprising emergence of the Association of South East Asian countries (ASEAN), especially after the American pullout from Vietnam. Hartland-Thunberg sees a bright future for this group over the coming years.

The ingredients of success for trading blocs seem to be the following: visionary leaders, a more-or-less equal level of development in economic and political institutions, and a willingness to subordinate nationalist to blocwide interests. This is indeed a tall order to fill. Hartland-Thunberg does not tell us how to bring about such a winning combination. Nevertheless, her book remains a valuable contribution to an understanding of the role of trading blocs in international economic relations.

K. V. NAGARAJAN
Susquehanna University
Selinsgrove
Pennsylvania

DONALD PHARES. *Who Pays State and Local Taxes?* Pp. xviii, 240. Cambridge: Oelgeschlager, Gunn & Hain, 1980. $20.00.

In recent years citizen frustration with the burdens and supposed inequities of state and local taxation has set in motion pressures for change. Taxpayer revolts, like that which produced California's Proposition 13, seek to deal with this problem through strategies to initiate tax and expenditure cuts and limitations. In contrast, other tax reformers try to find ways of making the cost of governmental operations more fairly apportioned among citizens; lawsuits challenging systems of school finance, legislative relief for special groups of taxpayers, local property tax reassessment, and national debate over shifting greater financial responsibility of state and federal governments all reflect the growing search for tax equity. It is mainly for the latter group that Donald Phares has written this high-quality analysis of the burden imposed by various state/local taxes and tax systems and the differential claims they make on individuals of different income levels.

The most innovative feature of this volume is that it provides accurate and useful information about tax burdens and equity within the context of all 50 states. Past studies of this subject have shared the limitation of providing little information about the distributional impact of taxes within the federal system; either they assumed that the pattern of equity and burden estimated for all 50 states was broadly representative of each state, or they suggested that the pattern in one state was indicative of that in others. Phares points out that there are wide variations in state and local tax policy within the federal system and that reform efforts should not ignore them. Only when each state's tax mix and particular tax provisions as well as such things as variations in spending patterns, income distribution, and spatial tax flows are taken into account can the impact of public policy on private income be understood.

Phares examines the tax burden in each governmental sector by income class and evaluates the equity of specific taxes and tax systems in each of the 50 states. In a clear and craftsman-like way he explores who pays the cost of state and local operations, how burdensome it is, and which income groups are likely to benefit from changes in the existing tax structure. Providing extensive statistical tables on equity for each state and major taxes within a state, he enables the reader to make comparisons among states or in reference to national averages on a tax-by-tax bases.

Although many findings confirm conventional wisdom, the author's careful attention to the impact of tax policy within the context of federalism reveals some highly interesting patterns. For example, his data show that the singular progressive influence in the entire state-local tax system derives from the state individual income tax. But here there is a range between considerable progressivity in California and marked regressivity in New Hampshire. Further, the federal governmental structure permits substantial geographical shifting of tax burdens among states as well as through the offset of state and local tax burdens by the national tax system. The latter federal offset amounted to a $13.5 billion decrease in the burden attributable to state and local taxation, mainly in favor of higher-income groups. Similarly, many states that made heavy use of the income and sales tax were successful in exporting substantial tax burdens. For instance, Texas was among the largest net exporters in dollar terms ($563 million), while others were major net importers, such as New Jersey ($245 million).

The volume concludes with a discussion of the implications of the findings for reform in state and local tax policy as well as an overview of recent developments in this area. Given the many interesting patterns uncovered earlier, many readers will find these concluding comments all to brief. Although Phares concedes that the question of the impact of tax policy is far from closed (particularly because the expenditure side of governmental operations is not examined here), his data raise many unexplored questions about the actual limits of tax equity at the state and local levels. If state and local governments are constrained to compete in order to promote their economic well-being, how far can tax policy be driven by considerations of equity? Is the federal system itself to blame for so many inequitable taxes? Despite this limitation, Phares's study is a useful resource for all who are interested in the problems of state and local taxation.

PAUL KANTOR

Fordham University
Bronx
New York

BRUCE M. SHEFRIN. *The Future of U.S. Politics in an Age of Economic Limits.* Pp. xiv, 251. Boulder, CO: Westview Press, 1980. $24.50.

Shefrin's book begins with a trenchant critique of the U.S. political system. He argues that consensus politics blocks the serious consideration of any attempt to redistribute wealth. He questions whether the lack of class consciousness on the part of the U.S. working class is a result of its acceptance of the system or of a false consciousness that is a product of "manipulative socialization and institutionalized repression."

Until now, economic growth has allowed the United States to avoid the contradictions inherent in capitalism and put off any serious challenge to the present unequal stratification system. Opposition to the economic status quo "takes the form not of 'change the rules' but, rather, of 'deal me in.'" Shefrin then examines the limits-to-growth arguments and concludes that the physical environment presents strict limits to the ability of the U.S. economy to continue to grow. The choice between preserving environmental quality and promoting economic growth must be

made, and the performance of the economy is unlikely to improve. He also concludes, along neo-Marxist lines, that the economic structure of corporate capitalism is unable to sustain further growth.

Given his conclusion that the U.S. economy will not be able to cope with the environmental limits and internal contradictions he posits, Shefrin speculates about how the U.S. political-economic system will respond. He presents four possible scenarios based on his examination of differing social philosophies and political ideologies.

1. His first scenario is a continuation of the present liberal ideology, despite the contradictions described in the first half of his book. This will result in an incremental change toward short-term improvement or slow deterioration, but will not solve the basic political and economic problems facing the country.

2. The neo-Marxist point of view presents a coherent critique of the status quo and has the ability to act as a rallying point for many of those disaffected by the inequities in the United States. But Shefrin is not optimistic about the ability of a leftist revolution to create a substantially more egalitarian alternative in the U.S. context or to solve the limits-to-growth dilemma.

3. Corporate conservativism would aim at redistributing wealth, but toward the rich rather than the poor. In its extreme form, this "friendly fascism" would probably not be able to sustain the degree of elite coordination necessary to enable such a system of domination to persist.

4. Ironically, Shefrin's scenario of traditional conservativism seems to present the best match to the imperatives of the limits-to-growth dilemma. It emphasizes social stability, scaled-down expectations, and the acceptance of social and economic stratification. At the same time, it would view the environment as part of the larger societal system and thus impose some limits on the economic elite. Its values are neo-nostalgic, antigrowth, and anti-big business.

Shefrin does not advocate any of these alternatives, though his analysis throughout the book reflects political values that are generally left of center in the U.S. context. Rather, he presents these scenarios to widen the consideration of alternatives and force the United States to confront openly the need to address the crisis in our political economy.

While the first half of the book repeats the leftist structural critique of U.S. society that has often been made before, he summarizes and synthesizes the arguments well. His contribution, however, is in bringing together the arguments from different perspectives: political, economic, philosophical, sociological, and biological. His purpose is to force the issue so that the future of U.S. politics will be explicitly confronted and chosen, rather than muddled into. He argues that the proponents of alternative views of the future present their own analyses as technological, economic, or environmental imperatives. This narrows the realm of politics and thought, and thus choice. Shefrin wants to open the debate by demonstrating that the United States can, and should, make explicit value choices about its political and economic future.

JAMES P. PFIFFNER
California State University
Fullerton

JOHN F. WITTE. *Democracy, Authority, and Alienation in Work: Participation in an American Corporation.* Pp. xii, 216. Chicago: University of Chicago Press, 1980.

RICHARD EDWARDS. *Contested Terrain: The Transformation of the Workplace in the Twentieth Century.* Pp. ix, 261. New York: Basic Books. Paperbound, $4.95.

These two books converge on the issue of industrial democracy, but differ radically in method, assumptions, and conclusions. Witte observes limited demand for industrial democracy, not enhanced by participation, and dubious

effects on productivity. Edwards claims the contrary. They serve as mutual antidotes.

Witte reports on a three-year case study, with references to related experience, mainly abroad, in the context of an extensive literature. It is a sophisticated and thought-provoking book. Experiments in the firm where he was a participant-observer included a worker-management central council, special-purpose committees, and shop-floor participation. His criteria for performance were (1) support for the idea of worker participation, (2) competence in decision-making, (3) ability to overcome obstacles of time and communication, and (4) realization of outcomes based on expectations. The experience clearly demonstrated worker competence. Support for participation did not increase, and other results were equivocal. The activists proved to be atypical workers with high ambitions and expectations who thus were not perfect representatives. Measures of alienation were uncorrelated with participation.

The dilemma of self-managing work groups is that complexity of the work environment increases the possibility of meaningful participation but also the need for coordination, the potential for conflict, and pressure to select a leader and defer to authority. The hierarchial and democratic systems of authority are in conflict. The former is meritocratic, stresses human differences, assumes that motivation is individual, and grants rewards and incentives on an individual basis. The latter is premised on political and considerable substantive equality and assumes group motives and rewards. But individual achievement remains the central value in this country.

As a mechanism for resolving conflicts arising from individual purposes, democracy is inapplicable to goal-oriented organizations. Democratic theory needs to be developed that recognizes the importance of achieving specific ends. Apathy and upward mobility are the deadly enemies of industrial democracy. The only, slim, prospect Witte sees is based on frustrated ambitions of educated workers and the possibility of a greater sense of community in the workplace.

Edwards's purpose is to "explore the dynamics of class conflict within the labor process." Relying heavily on the history and operations of nine large companies, he traces the evolution of corporate control of labor from simple entrepreneurial control—still characteristics of firms in the so-called periphery—to structural control operating either through the technology of production or through the bureaucratic structure of company rules. Aspects of this evolution are growth in size of firm, development of monopoly capitalism, the dialectic of worker resistance, reform movements, and the shift of the class struggle to the political arena as the "burden of suppressing labor shifted from individual employers to agencies of the federal government."

Technical and bureaucratic control replaced supervisor command after the failure of other attempts to obtain worker loyalty: corporate welfare programs, scientific management, company unions. Corresponding to the three types of control are three types of labor market: secondary, subordinate primary, and independent primary. These in turn match up with three fractions of the "working class"; the working poor, the traditional proletariat, and the middle layers. But bureaucratic control generates its own contradictions; by establishing job security and ladders of advancement to break up the sense of solidarity among workers, it creates conditions under which demands for workplace democracy flourish and "democracy at work requires socialism."

All this is interesting, much of it useful and often insightful. But its credibility is seriously prejudiced by the author's world view through the distorting prism of class struggle and the dubious and often mind-boggling attempt to reify its shopworn nomenclature in the American context. Labor troubles that peaked shortly after World War I were a titanic struggle whose outcome was a holocaust. Classes and class conflict in the Marxist sense are assumed, apparent evidence to the contrary is dismissed and lamented. Motives are by attribution, causal relations by assertion.

CHARLES T. STEWART
George Washington University
Washington, D.C.

OTHER BOOKS

AMOSS, PAMELA T. and STEVAN HARRELL, eds. *Other Ways of Growing Old: Anthropological Perspectives.* Pp. xxiv, 270. Stanford, CA: Stanford University Press, 1981. $18.50.

AUSTIN, M. M. and P. VIDAL-NAQUET. *Economic & Social History of Ancient Greece: An Introduction.* Pp. xv, 397. Berkeley: University of California Press, 1981. $27.50. Paperbound, $8.95.

AVENI, ANTHONY P. *Skywatchers of Ancient Mexico.* Pp. x, 355. Austin: University of Texas Press, 1980. $30.00.

BEDGGOOD, DAVID. *Rich and Poor in New Zealand.* Pp. 178. Winchester, MA: Allen & Unwin, 1980. $21.00. Paperbound, $11.50.

BELL, IAN. *The Dominican Republic.* Pp. xv, 392. Boulder, CO: Westview Press, 1981. $35.00.

BELL, ROBERT. *Contemporary Social Problems.* Pp. xiii, 559. Homewood, IL: Dorsey, 1980. $19.95.

BELOFF, MAX and GILLIAN PEELE. *The Government of the United Kingdom: Political Authority in a Changing Society.* Pp. x, 438. New York: Norton, 1980. $17.95. Paperbound, $6.95.

BENEVENISTE, GUY. *Regulation and Planning: The Case of Environmental Politics.* Pp. xvi, 207. San Francisco: Boyd & Fraser, n.d. No price.

BESSETTE, JOSEPH M. and JEFFREY TULIS, eds. *The Presidency in the Constitutional Order.* Pp. xii, 349. Baton Rouge: Louisiana State University Press, 1981. No price.

BEST, JOHN W. *Research in Education.* Pp. ix, 431. Englewood Cliffs, NJ: Prentice-Hall, 1981. $18.95.

BIALER, SEWERYN, ed. *The Domestic Context of Soviet Foreign Policy.* Pp. xviii, 441. Boulder, CO: Westview Press, 1981. $35.

BLOOM, MARTIN. *Primary Prevention: The Possible Science.* Pp. xi, 242. Englewood Cliffs, NJ: Prentice-Hall, 1981. No price.

BOUDON, RAYMOND. *The Crisis in Sociology: Problems of Sociological Epistemology.* Pp. vii, 285. New York: Columbia University Press, 1980. $25.00.

BOWKER, LEE H., ed. *Women and Crime in America.* Pp. vi, 433. New York: Macmillan, 1981. No price.

BRAYBON, GAIL. *Women Workers in the First World War: The British Experience.* Pp. 244. Totowa, NJ: Barnes & Noble Books, 1981. $24.50.

BROWN, E. RICHARD. *Rockefeller Medicine Men: Medicine and Capitalism in America.* Pp. xii, 283. Berkeley: University of California Press, 1981. $5.95.

BROWN, MERLE E. *Double Lyric: Divisiveness and Communal Creativity in Recent English Poetry.* Pp. xv, 236. Columbia University Press, 1980. $20.00.

BRUGGER, BILL. *China: Liberation and Transformation 1942-1962.* Pp. 288. Totowa, NJ: Barnes & Noble Books, 1981. $27.50.

BRUGGER, BILL. *China: Radicalism to Revisionism 1962-1979.* Pp. 275. Totowa, NJ: Barnes & Noble Books, 1981. $27.50.

BUCHANAN, JAMES M. and G. F. THIRLO, eds. *L.S.E. Essays On Cost.* Pp. 290. New York: New York University Press, 1981. $20.00. Paperbound, $7.00.

BURNS, JAMES MacGREGOR, J. W. PELTASON, and THOMAS E. CRONIN. *Government by the People.* 11th ed. Pp. xv, 830. Englewood Cliffs, NJ: Prentice-Hall, 1981. No price.

CARLSON, JOHN E., MARIE L. LASSEY, and WILLIAM R. LASSEY. *Rural Society and Environment in America.* Pp. xxii, 425. New York: McGraw-Hill, 1981. $18.95.

CARTY, R. KENNETH and W. PETER WARD. *Entering the Eighties: Canada in Crisis.* Pp. 160. New York: Oxford Unviersity Press, 1981. $5.95.

CHELF, CARL P. *Public Policymaking in America: Difficult Choices, Limited Solutions.* Pp. x, 406. Santa Monica, CA: Scott, Foresman, 1981. No price.

CHRISTENSON, REO M. et al. *Ideologies and Modern Politics.* Pp. x, 260. New York: Harper & Row, 1981. No price.

CHUDACOFF, HOWARD P. *The Evolution of American Urban Society.* Pp. viii, 312. Englewood Cliffs, NJ: Prentice-Hall, 1981. $11.95.

COFFIN, FRANK M. *The Ways of a Judge: Reflections from the Federal Appellate Bench.* Pp. xiv, 273. Boston: Houghton Mifflin, 1980. $10.95.

CROMPTON, MARGARET. *Repecting Children: Special Work with Young People.* Pp. 246. Beverly Hills, CA: Sage Publications, 1980. $20.00/ $9.95.

DAVIS, ALLEN F., ed. *For Better or Worse: The American Influence in the World.* Pp. xiv, 195. Westport, CT: Greenwood Press, 1981. No price.

de MACEDO, JORGE BRAGA, and SIMON SERFATY, eds. *Portugal Since the Revolution: Economic and Political Perspectives.* Pp. xiv, 217. Boulder, CO: Westview Press, 1981. $16.00.

DELUCA, ANTHONY R. *Great Power Rivalry at the Turkish Straits.* Pp. viii, 216. New York: Columbia University Press, 1981. $16.00.

DOENECKE, JUSTUS D. *The Presidencies of James A. Garfield & Chester A. Arthur.* Pp. xiii, 229. Lawrence, KS: Regents Press of Kansas, 1981. $15.00.

DONIA, ROBERT J. *Islam Under the Double Eagle: The Muslims of Bosnia and Hercegovina, 1878-1914.* Pp. xxii, 237. New York: Columbia University Press, 1981. $17.50.

DOUGHERTY, JAMES E. and ROBERT L. PFALTZGRAFF, Jr. *Contending Theories of International Relations.* Pp. xvi, 592. New York: Harper & Row, 1980. No price. Paperbound.

DU PREEZE, PETER. *The Politics of Identity: Ideology and the Human Image.* Pp. ix, 178. New York: St. Martin's Press, 1980. $25.00.

DYE, THOMAS R. *Understanding Public Policy.* Pp. xii, 401. Englewood Cliffs, NJ: Prentice-Hall, 1981. $16.95.

DYSON, KENNETH. *The State Tradition in Western Europe.* Pp. viii, 310. New York: Oxford University Press, 1980. $19.95.

EDDY, WILLIAM B. *Public Organization Behavior and Development.* Pp. xiii, 210. Englewood Cliffs, NJ: Prentice-Hall, 1981. $12.95. Paperbound, $8.95.

EIDLIN, FRED. *The Logic of Normalization.* Pp. iv, 278. New York: Columbia University Press, 1980. $20.00.

EMBER, CAROL R. and MELVIN EMBER. *Anthropology.* Pp. xxiii, 582. Englewood, NJ: Prentice-Hall, 1981. No price.

ENGELS, DONALD W. *Alexander the Great and the Logistics of the Macedonian Army.* Pp. xiv, 194. Berkeley: University of California Press, 1981. $4.95. Paperbound.

GARVIN, CHARLES D. *Contemporary Group Work.* Pp. xiv, 306. Englewood Cliffs, NJ: Prentice-Hall, 1981. $14.95.

GIBSON, JANICE T. *Psychology for the Classroom.* Pp. xxiv, 568. Englewood Cliffs, NJ: Prentice-Hall, 1980. No price.

GITTELL, MARILYN. *Limits to Citizen Participation: The Decline of Community Organizations.* Vol. 109, Sage Library of Social Research. Pp. 280. Beverly Hills, CA: Sage Publications, 1980. $20.00. Paperbound, $9.95.

GORDUS, JEANNE PRIAL. *Leaving Early: Perspectives and Problems in Current Retirement Practice and Policy.* Pp. ix, 88. Kalamazoo, MI: W. E. Upjohn Institute for Employment Research, 1980. $4.00.

GYSBERS, NORMAN C. and EARL J. MOORE. *Improving Guidance Programs.* Pp. x, 212. Englewood Cliffs, NJ: Prentice-Hall, 1981. $12.95.

HALPER, THOMAS. *Power, Politics, & American Democracy.* Pp. xxi, 458.

Santa Monica, CA: Scott, Foresman, 1981. No price.

HAMMOND, THOMAS H. and JACK H. KNOTT. *A Zero-Based Look at Zero-Base Budgeting.* Pp. xii, 135. New Brunswick, NJ: Transaction Books, 1980. $14.95.

HASKINS, RON and JAMES J. GALLAGHER. *Care and Education of Young Children in America.* Pp. viii, 216. Norwood, NJ: Ablex, 1980. $19.95.

HELLERSTEIN, ERNA OLAFSON, LESLIE PARKER HUME, KAREN M. OFFEN, eds. *Victorian Women: A Documentary Account of Women's Lives in Nineteenth Century England, France, and the United States.* Pp. xvi, 534. Stanford, CA: Stanford University Press, 1981. $27.50. Paperbound, $11.95.

MICKEY, D. J. and J. E. DOHERTY. *A Dictionary of Irish History Since 1800.* Pp. 615. Totowa, NJ: Barnes & Noble Books, 1981. $38.50.

HILLENBRAND, MARTIN J., ed. *The Future of Berlin.* Pp. 313. Montclair, NJ: Allanheld, Osmun, 1980. $27.50.

HIRSCHI, TRAVIS and MICHAEL GOTTFREDSON, eds. *Understanding Crime: Current Theory and Research.* Pp. 144. Beverly Hills, CA: Sage Publications, 1980. No price.

HIRSCMAN, ALBERT O. *National Power and the Structure of Foreign Trade.* Pp. xxii, 172. Berkeley: University of California Press, 1981. $15.50.

HOFFMAN, STANLEY. *Duties Beyond Borders: On the Limits and Possibilities of Ethical International Politics.* Pp. xiv, 252. Syracuse, NY: Syracuse University Press, 1981. $18.00. Paperbound, $9.95.

HOLZER, MARC and ELLEN DOREE ROSEN, eds. *Current Cases in Public Administration.* Pp. xvi, 352. New York: Harper & Row, 1981. No price.

HORNE, PETER. *Women in Law Enforcement.* Pp. xvii, 269. Springfield, IL: Charles C Thomas, 1980. $15.00. Paperbound, $10.50.

HORNER, MARTINA S. *The Quality of American Life in the Eighties.* Pp.

140. Washington, DC: U.S. Government Printing Office, 1980. No price.

HOWARD, DONALD S. and WALTER B. WRISTON. *Evolving Concepts of Bank Capital Management.* Pp. 64. New York: Citicorp, 1980. No price. Paperbound.

HOWARDS, IRVING, HENRY P. BREHM, and SAAD Z. NAGI. *Disability: From Social Problem to Federal Program.* Pp. xiii, 171. New York: Praeger, 1980. No price.

HUGHES, COLIN A. *The Government of Queensland.* Pp. xi, 322. Lawrence, MA: Queensland University Press, 1980. $19.25. Paperbound.

INCIARDI, JAMES A. and CHARLES E. FAUPEL, eds. *History and Crime: Implications for Criminal Justice Policy.* Pp. 288. Beverly Hills, CA: Sage Publications, 1980. $20.00. Paperbound, $9.95.

INLOW, E. BURKE. *Shahanshah: The Monarchy of Iran.* Pp. xxi, 279. Delhi, India: Motilal Banarsidass, 1979. No price.

IRISH, MARIAN D., JAMES W. PROTHRO, and RICHARD J. RICHARDSON. *The Politics of American Democracy.* Pp. x, 501. Englewood Cliffs, NJ: Prentice-Hall, 1981. No price.

JORDAN, DAVID P. *The King's Trial: Louis XVI vs. The French Revolution.* Pp. xx, 275. Berkeley: University of California Press, 1981. $14.95. Paperbound, $5.95.

KAUFMANN, GEIR. *Imagery, Language and Cognition.* Pp. 192. New York: Columbia University Press, 1980. $19.00. Paperbound.

KEDDIE, NIKKI. *Iran: Religion, Politics & Society: Collected Essays.* Pp. x, 243. Totowa, NJ: Frank Cass, 1980. $29.50. Paperbound, $9.95.

KEDOURIE, ELIE and SYLVIA G. HAIM, eds. *Modern Egypt: Studies in Politics and Society.* Pp. 136. Totowa, NJ: Frank Cass, 1980. $25.00.

KEDOURIE, ELIE and SYLVIA G. HAIM, eds. *Towards a Modern Iran: Studies in Thought, Politics, and*

Society. Pp. ix, 262. Totowa, NJ: Frank Cass, 1980. No price.

KONRAD, HERMAN W. *A Jesuit Hacienda in Colonial Mexico: Santa Lucia, 1576-1767.* Pp. xii, 455. Stanford, CA: Stanford University Press, 1980. $28.50.

KUEHN, THOMAS J. and ALAN L. PORTER, eds. *Science, Technology, and National Policy.* Pp. 530. Ithaca, NY: Cornell University Press, 1981. $35.00. Paperbound, $9.95.

LA GORY, MARK and JOHN PIPKIN. *Urban Social Space.* Pp. xii, 356. Belmont, CA: Wadsworth, 1981. No price.

LABAW, PATRICIA. *Advanced Questionnaire Design.* Pp. xiv, 183. Cambridge, MA: Abt Books, 1980. No price.

LAMB, ROBERT, WILLIAM G. ARMSTRONG, Jr., and KAROLYN R. MORIGI. *Business, Media, and the Law: The Troubled Confluence.* Pp. xiii, 137. New York: Columbia University Press, 1980. $15.00.

LERNER, JANET, CAROL MARDELL-CZUDNOWSKI, and DOROTHEA GOLDENBERG. *Special Education for the Early Childhood Years.* Pp. xii, 368. Englewood Cliffs, NJ: Prentice-Hall, 1981. $17.95.

LEVINE, MURRAY. *From State Hospital to Psychiatric Center.* Pp. xx, 139. Lexington, MA: D. C. Heath, 1980. No price.

LEWIN, LEIF. *Governing Trade Unions in Sweden.* Pp. vi, 180. Cambridge, MA: Harvard University Press, 1980. $20.00.

LIDZ, CHARLES W. and ANDREW L. WALKER. *Heroin, Deviance and Morality.* Vol. 112, Sage Library of Social Research. Pp. 269. Beverly Hills, CA: Sage Publications, 1980. $20.00. Paperbound, $9.95.

MANSFIELD, EDWIN, ed. *Economics: Readings, Issues and Cases.* Pp. xviii, 440. New York: Norton, 1980. $5.95.

McWHINNEY, EDWARD. *Conflict and Compromise: International Law and World Order in a Revolutionary Age.* Pp. 160. New York: Holmes &

Meier, 1981. $17.50. Paperbound, $8.50.

MISHAN, E. J. *Introduction to Normative Economics.* Pp. xxi, 548. New York: Oxford University Press, 1981. $14.95. Paperbound.

MOMMSEN, WOLFGANG J. *Theories of Imperialism.* Pp. x, 180. New York: Random House, 1981. $9.95.

MOREHOUSE, SARAH McCALLY. *State Politics, Parties and Policy.* Pp. xiii, 527. New York: Holt, Rinehart & Winston, 1980. No price.

MYERS, LENA WRIGHT. *Black Women: Do They Cope Better?* Pp. x, 118. Englewood Cliffs, NJ: Prentice-Hall, 1980. $9.95. Paperbound, $4.95.

PALEN, J. JOHN. *City Scenes: Problems and Prospects.* 2d ed. Pp. ix, 300. Boston: Little, Brown, 1981. No price.

PALM, RISA. *The Geography of American Cities.* Pp. xiii, 365. New York: Oxford University, 1981. $18.95.

PAIVIO, ALLAN and IAN BEGG. *Psychology of Language.* Pp. xiv, 417. Englewood Cliffs, NJ: Prentice-Hall, 1981. $19.95.

PATSOURAS, LOUIS and JACK RAY THOMAS, eds. *Varieties and Problems of 20th Century Socialism.* Pp. xxi, 189. Chicago: Nelson-Hall, 1981. $15.95. Paperbound, $8.95.

PETERSON, SIDNEY. *The Dark of the Screen.* Pp. 174. New York: Columbia University Press, 1980. $22.50. Paperbound, $9.00.

PHILLIPS, PAUL. *Marx and Engels on Law and Laws.* Pp. xiii, 238. Totowa, NJ: Barnes & Noble Books, 1981. $27.50.

PIERSON, FRANK C. *The Minimum Level of Unemployment and Public policy.* Pp. vii, 194. Kalamazoo, MI: W. E. Upjohn Institute for Employment Research, 1980. $8.50. Paperbound, $5.50.

PIPPIN, JAMES A. *Developing Casework Skills,* Vol. 15, Sage Human Services Guides. Pp. 159. Beverly Hills, CA: Sage Publications, 1980. $8.00.

PLANT, RAYMOND, HARRY LESSER, and PETER TAYLOR-GOOBY. *Political Philosophy and*

Social Welfare: Essays on the Normative Basis of Welfare Provision. Pp. xiii, 260. London, Boston, and Henley: Routledge & Kegan Paul, 1980. $27.50. Paperbound, $15.00.

Politics and Power Editorial Board. *New Perspectives on Socialist Politics.* Pp. vi, 232. Boston: Routledge & Kegan Paul, 1980. $12.50. Paperbound.

RAPTIS, MICHAEL. *Socialism, Democracy & Self Management.* Pp. 208. New York: St. Martin's Press, 1980. $22.50.

Report of the Panel on the Quality of American Life. *The Quality Of American Life In The Eighties.* Pp. 140. Washington, DC: Superintendent of Documents, 1980. No price.

ROBINSON, JOAN. *What Are the Questions? and Other Essays.* Pp. xiv, 202. Armonk, NY: M. E. Sharp, 1981. $15.00. Paperbound, $6.95.

ROBINSON, PAUL W. *Fundamentals of Experimental Psychology.* 2d ed. Pp. xv, 415. Englewood Cliffs, NJ: Prentice-Hall, 1981. No price.

ROSENTHAL, ALAN. *Legislative Life: People, Process, and Performance in the States.* Pp. xiii, 354. New York: Harper & Row, 1981. No price.

RUBINSTEIN, ALVIN S. *Soviet Foreign Policy Since World War II.* Pp. viii, 296. Englewood Cliffs, NJ: Prentice-Hall, 1981. $15.00. Paperbound, $9.95.

SACK, ROBERT DAVID. *Conceptions of Space in Social Thought: A Geographic Perspective.* Pp. ix, 231. Minneapolis: University of Minnesota Press, 1981. $27.50. Paperbound, $9.95.

SAFFELL, DAVID C. *The Politics of American National Government.* Pp. xvi, 584. Englewood Cliffs, NJ: Prentice-Hall, 1981. $12.95.

SAGARIN, EDWARD, ed. *Taboos in Criminology.* Pp. 149. Beverly Hills, CA: Sage Publications, 1980. $15.00. Paperbound, $7.50.

SAMUEL, RAPHAEL, ed. *People's History and Socialist Theory.* Pp. lvi, 417. Boston: Routledge & Kegan Paul, 1981. $32.50. Paperbound, $19.95.

SANDELOWSKI, MARGARETE. *Women, Health, and Choice.* Pp. ix, 278. Englewood Cliffs, NJ: Prentice-Hall, 1981. $11.95. Paperbound.

SARKESIAN, SAM C. *Combat Effectiveness: Cohesion, Stress, and the Volunteer Army.* Pp. 305. Beverly Hills, CA: Sage Publications, 1980. $22.50. Paperbound, $9.95.

SCANZONI, JOHN and MAXIMILIANE SZINOVACZ. *Family Decision Making: A Developmental Sex Role Model,* Vol. III, Sage Library of Social Research. Pp. 309. Beverly Hills, CA: Sage Publications, 1980. $20.00. Paperbound, $9.95.

SCHAEFFER, K. H. and ELLIOTT SCLAR. *Access for All.* Pp. xi, 182. New York: Columbia University Press, 1980. $15.00. Paperbound, $5.00.

SCHERER, ROSS P. *American Denominational Organization: A Sociological View.* Pp. viii, 378. Pasadena, CA: William Carey Library, 1980. $14.95.

SCHUMAN, DAVID. *A Preface to Politics.* Pp. xx, 250. Lexington, MA: D. C. Heath, 1981. No price.

SCHWAB, GEORGE, ed. *Eurocommunism: The Ideological and Political-Theoretical Foundations.* Pp. xxvi, 325. Westport, CT: Greenwood Press, 1981. $25.00.

SCOTT, W. RICHARD. *Organizations: Rational, Natural, and Open Systems.* Pp. xviii, 381. Englewood Cliffs, NJ: Prentice-Hall, 1981. $18.95.

SHAVER, KELLY G. *Principles of Social Psychology.* Pp. xvi, 572. Englewood Cliffs, NJ: Prentice-Hall, 1981. $19.95.

SHEHADEH, RAJA with JONATHAN KUTTAB. *The West Bank and the Rule of Law.* Pp. 128. New York: International Commission of Jurists, 1980. No price.

SHOTOKI, JINNO OF KITABATAKE CHIKAFUSA. Translated by H. Paul Varley. *A Chronicle of Gods and Sovereigns.* Pp. 300. New York: Columbia University Press, 1980. $22.50.

SHRIVASTAVA, B. K. and THOMAS W. CASSTEVENS, eds. *American*

Government and Politics. Pp. xii, 328. Atlantic Highlands, NJ: Humanities Press, 1981. $20.00.

SHUMELDA, J. *Quo Vadis Homine: Where Do You Go?* Pp. v, 196. San Francisco: Alchemy Books, 1980. No price.

SILVERMAN, SYDAL, ed. *Totems and Teachers: Perspectives on the History of Anthropology.* Pp. xv, 322. New York: Columbia University Press, 1981. $22.50. Paperbound, $8.00.

SIMON, HERBERT A. *The Sciences of the Artificial.* 2d ed. Pp. xiii, 247. Cambridge, MA: MIT Press, 1981. $4.95. Paperbound.

SIMON, MAURICE D. and ROGER E. KANET, eds. *Background to Crisis: Policy and Politics in Gierak's Poland.* Pp. xviii, 418. Boulder, CO: Westview Press, 1981. $27.50.

SINGH, ELEN C. *The Spitsbergen (Svalbard) Question: United States Foreign Policy, 1907-1935.* Pp. iv, 244. New York: Columbia University Press, 1981. $23.00.

SMITH, JOAN. *Social Issues and the Social Order: The Contradictions of Capitalism.* Pp. xiii, 381. Englewood Cliffs, NJ: Prentice-Hall, 1981. $11.95.

SPEIER, HANS. *From the Ashes of Disgrace: A Journal from Germany, 1945-1955.* Pp. 336. Amherst: University of Massachusetts Press, 1981. $20.00.

STANKOVIC, SLOBODAN. *The End of the Tito Era: Yugoslavia's Dilemmas.* Pp. xiv, 154. Stanford, CA: Hoover Institution, 1981. $9.95.

STEIN, THEODORE J. *Social Work Practice in Child Welfare.* Pp. viii, 279. Englewood Cliffs, NJ: Prentice-Hall, 1981. No price.

STEINER, KURT, ELLIS S. KRAUSS, and SCOTT B. FLANAGAN, eds. *Political Opposition and Local Politics in Japan.* Pp. ix, 486. Princeton, NJ: Princeton University Press, 1981. $30.00. Paperbound, $9.95.

STROMBERG, ROLAND N. *European Intellectual History Since 1789.* 3d ed. Pp. xii, 386. Englewood Cliffs, NJ: Prentice-Hall, 1980. $13.95. Paperbound.

STROUT, CUSHING. *The Veracious Imagination: Essays on American History, Literature, and Biography.* Pp. xiv, 301. Middletown, CT: Wesleyan Press, 1981. $17.50.

SUDA, ZDENEK. *Zealots and Rebels: A History of the Ruling Communist Party of Czechoslovakia.* Pp. xiv, 412. Stanford, CA: Hoover Institution Press, 1980. $8.95. Paperbound.

SULLIVAN, JOHN L., ed. *Applied Regression: An Introduction.* Series: Quantitative Applications in the Social Sciences. Vol. 22. Pp. 79. Beverly Hills, CA: Sage Publications, 1980. $3.50. Paperbound.

SULLIVAN, JOHN L., ed. *Interrupted Time Series Analysis.* Pp. 96. Beverly Hills, CA: Sage Publications, 1980. $4.00. Paperbound.

SULLIVAN, JOHN L., ed. *Log-Linear Models:* Pp. 80. Beverly Hills, CA: Sage Publications, 1980. $4.00. Paperbound.

TAFT, PHILIP. *Organizing Dixie: Alabama Workers in the Industrial Era.* Pp. xxv, 228. Westport, CT: Greenwood Press, 1981. $35.00.

The Three Per Cent Solution and the Futures of NATO. Pp. xv, 118. Philadelphia, PA: Foreign Policy Research Institute, 1981. $6.95.

THIMM, ALFRED L. *The False Promise of Codetermination: The Changing Nature of European Workers' Participation.* Pp. xiv, 301. Lexington, MA: D. C. Heath, 1980. $27.95.

TIVEV, LEONARD, ed. *The Nation-State: The Formation of Modern Politics.* Pp. x, 214. New York: St. Martin's Press, 1981. $27.50.

TRAVERS, JEFFREY and BARBARA DILLON GOODSON. *Research Results of the National Day Care Study.* Pp. 256. Cambridge, MA: Abt Books, 1981. $20.00.

TREFOUSSE, HANS L., ed. *Germany and America: Essays on Problems of International Relations and Immigration.* Pp. xiv, 247. New York: Columbia University Press, 1981. $23.00.

TRIBBLE, EDWIN, ed. *A President in Love: The Courtship Letters of Woodrow Wilson & Edith Bolling Galt.* Pp. xxiv, 225. Boston: Houghton Mifflin, 1981. $11.95.

Publisher's Note: The following information is printed in accordance with U.S. postal regulations: Statement of Ownership, Management and Circulation (required by 39 U.S.C. 3685). 1. Title of Publication: THE ANNALS OF THE AMERICAN ACADEMY OF POLITICAL AND SOCIAL SCIENCE. 1A. Publication No.: 026060. 2. Date of Filing: October 2, 1981. 3. Frequency of Issue: Bimonthly. 3A. No. of Issues Published Annually: 6. 3B. Annual Subscription Price: institutions, $35.00 (paper), $41.00 (cloth); individuals, $20.00 (paper), $26.00 (cloth). 4. Location of Known Office of Publication: 3937 Chestnut Street, Philadelphia, PA 19104. 5. Location of the Headquarters or General Business Offices of the Publishers: 3937 Chestnut Street, Philadelphia, PA 19104. 6. Names and Complete Addresses of Publisher, Editor, and Managing Editor: Publisher: The American Academy of Political and Social Science, 3937 Chestnut Street, Philadelphia, PA 19104; Editor: Richard D. Lambert, 3937 Chestnut Street, Philadelphia, PA 19104; Managing Editor: None. 7. Owner (If owned by a corporation, its name and address must be stated and also immediately thereunder the names and addresses of stockholders owning or holding 1% or more of total amount of stock. If now owned by a corporation, the names and addresses of the individual owners must be given. If owned by a partnership or other unincorporated firm, its name and address, as well as that of each individual must be given.): The American Academy of Political and Social Science, 3937 Chestnut Street, Philadelphia, PA 19104. 8. Known Bondholders, Mortgagees, and Other Security Holders Owning or Holding 1% or More of Total Amount of Bonds, Mortgages or Other Securities: None. 9. For Completion by Nonprofit Organizations Authorized to Mail at Special Rates (Section 132.122, PSM): Has not changed during preceding 12 months.

	Av. No. Copies Each Issue During Preceding 12 Months	Actual No. of Copies of Single Issue Published Nearest to Filing Date
10. Extent and Nature of Circulation		
A. Total no. copies printed (net press run)	11,142	11,142
B. Paid circulation:		
1. Sales through dealers and carriers, street vendors and counter sales	4,473	4,473
2. Mail subscriptions	3,741	3,741
C. Total paid circulation (sum of 10B1 and 10B2)	8,214	8,214
D. Free distribution by mail, carrier or other means: samples, complimentary, and other free copies	268	268
E. Total distribution (sum of C & D)	8,482	8,482
F. Copies not distributed:		
1. Office use, left-over, unaccounted, spoiled after printing	2,660	2,660
2. Returns from news agents	0	0
G. Total (sum of E, F1 and 2—should equal net press run shown in A)	11,142	11,142

11. I certify that the statements made by me above are correct and complete. (Signed) Ingeborg Hessler, Business Manager. 12. 39 U.S.C. 3626 provides in pertinent part: "No person who would have been entitled to mail matter under former section 4359 of this title shall mail such matter at the rates provided under this subsection unless he files annually with the Postal Service a written request for permission to mail matter at such rates." In accordance with the provisions of this statute, I hereby request permission to mail the publication named in item 1 at the reduced postage rates presently authorized by 39 U.S.C. 3626. (Signed) Ingeborg Hessler, Business Manager.

INDEX

AMERICAN JOURNAL OF

POLITICAL

SCIENCE

Herb Asher and Herb Weisberg, Editors

One of the leading journals of political
science in the country, publishing works
in American Politics, and methodology,
international politics, comparative
politics and political philosophy.

JOURNALS DEPARTMENT
UNIVERSITY OF TEXAS PRESS
Box 7819
Austin, Texas 78712

RATES:
Individuals $15.00
Institutions $30.00

THE ANNALS

of The American Academy *of* Political *and* Social Science

RICHARD D. LAMBERT, *Editor*   **ALAN W. HESTON,** *Associate Editor*

TECHNOLOGY TRANSFER: New Issues, New Analysis
   Guest Editors: Alan W. Heston and Howard Pack
   THE ANNALS Volume 458 November 1981

THE ENVIRONMENT AND THE QUALITY OF LIFE: A World View
   Guest Editor: Marvin E. Wolfgang
   THE ANNALS Volume 444 July 1979

ETHNIC CONFLICT IN THE WORLD TODAY
   Guest Editor: Martin O. Heisler
   THE ANNALS Volume 433 September 1977 – in paper only

AFRICA IN TRANSITION
   Guest Editor: Marvin E. Wolfgang
   THE ANNALS Volume 432 July 1977 – in paper only

INDUSTRIAL DEMOCRACY IN INTERNATIONAL PERSPECTIVE
   Guest Editor: John P. Windmuller
   THE ANNALS Volume 431 May 1977 – in paper only

Single volumes of THE ANNALS are ideal classroom supplements and texts—authoritative, accessible, and inexpensive. Single volumes quickly become standard reference works on the subjects addressed and are widely cited in scholarly research. In THE ANNALS, some of the most brilliant minds of the time are applied to emerging issues of international importance, exploring a full range of factors influencing and being influenced by the subject in question.

THE ANNALS

of The American Academy *of* Political *and* Social Science

RICHARD D. LAMBERT, *Editor*   **ALAN W. HESTON,** *Associate Editor*

JAMES F. SHORT, Jr., editor
The State of Sociology: Problems and Prospects
An exciting set of specially commissioned essays on the progress, problems, and prospects of contemporary sociology.
1981 / 304 pages / hardcover $22.50 / softcover $9.95

MICHAEL QUINN PATTON
Creative Evaluation
Provides a large repertoire of creative techniques for overcoming inertia and complacency in evaluation, keeping evaluation processes fresh and meaningful, and maximizing effectiveness in evaluation consultations.
1981 / 296 pages / hardcover $20.00 / softcover $9.95

BENJAMIN H. GOTTLIEB, editor
Social Networks and Social Support
A stimulating collection of original essays exploring the many facets—and advantages—of human attachments as natural support systems. An invaluable guide for scholars and practitioners in a wide variety of human services.
1981 / 304 pages / hardcover $20.00 / softcover $9.95

GEORGE W. BOHRNSTEDT and
  EDGAR F. BORGATTA, editors
Social Measurement: Current Issues
This compilation of up-to-the-minute measurement techniques will stimulate more empirical and theoretical work, and provide new practical applications, in the social sciences.
1981 / 256 pages / hardcover $22.50 / softcover $9.95

LEONARD SAXE and MICHELLE FINE
Social Experiments: Methods for Design and Evaluation
    Introduction by Donald T. Campbell
The authors take an unconventional look at the many aspects of social experimentation and the principles of social research and application, demonstrating how traditional and innovative methodology can be applied to real-world problems in such areas as education, health care, and criminal justice.
1981 / 272 pages / hardcover $20.00 / softcover $9.95

SAGE PUBLICATIONS
The Publishers of Professional Social Science
275 South Beverly Drive • Beverly Hills, California 90212